My Life
as Me

Barry Humphries

My Life as Me

A Memoir

I do not know
whether to put in the things I do not remember
as well as the things I do remember

Gertrude Stein

MICHAEL JOSEPH
an imprint of
PENGUIN BOOKS

~

To Tessa and Emily, Oscar and Rupert
In the hope
That somewhere in these pages
They might recognise
Their father

MICHAEL JOSEPH

Published by the Penguin Group
Penguin Books Ltd, 80 Strand, London WC2R ORL, England
Penguin Putnam Inc., 375 Hudson Street, New York, New York 10014, USA
Penguin Books Australia Ltd, 250 Camberwell Road,
Camberwell, Victoria 3124, Australia
Penguin Books Canada Ltd, 10 Alcorn Avenue, Toronto, Ontario, Canada M4V 3B2
Penguin Books India (P) Ltd, 11 Community Centre,
Panchsheel Park, New Delhi - 110 017, India
Penguin Books (NZ) Ltd, Cnr Rosedale and Airborne Roads,
Albany, Auckland, New Zealand
Penguin Books (South Africa) (Pty) Ltd, 24 Sturdee Avenue,
Rosebank 2196, South Africa

Penguin Books Ltd, Registered Offices: 80 Strand, London WC2R ORL, England

www.penguin.com

First published in Australia by Penguin Books 2002
First published in Great Britain by Michael Joseph 2002

1

Copyright © Oceania Investments BV, 2002

The moral right of the author has been asserted

Frontispiece: Father and son on the beach: Eric Humphries with Barry

Set in Aldus
Printed in Great Britain by Clays Ltd, St Ives plc

A CIP catalogue record for this book is available from the British Library

ISBN 0-718-14541-0

CONTENTS

~

PROLOGUE

~

TEN YEARS AGO, at a publisher's request, I wrote a brief account of my life. Brief, that is, in comparison with what I might have written, but Voltaire was right when he defined a bore as a man who leaves nothing out, and I hoped to avoid that epithet. When I sent my book to the publisher, he protested that it was too short; indeed the story ended when I was forty years of age, since I intended to resume the narrative in a second volume if it were called for.

'But', he protested, 'we have already announced that your memoir takes us up to the *present day*. It's even printed on the dust jacket. You must quickly extend it.'

'How long have I got?' I asked.

'We can give you two more weeks.'

Hence my autobiography *More Please* suddenly and almost comically goes into fast-forward, and the events of the seventies and eighties seem to dance across the page with the elliptical speed of a Keystone Cops' movie.

Most of my life I have been convalescing from the long illness of youth, and only after the publication of my recollections did I realise I had completely forgotten to include some of the most significant events of that interminable recovery. In offering a second volume, I have thus decided to begin once more at the beginning and write a parallel memoir.

Here and there readers may recognise a coincident event or personage from my earlier volume, for this is a cubist, even a futurist, self-portrait that I offer the reader, observing myself from many angles at once as in the hall of mirrors at a fairground, and with whiffs of scent, incoherent voices, shards of music.

I have changed the names of several of my dramatis personae who are still living, especially where their portrayal is of such accuracy as might inspire foolhardy litigation. I have honoured the dead by calling them by their real names.

Barry Humphries

Sunny Sam

~

*Each of us has a beach
somewhere to look back on*
C.H.B. Kitchin

Towards me, whistling, my father strides along the beach. Arms outstretched, he snatches me off my feet and hoists me above his head, a swaddled chortling cherub: little Sunny Sam. His lips under the marmalade Melvyn Douglas moustache are still chirping a version of that jaunty novelty number of 1934, 'The Whistler and His Dog' by Arthur Pryor. On the beach at Frankston, on that sparkling January morning, five years into the Great Depression, I am adored.

'I wish your father wouldn't try to whistle,' my mother often said ruefully. 'If he could only hear himself, he most certainly wouldn't.'

I fell in love at the age of five with a tall girl with slim brown legs and bobbed brown hair. Her name was Rosemary. It is strange to think that somewhere in a small office, off a long and ill-frequented corridor of my brain, is a locked cabinet containing her file: her real name, her eye pigmentation and the colour of her ruched bathing suit. She was old, perhaps even twelve years old, and feline, like a drawing by Balthus. She was on holiday with her father: no mother apparent. They were my first one-parent family.

We were staying at Erskine House in Lorne, a rambling, white, weatherboard guesthouse right on the sea. All night the breakers of Bass Strait crashed outside our chalet, if a sparsely furnished outhouse could be so described – although we had the best accommodation that famous prewar resort could provide, a short walk across a sandy lawn of tough buffalo grass to the main house and the 'facilities'. It was at least, as my mother said, 'secluded'.

The window of my bedroom – a mere cubicle – wore a sagging flywire screen, brittle with rust, and had a view of the marbled waves thunderously breaking and creaming up the beach: almost, it seemed, to the door of our flimsy abode. Across those miles of sea, beyond the deep Prussian-blue stripe at the horizon, lay the mysterious realm of Tasmania.

Except for 'rough' older boys who bobbed around beyond the breakers with their surfboards and yelled at each other in common voices, the surf was out of bounds for children, and to deter the most intrepid there were many cautionary tales of toddlers sucked out to sea. Instead we hopped about at the water's edge, laughing with a pleasurable terror, and ran screaming to higher ground and the safety of rugs and umbrellas as the great fans of foam sped up the beach demolishing sandcastles, confiscating spades, buckets and the occasional Thermos flask, and triumphantly reclaiming collections of shells and cuttlefish.

Beyond the wide beach and across the main road were a few shops selling cakes, pies, sandwiches and newspapers, and a popular milk bar that exhibited on its fascia a large picture of a polar bear eating an ice-cream cone.

I had, I suppose, been courting the indifferent Rosemary; that is to say, I had been loitering on the beach a short distance from her whenever possible, and I was on shyly nodding terms with her father, who usually lay on the sand, propped up on one elbow, smoking a pipe and reading. My adored one barely glanced in my direction, and when she did it was mostly a glance of amused disdain. However, this beautiful, long-limbed creature whom I watched each day as she emerged from the sea, peeling off her white rubber bathing cap and shaking out her seductive bob, must surely have tossed me a few crumbs of encouragement.

I had observed her one morning reclining on a beach rug, idly chafing her unsandalled, sun-lozenged insteps. She was eating a new kind of ice-cream, called a Butterscotch Pie. It was an ice-cream paddle covered with a delicious and brittle shell of butterscotch, which enjoyed a short-lived vogue in the late thirties. Accordingly I asked my parents for the money for one of these exquisite confections and next day paid an unsupervised visit to the milk bar.

The day was hot and the walk back across the scorching sand was painful. I had peeled off the wrapping, and held my gift at arm's length as I approached its intended recipient. She was standing with a delicious negligence, frowning slightly and brushing sand off her butterscotch-coloured thighs, already brailled by the sea's chill. Suddenly she looked up and saw me with my sweet offering extended; its frosty bloom had melted and there were already ominous trickles over my knuckles. Her face lit up and I thought I saw something like ardour in her gaze as she reached towards me, but what I had not seen was the half-submerged yellow spade in my path. In the next second I tripped over it, sending the Butterscotch Pie flying irretrievably into the sand. I lay there, face down, weeping with shame, and dared not look up. I could only hear her laughter as she ran off for another swim.

The next day father and daughter were gone.

WHILE at Lorne my dad took me to the ruins of a house that had been recently engulfed by a small bushfire. It was a little up the hill from the township, standing amongst blackened gums, and it was something of a miracle that the conflagration had not descended to that small parade of wooden shops on the Great Ocean Road, where it would have melted many a Butterscotch Pie and overheated countless pasties and sausage rolls.

The gutted house with its lone brick chimney, its scorched walls and the charred remnants of furniture made a profound impression on me, and the acrid stench stayed in my nostrils for weeks. One horrifying detail remains unforgotten: a small carbonised shoe – the shoe of a child – half buried in blackened rubble.

I had seen many houses in the process of construction

when I visited my father's building sites, but I had never before seen a house destroyed. I already suffered the obscure terrors of the night, but now the thought that what was once a safe and comfortable domicile could suddenly be devoured by fire gave me nightmares that lasted long thereafter.

At home in my bed with the door to the upstairs hallway ajar, I would wake and imagine I could see the wavering ruddy light of flames consuming the stairway and barring my flight. I would look out my window and vainly try to calculate how to escape by jumping down two floors to the back terrace without incurring multiple fractures. In the sleepless hours I rehearsed, over and over again, my perilous evacuation from the blazing house.

The fire station was only fifteen minutes' walk away from Christowel Street, down Camberwell Road, and I took a new interest in its reassuring proximity and its brass-helmeted inhabitants. The greasy pole was visible from the street, and down this I imagined the firemen sliding when the urgent summons from our combusting residence roused them from sleep. But would they respond? I fearfully wondered. I saw them hearing our urgent mayday and assuming it to be a hoax. Who would believe that a big, solid, neo-Georgian brick house at the top of the hill could be going up in smoke, even with bouquets of flame at every window and the sound of a screaming child trapped in his bedroom?

But our house was not designed for easy escape. There was something intangibly wrong with the design of this 'home beautiful', as the title of a still-popular magazine coyly inverted the adjective and noun. Enviably large though it was, and filled with so many nice things, the house had an inhospitable geometry.

Today one might perhaps say that its feng shui needed radical adjustment. In spite of the care and costly materials my father had lavished on the construction of our family residence, there were somehow too many windows; and the rooms failed to flow comfortably from one to the other. Moreover downstairs there was a dark hallway leading to my father's den, which was meant to segregate him from the rest of the family when he was working, but seemed like a gloomy and baffling cul-de-sac.

Even in the daytime the house possessed an aura of unease, for all its apparent comfort and amenity, so that if I sometimes returned from school when there was nobody at home, I found it impossible to stay indoors with any sense of security. Absurd as it sounds, I often had to run out into the garden and loiter there amongst the trees and shrubs, beyond the reach of something vaguely inimical within. But when my parents returned and lamps were lit, kitchen smells ignited and the radio resumed its cosy susurration, the demons fled.

Of course, the house was not really haunted: preposterous to imply that such a new building in an Australian suburb might harbour ghosts. But it was *potentially* haunted, by spirits yet unbidden – one day, perhaps, by me!

NAROOMA

~

Out of the complicated house, come I
To walk beneath the sky

FRANCIS CORNFORD

MY MOTHER often spoke of a beautiful place. It was a place she
had been to once and experienced some kind of great happiness.
A wistful memory of that happiness infused her conversation
whenever we asked her about it. The place was called Narooma.
Although we were never shown it on a map and it was never
described, I somehow knew it was by the sea. It was just a place
that glowed in her memory – almost mythological like the
island of Cythera – and I suppose I liked to hear her say its
name: so euphonious, like a mantra, 'Narooma'. When I was
very young I needed to know what made my mother happy;
hopeful, perhaps, that I too might one day be able to provide her
with something of that elusive joy. I sensed that Narooma was a
place where, long ago, she had felt persuaded by love.

My parents' habitual name for me, Sunny Sam, stayed
with me until I was at least six or seven years of age. Even the
advent of my sister, Barbara, did not seem noticeably to depress

the ebullient spirits that had earnt me that cheerful soubriquet.

My new sister's countenance seemed to wear a perpetual scowl. 'What a disappointing contrast she is to me!' I seemed to be telling my parents. But poor Barbara's ill-humour was probably due in no small measure to secret torments inflicted by me.

When Santa Claus brought Barbara her first doll, it was a miraculously chubby homunculus of rubber and celluloid, with rouged cheeks and big blue eyes. When my sister laid her down, the eyes closed; and when she picked her up, the eyes clicked open and the long sable lashes fluttered.

'What will we call her, Barbara?' my mother asked on that far-off Christmas Day.

'Rosebud,' I at once interposed, and Rosebud she became thereafter. It was long before I saw *Citizen Kane*, but the name Rosebud – and its rosaceous variations – have haunted my life like a refrain.

What I loved most of all as a child was to visit department stores in town with my mother and building sites with my father, the Master Builder. The excursions with my mother often involved tasty luncheons at the Wattle or the Wild Cherry tea rooms or those other subterranean oases the Russell Collins and Elizabeth Collins cafés, where we were always greeted by a 'refined' young receptionist in black, with a starched white collar, who would show us to a secluded booth decorated with poppies and gum tips. But my favourite was Ernest Hillier's in Collins Street, which offered banana and pineapple sundaes, followed by a chocolate 'frappé' (pronounced 'fraip') – a chocolate milkshake with marshmallows. In later years Raffles, also in

Collins Street, was a regular haunt of mine, where we would adjourn after a symphony concert in the Town Hall for those two sophisticated staples of the early fifties, coffee and toasted raisin bread.

When I was still Sunny Sam, I was inducted into the exciting world of my father's business. In those early years, before he had an office and builder's yard down at Hartwell, he worked entirely from his den at home. The den had its own entrance at the side of the house, which tradesmen used. In this small office he had his drawing board and draftsman's accoutrements: compass, set square, protractor, scale rule and a set of French curves. In a drawer he kept his beautiful boxes of blue pencils by Staedtler, as well as coloured pencils made in Bavaria and Czechoslovakia. It was strange, in 1940, to watch my father drawing up plans for people's houses with instruments that bore the legend 'Made in Germany'.

In our front lounge my father interviewed couples who wanted him to build them a home – 'clients' my mother called them – and I often watched them, through the glass doors, poring eagerly over blueprints or looking through catalogues and books on domestic architecture, choosing a style: Spanish Mission, Tudor, Georgian, Jazz Moderne. He owned a very interesting book called *The Modern House*, which must have been published in the thirties. It was bound in coarse fawn linen and the title was in a stately art deco typeface. It was printed on glossy paper and filled with photographs of ultra-modern houses in Europe. Each section bore the name of a country that had become all too terribly familiar because of the war. There were modern houses in Holland, Germany, Poland, Denmark and Czechoslovakia, of which I had seen very different images in *The Sun News-Pictorial*. These houses in the book were not in ruins. There were no snipers crouching amongst their rubble or frightened children fleeing. These houses, with their flat roofs and corner windows, were white and serene and stood beside birch forests and lakes. Yet there were no people sitting on the chrome chairs by Marcel Breuer or housewives pottering in the stainless-steel kitchens, so like our own in Melbourne. As I turned the shiny pages, with my father's permission, I imagined the war that must now be raging around those ineffably civilised habitations. Was that why there were no people to be seen? I wondered. Were they dead?

The object I admired most in my father's office was his majestic black Underwood typewriter, which he carefully covered every night with its mackintosh hood. There was a contrivance on the carriage that rang a tiny bell when the typist reached the end of a line. Often late at night in the quiet house I would hear this distant tintinnabulation, and I knew that my father was downstairs jabbing away with two fingers at the instrument in order to complete a building specification, or to lodge a late tender. It was on this stately machine that I typed my first poems and essays, in triplicate using lots of carbon paper.

Sometimes my father would invite Pat Baggot, our handyman and gardener, or Alec Gibson, his head carpenter, into his den for a chat after work. The door was always closed, but now and then I barged in on one of these grown-up meetings. There was usually a cloud of cigarette smoke – Alec rolled his own –

and not seldom I surprised my father in the act of concealing something on the windowsill. Later when I peered behind the curtain, I noticed that it was a glass of amber-coloured fluid with a frothy collar: beer. I never commented on this inexplicable secrecy, although I instinctively knew that the beer must never be mentioned to my mother. 'If you must have the occasional glass, Eric,' I once overheard her whisper, 'please not in front of the children.'

MY FATHER had relocated his parents, Jack and Sarah, in a new cream-brick villa that he had specially built for them in the nearby suburb of Canterbury, saving us the long Sunday drive to their pre-Depression bungalow in the distant suburb of Thornbury. Their old house was in a diluted Spanish Mission style with pargeted caramel stucco. Small within, it was dark, very dark, and smelt of furniture polish, a distant whiff of gas from the kitchen, and an unfamiliar soap. Objects glinted in the dimly lit rooms. Everything had been burnished and dusted and embalmed.

To get to Nana and Papa's old abode, we had to drive up hill and down dale across Melbourne, past Ivanhoe and Eaglemont where the Australian impressionists had camped in the early eighteen-nineties and painted their romantic landscapes on the lids of cigar boxes. This idyllic riverland is now almost filled with lovely homes, its gums and willows deracinated, and what remains of space-wasting meadow and riverbank is blighted with a teeming freeway.

Beyond Eaglemont, already subdivided in the thirties, we entered the fringes of an older suburb, its streets meaner, yet paradoxically wider, with peppercorn trees, barefoot children and joined-together Victorian houses. In the back seat I felt my heart beating wildly in the hope of an exciting glimpse of the Poor. There was a High Street along which the mulberry-coloured cable trams rumbled, and across the railway line my grandparents' old home. They lived, literally, on the wrong side of the tracks.

The most memorable feature of the house was its fernery in the backyard. This was a latticed structure full of hanging baskets of staghorns, Rex begonias and maidenhair ferns. Many houses of that period boasted a fernery, with its dim green light, cool mossy smell and perpetual drizzle of water.

WHILE visiting my grandparents on hot days, I would often play with my cousin Don in the fronded seclusion of Nana's fernery. My mother insisted that Don was an excellent artist, and she absolutely refused to hear my outraged protests that he only *copied* Walt Disney characters such as Donald, his name-sake, or Mickey or Goofy, whereas my own drawings were at least *original* – although I doubt I used that epithet. At a very early age I had formed a strong antipathy to cartoons, and indeed the entire oeuvre of Walt Disney, and never saw the point of all those anthropomorphic vermin beating each other up or singing their squeaky songs. Even worse than the cartoons were the mawkish, attenuated films about cute deer, lovable elephants and those terpsichorean hippos who pranced through the kitschy *Fantasia*.

I did, however, subscribe to some comics, particularly *Knockout* and *Film Fun*, which were published in England and found their way to Australia months later across perilous wartime seas. Once a week these gaudy little booklets on cheap paper, from faraway blitzed London, arrived on our front lawn, rolled up and tossed over the fence by a newsboy on a bicycle. In *Knockout* I followed the adventures of Deed-a-Day Danny, the boy scout, and Sexton Blake and his sidekick, Tinker, who lurked behind bushes and spied upon German slave labour camps, for the war had already percolated into the innocent world of comic cuts. My sister, Barbara, meanwhile subscribed to *Chicks' Own*, upon which I looked with the greatest disdain.

Film Fun and its companion comic *Radio Fun* were filled with the adventures of popular British entertainers we knew little or nothing about in Australia: Arthur 'Hello Playmates' Askey, the Western Brothers with their top hats and monocles, and Will Hay and Tommy Handley. Most of the jollity of these childish cartoon narratives was firmly anchored in a prewar London society of toffs and cockney wags, blimps and East End ragamuffins.

Graham Coles, who lived halfway down Marlborough Avenue, and whose father had a First World War German helmet with a spike on top in his wardrobe, subscribed to *The Champion*, which was more reading than pictures. There was always a cover illustration of a foppish Nazi being bayoneted or garroted by an English officer with a public-school profile, but my mother had forbidden me to order this 'unsuitable' publication from the newsagent's. Graham also owned a Donkey engine and a billycart, two fervently desired, but again prohibited, possessions: Donkey engines could explode and billycarts had been known to propel a kiddie under a truck.

Rescued by my forever rescuing father, my grandparents settled into their new, vaguely Tudor, even *Tudoid* dwelling, where their old-fashioned possessions looked rather out of place. The upright piano, with its brass sconces and hymn-stuffed stool, stood resentfully in the lounge, beneath a brand-new, fashionably peach-tinted mirror. On the top of the piano my grandmother displayed framed family photographs, mostly from the famous studio of Maxwell Porteous. His florid signature in white ink embellished these artfully retouched studies of my innumerable cousins.

I rather missed the long drive to Thornbury to visit my grandparents in their old house. Whenever we called on them in their Canterbury dwelling, there was always a long pause before Nana responded to the recently installed electric chimes. With a knowing smile, my mother once told me that Nana, having glimpsed our arrival in the driveway through her new Venetians, quickly rearranged the photos on the piano, demoting the previous family visitors and replacing them with pictures of us.

I was so sure of my position as most favoured grandchild that I dismissed my mother's cynical theory, until one afternoon when we decided to pop in on Nana and Papa unexpectedly. There was a particularly long delay before my grandmother opened the front door and we had barely sat down when we were startled by a terrible clatter. Our framed photographs, so hastily reshuffled on the piano, had toppled like dominoes and cascaded onto the mushroom wall-to-wall. Fortunately Nana was in the kitchen, hastily improvising one of her lavish afternoon teas, and failed to notice the giveaway avalanche.

Cakes had always been her speciality, particularly sponges and pavlovas, and we never left without our grandmother pressing upon us platefuls of food to take home. She had acquired her proficiency as a country girl, helping her mother and sisters in the Coffee Palace at Benalla, in northern Victoria, and afternoon tea at Nana's place was always a Lucullan event. On our arrival Papa would invariably offer us a glass of fortified red wine or sherry, which particularly riled my mother, who regarded this kind of old-fashioned hospitality as 'uncalled for', especially in front of the children. My grandparents politely ignored, or perhaps even failed to notice, my mother's almost palpable hostility to the proffered beverages and continued to serve 'a drop of something' to visitors for the rest of their lives.

But something quite sinister had started happening in my grandmother's lovely new home. When she came into her kitchen one morning, Nana noticed small cones of the finest buff-coloured sawdust on her beautiful 'surfaces'. Exactly above these miniature pyramids, in the overhanging cream-painted cupboards, could be discerned some tiny black holes. My father was summoned and made the terrible diagnosis: borer!

My mother blamed Mr Freedman, who had supplied all the timber. He was after all Jewish, and a prime suspect. It seemed that Nana's kitchen was *infested* with these invisible yet industrious insects, which produced at least half a cup of fine sawdust every morning. An exterminator was called, who brought in his equipment and over several days injected a lethal syrup into every perforated surface.

The smell of this powerful insecticide, which resembled Fernet-Branca in colour, odour and viscosity, took many days to disperse, yet finally the infestation was extirpated and the kitchen duly repainted by my father's men. But Nana's cakes were never the same again. Forever after there was the slightest taint of the exterminator's potion in her fluffy sponges and iced pastries. Always after a visit, at my mother's insistence, and in spite of our protests and my father's intense pain, we would have to furtively dump Nana's lovingly prepared confections by the roadside.

I was the apple of my grandmother's eye until her death in the late sixties and she would never hear a word against me, although by then there were many such words from family members dismayed by my moral decline.

'Well, Barry,' my mother would say, shaking her head, 'at least Nana won't hear a word against you', as though this were incontrovertible evidence of her mother-in-law's senility.

MELBOURNE in the early forties was not untouched by far-off wars. We had dug up our verdurous back lawn – 'It's not a backyard,' insisted my mother. 'They're common. Always remember ours is a *back lawn'* – and planted peas, beans, lettuce and potatoes. And against a high trellised wall, or what then seemed to me to be a high wall, between our garden and that of our neighbours, the Misses Train, my father and Pat Baggot had pleached apricot and plum trees.

My parents listened every evening to the news broadcasts with an almost romantic intensity. Idiosyncratically pronounced by Australian newsreaders such as Monty Blandford and Dick Cranbourne, the European names and places had a sinister yet seductive force. The personage most often mentioned on the radio and in *The Sun News-Pictorial* after Hitler, Churchill and the ludicrous Reichmarshal Göring, and the one I liked best having seen photographs of him in his self-designed, operetta-like uniforms, was Joachim von Ribbentrop, the egregious Nazi foreign minister. I vaguely knew he was on the wrong side, but I loved the euphony of his name: the dainty undulation of the 'ribben' ending with that unexpected and abrupt whiplash of 'trop'. Press photographs of him in mufti shaking hands with Molotov made him seem positively genial and a bit like a well-to-do member of the Riversdale Golf Club; even his broad-lapelled suits looked as if they might have been made by Arthur Warner, my father's tailor.

In some snapshots of myself at this time, I recognise in my affected pose and supercilious mien the absurd object of my misplaced adulation. Reinhard Spitzy, who was Ribbentrop's aide before the war and is now in his eighties and living in agreeable retirement in a valley outside Salzburg, has a fund of stories about the Führer's former foreign minister, all of which confirm that far from merely being an odious buffoon Ribbentrop was one of the most dangerous monsters in Hitler's bestiary.

Many years later, sometime in the mid-sixties in London, the food editor of *The Daily Express* asked me to the Savoy Grill for lunch. She was going to write a story about it and invited me to choose my own menu. I love oysters and I had read somewhere of an exotic combination called Oysters Tsarina: oysters smothered with beluga caviar, dipped in cream, with a dash of shallots and chopped parsley, and conveyed hastily to the mouth. The waiter had never heard of this delicacy, but after a short delay the elderly head chef of the Savoy appeared at our table with a magnificent plateful of Oysters Tsarina.

He looked at me gravely. 'I wish to tell you, sir, that you are the first gentleman to have ordered this dish since Ambassador Ribbentrop.'

My impious fascination with a Nazi buffoon apart, it was my Uncle Wilf who, in the first ten years of my life, I loved more than any living being. He and my father were such good friends: always laughing, joshing each other and sharing incomprehensible jokes. Together they had built 'the shack' at Healesville, forty miles from Melbourne, where we spent so many happy bushland holidays. Uncle Wilf had been outside Australia in the First World War and, although I believe he had not seen active service, there were gleaming brass shell cases on his mantelpiece, which Aunty Violet diligently burnished with Brasso. He also had medals with rainbow-hued ribbons, which he wore at the March on every Anzac Day.

Uncle Wilf did things and knew things that my parents never did or seemed to know. He occasionally rode in taxis, he smoked pipes, and he read racy English periodicals such as *Lilliput* and *London Opinion*, which found their way to Australia across dangerous seas, months after publication. Apart from the occasional 'artistic' photograph of the female nude posed in silhouette amongst reeds by sparkling lakes, *London Opinion* featured jokes by cartoonists of the period such as Osbert Lancaster and 'Anton', whose styles I began to recognise, although their jokes remained occult. The men in all the jokes were in uniform.

Uncle Wilf also possessed a fine old musical box with scrolly gilt writing in a foreign language inside its mahogany lid. By cranking an elegant handle you could make the brazen cylinder within, prickled like a cactus, revolve against a row of brass teeth, combing out tinkling airs from Bizet's *Carmen*.

When Wilf Gatliff died of a brain tumour in 1944 it was a desolating experience for us all. Forbidden to go to the funeral, I had to mourn my beloved uncle in private. Funerals were considered highly 'unsuitable' for children, so that mourning never really ever came to an end but just faded away.

The only other death I was to experience as a child was that of Roslyn Forbes. Ann and Roslyn Forbes were two of my sister's best friends, and mine also; they lived in a cream-brick Moderne house at the bottom of Lansell Crescent. There is a grainy home movie of us playing together at one of Roslyn's birthday parties. She was killed at the age of nine: knocked down by a car as she jumped off the tram and ran across Camberwell

Road. The death of Roslyn was one of the terrible events of our childhood. We did not attend her funeral, just as we did not attend Uncle Wilf's.

In the weeks that followed Wilf's death, I overheard many muttered conversations between my parents about the penurious condition in which Uncle Wilf's sudden and unforeseeable death had left my mother's sister Violet, and their severely spastic son, John. Something had to be done and, as usual, it fell to my father to do it.

Certainly the shack had to be sold to augment Aunty Vi's meagre increment. The rambling house of 'fibro' sheeting, with a corrugated iron roof, was of no great value. It had been cobbled together in the thirties of leftover timbers and a mishmash of orphaned and ill-matched fixtures and furbishments, but it stood in an idyllic setting in thirty acres of bushland, looking out across paddocks towards the perennially blue foothills of the Yarra Ranges. It was, moreover, ideal for a young family, since amongst its outbuildings was my rustic fort, and high in an old messmate (*Eucalyptus obliqua*), camouflaged with leaves, perched my luxurious eyrie: a magnificent tree house, linked to the main house by telephone and erected specially for me.

I believe the reason for selling the shack was much more sentimental than financial; its associations with Wilf would have made the continuing use of it too painful for the family, particularly for my grieving father.

We returned to the shack for one last visit when everything was being packed up, and I wandered off into the familiar bush by a secret path I knew and concealed under the bark of

a tree a valedictory poem. I can only remember a couple of
doggerel lines:

> *... the little creek is turning into a waterfall*
> *but this heaven I am leaving, far from the magpie's call ...*

My mother did not accompany us on this last, sad journey
to Healesville, but my father took Barbara and me with him as
he 'finalised' the sale arrangements with the agent in the township (this was the year when the word 'finalised' was invented,
and it was an invention that my father celebrated at every
opportunity).

The day was grey – or memory has coloured it so – but
my father proposed a picnic before we drove back to Melbourne.
He was clearly very dejected, and a picnic was about the last
thing any of us were in the mood for, but we bought a few pro-
visions and stopped the car beside a particularly bleak, scrubby,
wind-vexed paddock about a mile from our already forsaken
country home. My father, looking terribly sad, managed to
kindle a small, reluctant fire on which he, my small sister and I
attempted to grill some very unwieldy lamb chops. The fire
went out twice, the chops, tough and underdone, proved ined-
ible, and the vanilla slices he had bought from the little
homemade-cake shop in Healesville were so fresh and oozy
our thumbs stuck to the icing and the custard dribbled down our
chins. It was the most mournful repast I can remember: a wake
for the lost Arcadia of our childhood.

Soon after, my father found a nice flat for Aunty Vi and

John in an apartment building he owned in Riversdale Road, and he also persuaded Imperial Chemical Industries, for whom Wilf had worked for many years, to provide his widow with a small pension, which I have no doubt my father augmented.

ABOUT ten years ago I returned to Healesville to visit a friend who had built a modern house near the new golf course and country club. I still retained a precise recollection of the journey that I had made so often and so impatiently in my childhood. *Are we nearly there yet?* was my constant refrain from the back seat. This time, embarking upon the same road nearly fifty years later, I was prepared for dramatic, even brutal transformations to the landscape; but nothing prepared me for what I now saw. Vast suburbs had spilt out across the countryside; farms had been swallowed up and swathes of bush extirpated to make way for more suburbs, malls, McDonald's, service stations and Kentucky Fried Chicken dispensaries. I found myself on an unfamiliar highway, flanked by used-car lots with their gaudy fluttering pennants, and wondering if the city of Melbourne would ever come to an end, and whether the little township of Healesville still existed or had been irretrievably engulfed by the lava flow of lovely homes.

Amazingly the township had not been so devastated by progress as to be unrecognisable, so I decided on a brief detour to take a look at the old shack. The Don Road seemed vaguely familiar as I drove up it, and after about a mile I began peering to my right in search of that heart-stopping gap in the trees where the unnamed and dusty track to our former holiday home began. There I thought I recognised a few decaying pine trees; perhaps the ones my cousins Ken and Trevor had bravely climbed while I stood beneath them, amongst the cones and needles, gazing up in admiration for I was too much of a sissy to climb trees. My mother, of course, would have been appalled had I done anything so dangerous, but when she heard of my cousins' arboreal exploits she could never resist saying with a whimsical laugh, 'Ken and Trevor are *real boys*, there's no doubt about it.'

I continued motoring up the Don Road until I realised that something was wrong. Although Mount Riddell on my left still raised its blue hump, piebald here and there where fires had raged long ago, the bush on my right had petered out. I had heard that our old picnic spot on a ferny knoll beside Badger Creek – where many a platypus lurked, but never a badger – had become 'wheelchair accessible', with appropriate concrete barbecue facilities and handicapped restrooms. Now a tawdry new housing estate swung into view through my rented windscreen: 'prestige town houses', I surmised – a prestige town house in Australia can be any house within a forty-mile radius of a town. There were garish signs inviting inspection, and, it seemed, a 'display home' of transcendental dullness. I could look no longer. It served me right. One should never go back.

As I recklessly turned the car around, not even daring to grieve for that lost idyll of childhood, I saw a sign outside the display home. It exhibited, in an enlarged photograph, the developer himself, Wayne Acropolis, in natty suit and tie, extending a fat, foreshortened hand of welcome to the passing motorist, and from his lips a large balloon framed these words:

HAPPENING HEALESVILLE

WELCOME TO PLATYPUS PLAZA

YOU COULD BE HAPPY HERE!

Turps

~

My parents kept me from
children who were rough

Stephen Spender

After my father had built us our own seaside holiday house at Mornington, on the peninsula of the same name near Melbourne, with our own sandy cove on which the clear waters of Port Phillip Bay lapped with an almost Homeric limpidity, we ceased visiting perilous beaches and guesthouses, with their porridgy mattresses and dinner gongs, and enjoyed the small comforts and pleasures that my father's post-war prosperity had brought us. At Mornington we had our own tennis court and a short walk away, on Beleura Hill, a long bluff overlooking the sea, there was a new links and golf club in which my father immediately enrolled me, with his usual poignant optimism that I might, after all, take up some sporting interest.

I had received not only swimming lessons from a Berlin Olympics champion, but also golf lessons from a famous professional and endless coaching on the tennis court. However, I could never participate with the least pleasure or success in any recreation that involved other players. My childhood was filled with reproachful voices saying, 'I'll never play tennis/golf/canasta/mah-jong/ping-pong with you again, Barry – *ever*!'

Perhaps the most horrible gift I ever received from my father, apart from a cricket bat, was a pair of boxing gloves.

'It's important that Barry learns to defend himself,' he said, although he never mentioned against whom. I had a brief vision of all those people out there waiting to hit me. I was not ten years of age and yet my father, normally a gentle man, was taking a bloodthirsty pleasure in organising backyard boxing matches in which I was expected to spar with neighbourhood boys. We had been taught the rudiments of boxing by Scottie, the bald bully who ran the gymnasium at my junior school, Camberwell Grammar, but I detested it then, and what still seems to me now to be a perfectly natural aversion to pain and facial injury earnt me the shaming nickname of 'Granny Humphries'. Whenever I was thrown into the ring with some keen young lout, I always concentrated on losing the match without loss of blood.

The backyard boxing matches were short-lived. My mother put a stop to them forever after I gave Graham Coles a bloody nose, by accident rather than design. The poor boy fled home in tears, a crimson handkerchief pressed to his face, but I was ashamed to observe my father's mood of quiet triumph. Was this what was expected of me? I wondered. Was this what it took to be a real man?

Down at Mornington for the long summer holidays, the recreations were mostly swimming, reading and, for me, painting.

I had loved colour since earliest childhood, probably because my mother often carried my basinet into the garden, where through my gauzy veil I could enjoy the brilliant hues of phlox and pansies, marigolds, zinnias, snapdragons, anemones and the big Wedgwood-blue pompoms of the hydrangeas. Only the dissolute rose was excluded from my mother's flowerbeds. In my first paintings I tried to recapture the gem-like intensity of her summer garden.

I became an avid post-impressionist. I persuaded my parents to buy me the Phaidon books on Cézanne, Van Gogh and Gauguin for my twelfth birthday and I tried to paint the cliffs and coves in their exuberant manner, using enormous amounts of pigment, much of it applied with a palette knife. My mother would drop me off in her cream 'baby' Austin convertible at a picturesque vantage point and I would set up my easel and folding chair, anointing my nose against sunburn with the compulsory impasto of zinc cream.

By lunchtime another gaudy picture was finished and when my mother came back to collect me and my latest masterpiece there was often a small crowd of curious bathers clustered behind me, gazing with awe and amusement at my rather capricious version of the scene before us.

'Look, Kev,' I heard one father say to his appallingly sunburnt child. 'Look at the photo this boy's paintin' of our beach!'

It was the first time that I had observed the Australian working-class custom of calling any pictorial image, however wrought, a photo, and it was also the first taste I had had of celebrity. To be sitting there on a cliff top beside the dazzling bay with a small audience behind me watching every flamboyant brush stroke was rather thrilling, but it was also slightly disturbing to be talked about – sometimes quite loudly – as though I wasn't there.

Today, because of television, I am occasionally recognised in the street and I hear people say to each other at the top of their voices, 'Look, there's Barry Humphries!', after which they often fall about laughing. They mean no harm – on the contrary – but they give one a disquieting sense of being somehow outside the human race.

There was a wonderful old convent at Mornington, buff-stucco'd and red-roofed, which I loved to paint in my Cézanne style. It stood amongst conifers and sheoaks on a steep, tawny hillside, and in the needle-sweet shade of a dusty pine tree I drew and painted it from every angle.

I was very proud of my convent pictures but surprised that they never elicited much enthusiasm from my mother. The rather obvious reason for this failed to dawn on me until one day when I propped a particularly successful canvas up on the mantelpiece and bluntly invited her comments. She looked at the picture with a slightly pained expression.

'Barry,' she said, 'your father and I have been quite worried for some time . . .' My mother invoked my father, usually without his knowledge, in all matters of grave moral import. 'I hope you know that place you're always painting is a Roman Catholic convent. *Why can't you paint something nice?*'

Most of my paintings and drawings were posted off to Sydney to the Argonauts' Club to earn me certificates of merit and occasionally a thrilling word of praise on my favourite radio

The convent, Mornington, c. 1949 (author's sketch)

programme, although my identity was modestly concealed by the Greek pseudonym Ithome 32. We were all meant to be rowers in Jason's fleet and this popular and edifying session on the national station played a rousing ditty to encourage its youthful listeners to pull their oars:

> *Row! Row! Merry oarsmen, Row!*
> *That dangers lie ahead we know, we know.*
> *But bend with all your might*
> *As you sail into the night*
> *And wrong will bow to right.*
> *'Jason' cry, adventure know,*
> *Argonauts Row! Row! Row!*

I loved the Argonauts' Club, and even before I had reached the age of ten I kept a journal that chronicled all my contributions in paint, prose and verse to this popular children's show. It was an outlet for my drawings and doggerel; a chance to win those multi-coloured certificates and, above all, a frisson of fame, which I experienced each time they called out my name over the airwaves.

I recently discovered my old Argonauts scrapbook in a box of miscellaneous juvenilia salvaged from our family home.

Every Friday after school
I keep up to my weekly rule
And write in to the Argonauts
With contributions full of thoughts
And when they ask me I proudly tell
Of the Argonauts badge on my coat lapel.

So I artlessly wrote on the fourteenth of October 1944.

I signed all my paintings simply 'Barry', just as Van Gogh had signed his works 'Vincent', and as I shipped each carefully packed canvas off to the Argonauts and, inevitably, the furnaces of the Australian Broadcasting Commission, I felt I knew how the unhappy and uniauricular Dutchman must have felt as he dispatched his masterpieces to his brother Theo in far-off Paris.

Yet I wanted so much to be an artist that I wrote to a Sydney post-office box number seeking the vocational advice of Joe, who gave weekly radio chats to the Argonauts on artistic matters and judged all pictures submitted. He kindly replied, but suggested a career I had never heard of: commercial art. It sounded so business-like, so prosaic and uninspired that I thought it could only delight my parents, so I proudly informed them that I had found my vocation.

They took it very well at the time, although had I announced that I wished to become a train driver or a venereologist they would probably have been equally understanding. The career decisions of a twelve-year-old need rarely be taken seriously.

Barry is just going through a phase, my mother would say with amused tolerance, confident that nearly a decade lay ahead before I slipped effortlessly into my father's business. But I had a real gift for caricature, as many schoolmasters discovered as they confiscated scurrilous drawings clandestinely executed beneath classroom desks. I even caricatured my parents, and a sketch of my father survives, drawn when I was eleven, which I managed to hide when my mother was conducting one of her purges of improper drawings. I am still a caricaturist, but of the theatre.

In the back pages of *Pix* and *The Australasian Post*, two periodicals to which my parents subscribed, and wedged between the announcement of an 'AMAZING HAIR DISCOVERY' and advice on 'HOW TO BE REGULAR IN TEN DAYS' was a striking advertisement. It was a stylish ink drawing of a leggy blonde in a bathing costume and high-heeled shoes, looking rather like Rita

31

Hayworth. Leering at her, with a sketchbook in his hand and a pencil poised, was a brilliantined man with a Ronald Colman moustache. 'ANYONE CAN DRAW!' ran the rubric, in an arresting penman's script. Readers were invited to fill in a coupon and to post it, obligation-free, to the Brodie Mack Correspondence Art School at a post-office box number in Sydney.

I was interested in moving from landscape painting to a portrayal of the human figure, either in or out of a bathing costume, and the advertisement suggested that this could well be Brodie Mack's speciality. I was not prepared for the avalanche of printed matter that arrived on our doorstep. The Brodie Mack School bombarded me for weeks and months with aptitude tests, brochures, newsletters, special offers and, as might be expected, demands for money. All of this material – or what Americans would call 'literature' – was embellished by Brodie's adroit caricatures and 'glamour' sketches of winking and pouting Betty Grable look-alikes.

I remember a series of drawings showing the various stages in the creation of a caricature. The caption read 'Delight your friends. Draw Goebbels.' On the brochure a young man smoking a pipe and wearing a beret, remarkably like Brodie Mack himself, was displaying a caricature of the recently incinerated Nazi propaganda minister to a group of excited and convulsed young women in tight clothing. Had I but apprehended it then, this was my first encounter with the idea of art as an instrument of arousal and seduction, although few but Brodie Mack and a handful of German platinum-blonde Ufa starlets could have discerned the aphrodisiacal qualities of Dr Goebbels.

I had applied for the Brodie Mack course without the knowledge of my parents, but as the junk mail poured in (although with the original extortionate fees reduced to 'a once in a lifetime opportunity'), I was forced to confide in my mother, who wrote a stiff letter to Brodie Mack, after which the bombardment ceased. I was left with vague feelings of guilt, as I always was when my parents fixed things up. I recognised that Brodie Mack's art was not really art as I had precociously come to appreciate it, but it was a *kind of art*, to which pop artists such as Roy Lichtenstein, Andy Warhol and Alan Jones have since given respectability. By not enrolling I had probably got myself onto a blacklist somewhere; and if I ever wanted to be a real artist one day, they'd point at me and say, 'There's the mother's boy who cost Brodie Mack a fortune in stamps.'

One September, at the time of the Royal Melbourne Show, the Argonauts came to town. They told us over the air before-hand that they were coming. They were going to do one of their sessions in a soundproof glass booth at the Royal Show, and would be happy to greet any 'rowers' who turned up. I was agog.

I had to go and see my idols. What picture of them I had formed in my imagination I cannot now recall, but I had invested those voices on the radio with corporeal splendour; they were, after all, my preferred family, my cultural mentors and pre-ceptors. From them I learnt English folk songs and the names of trees and the mystery of jokes. They had an almost super-natural beauty.

It was not easy to persuade my father to take me to meet these paragons. The Royal Show had been out of bounds for some years since he had once taken me there for the day and left me outside the tent while he went in to see the Tattooed Lady. Disingenuously, I am afraid, I had reported this to my mother, although it seemed that my father's interest in the embellished woman concerned her more than my banishment from this curious attraction.

Howbeit, strong assurances must have been offered and accepted for we went, my father and I, to the Showgrounds in Flemington on the appointed day. It was a wonderful place, milling with farmers and their wives, oddly dressed in their old-fashioned best and examining the new agricultural equipment. There was a smell of dust and burnt pink fairy floss, and there were sample bags to buy full of miniature cereal packets and little bottles of tomato sauce. These bags had formerly been my preoccupation at the Royal Show but now, older and wiser, I made a beeline for the pavilion of the Australian Broadcasting Commission. There was a small crowd looking up through the large glass windows into the studio, where technicians wandered about setting up microphones as though unobserved. My heart was pounding, When would Jason appear? I wondered. And Elizabeth?

An orchidaceous youth with long hair and crêpe-soled green suede shoes walked, or rather waltzed, across the studio and tapped on the microphone. I noticed he was wearing a large Frank Sinatra Swoon Club badge on his corduroy lapel. 'Testing . . . testing,' he said, and the 's' in 'testing' made a little hiss. There were a few children of my own age craning their necks beside me. Fellow Argonauts, I surmised.

We seemed to wait a long time, during which other people entered the studio, through a door lined with perforated acoustic panels. An older man in a rumpled suit, with a ginger moustache, sat down and rather crossly examined some papers. A fat, bald fellow wearing an old cardigan lit a cigarette and glanced casually through the glass windows at the crowd. A fair-haired woman in a beige twin-set came in and started talking to one of the technical people. Outside in the crowd we could almost hear her words. Was that a familiar voice? Could she be Elizabeth, the beautiful star of the programme? She was pretty certainly, but disappointingly, well . . . human. One of her stockings had even run a little.

The effeminate youth now sat down behind a desk, a red light went on and suddenly the theme music of the Argonauts blared from overhead speakers:

. . . It's time for the Session, it's time for the fun.

The nondescript trio had meanwhile shuffled towards the microphone and were standing in a slovenly triangle, holding bunches of paper.

'Hello, boys and girls,' said the old man with the moustache. 'Welcome to our special edition of the Argonauts from Melbourne. Oh and here's Elizabeth coming into the studio. Hello, Elizabeth!'

'Hello, Mac! Hello, Joe!' said Elizabeth, for it was she. But she had not come into the studio just then, she had been there for some time! And why were they reading all this? Had those funny, friendly exchanges I had listened to with such pleasure at home been written by someone else and typed out?

There were tears of disappointment in my eyes as I watched these very ordinary, even somewhat shabby people – they had probably travelled all night by rail from Sydney – prosaically reciting their lines. It was not that they were merely actors doing a job, dutiful employees of the ABC, but (and I blush to recall this precocious, yet probably accurate twelve-year-old's observation) that they looked – underpaid. It was a bitter day of disillusionment; far worse than the day when I discovered that my parents wore dentures.

THROUGHOUT my life I have continued to paint; a cheerful amateur perched on Peloponnesian cliff tops with a wind-buffeted easel, in the shade of Italian cypresses, on the battlements of Portuguese castles or amongst the spinifex on the flat, red earth of north-west Australia. The things I paint are a far cry from the pictures I like and occasionally collect, and if a dealer offered me one of my own bravura works I would probably never speak to him again.

I always travel with my painting equipment, and a few years ago, on a flight from Melbourne to Sydney, I noticed a fleck of bright yellow oil paint on the lapel of my jacket. Remembering that some of my painting kit was stowed in the overhead compartment, I stood up and rummaged through my gear for a bottle of turpentine and a rag. After a little gentle rubbing the stain was gone and I returned, immaculate, to my seat.

Barely a minute later the chief steward accosted me in a less than cordial manner. He wanted to know what it was everyone could smell at that end of the plane. I had reached that happy position in life and fortune when, on entering an aircraft, I habitually turned left.

'It's only turpentine,' I replied brightly. 'Isn't it a marvellous smell?'

'Are you aware, sir, that turpentine is highly hazardous in terms of inflammable, and having it in your possession is in serious violation of the law in terms of the Australian Airline Security Commission?' At this period, the locution 'in terms of' had infested everyday speech in Australia with the virulence of a plague.

I told him politely that I had not known, that I was stupid and that I would never do it again. I thought this would be the end of the matter, but it was not. There were some quick, excited colloquies at the front of the plane, and the turps was confiscated and put in a locker in the galley. For the rest of the flight the once-smiling, even fawning cabin crew looked at me with expressions of contempt.

When we arrived in Sydney, I was met by a senior airline official who solemnly escorted me to a private room wherein he reiterated the gravity of my offence. 'In terms of irresponsible behaviour, Mr Humphries, what you did today in terms of possessing a toxic and volatile substance on board a passenger aircraft is, in terms of seriousness, a bloody disgrace.'

I wrung my hands, I begged for mercy. Had I ashes, I would have poured them on my head, but the official was intransigent.

'You haven't heard the end of this, Mr Humphries. This offence is punishable in terms of a prison term. Airline safety is a big concern, and we want to bring this home to the public. A high-profiled individual like you in terms of celebrity is just what we need to get our message across.'

Although I was the very picture of abject contrition, it didn't seem to wash. He sent me home, but with a warning that he would be in contact as soon as Management had met and they had decided whether or not to make an example of me in terms of prosecution and a jail sentence. Cursing my stupidity, I spent a nervous week awaiting Management's decision, until I finally received a call from a very senior airline official indeed.

'Is that Brian Humphrey?' I didn't argue.

'Captain Gerard Doig speaking, Australian Airline Security Commission. As you are aware, we are treating your offence with the greatest seriousness, and I hope you know that this is a crime that could land you in the slammer for a considerable period in terms of time.'

I croaked yet another ineffectual apology as the commissioner resumed.

'I am calling you from my own home in Sutherland so our conversation is off, in terms of the record. There is no scintilla in my mind that you could go for the jump on this one, but I doubt that someone in your position would appreciate a vertical suntan. There is another course of action, which I would suggest to you, sir, as a way out of the deep shit in which you find yourself.'

By now I was listening attentively.

'My good lady wife, Corinne, happens to be a big fan of Dame Enid, which is, I believe, one of your skits. God help her, she actually *loves* Dame Enid. We would be prepared . . . I would be prepared . . . to overlook this incident if Dame Enid could have a talk to my wife on the phone. It would have to be a talk of no less than thirty minutes' duration, Mr Humphrey, and believe you me, sir, it would have to be funny – *very, very funny*!'

So it was that for something like forty minutes, with the receiver clamped to my ear and sweat pouring from my brow, I gave the most difficult performance of my life. I could barely hear so much as a titter from Corinne Doig on the other end of the line, but my freedom depended on it and I improvised wildly and not without that inspiration born of fear and adrenaline. I was just beginning to falter, my mind blank, my throat dry and Edna's voice a husky baritone, when a stern voice interrupted me.

'Gerry Doig here. You can knock it off now. She's laughin' – not much, but she's laughin'. We will overlook that aircraft incident at the present period of time, but we'll be watching you from now on, Brian. You're a very lucky bastard.'

Sweetcorn and Solyptol

~

It has long been an axiom of mine that
the little things are infinitely the most important

Sherlock Holmes

In spite of being appallingly spoilt, I soon became dissatisfied with my parents. Indeed the dissatisfaction was in later years reciprocal and my mother was fond of saying in my presence to whomsoever cared to listen, although not without a hint of pride, 'Eric and I don't know where Barry comes from.' In tortured adolescence I would sometimes wait outside our house for hours hoping that my real parents might one day turn up and rescue me.

At Camberwell Grammar I had befriended a boy called Rodney Tipping, whose mother and father were considerably more interesting than my own. He was a tall, reserved lad with an air of aloofness and the habit of flicking back a blond forelock, a schoolboy mannerism that I have noticed some men retain into bald old age. Rodney's clothes always seemed better than everyone else's and I later learnt that they had been specially tailored for him, an unheard-of luxury in a preparatory school during wartime, and possibly unique in Australia.

Rodney's home was not far from the school and it seemed to me then like a mansion. Driving past it recently I was surprised by its rather modest proportions. It was a late-thirties two-storey brick house in a watered-down modernistic style, but it had two unusual and luxurious features: a high front fence and a tennis court at the back. All the houses my father built had low fences and my mother viewed with suspicion anyone with an unnecessarily lofty parapet.

'*They* must have something to hide,' she opined.

Mr Tipping made Krunchies, a breakfast cereal that for some time rivalled Kellogg's products in popularity. Many of us favoured Krunchies because each packet contained a small card depicting a military vehicle, which we all avidly collected. It must have been a profitable business for Rodney seemed to have an endless stream of enviable possessions: a microscope, a small hand printing press, golf clubs, and a complete set of Windsor and Newton's student-quality oil paints with brushes, canvases and easel. I was most covetous of these last, and besought my father for the same. It was only a matter of time before my desire was gratified, as usual, and Rodney and I would set out by tram on weekends with our artist's equipment to the gorse-covered hills of North Balwyn, soon to be subdivided and turned into what was then called, inexplicably, a 'dress-circle suburb'. We would alight at the terminus, clamber through a fence, cross a couple of paddocks, now mercilessly developed, and daub our impressions of the distant Dandenong Ranges.

After a Saturday at the easel, we would take the tram back to Rodney's place, stopping off at a milk bar in Whitehorse Road for a crème de menthe sundae. It was the only ice-cream parlour in Melbourne that served this exotic concoction and we could sit at the bar while the girl behind the counter drizzled the emerald, peppermint-flavoured imitation liqueur over two scoops of Swallow's Ice Cream, into which she would finally jab an isosceles McNiven's wafer.

Rodney's mother and father possessed virtues with which my parents' could only be unfavourably compared. For instance, Mr Tipping drove an English car – I think an Alvis – whereas my father preferred flashier American models. He also boasted a library, and in their large drawing room were at least four shelves filled with books. I can remember titles such as *Van Loon's Lives*, Lord Wavell's anthology *Other Men's Flowers*, an illustrated edition of *The White Cliffs of Dover*, *The Silver Jubilee Book*, Elbert Hubbard's *Scrapbook*, a row of chubby brown *New World* encyclopaedias, probably bought – as we bought ours – from a door-to-door salesman, and that celebrated soporific of the period, which I once attempted to read, *Letters of an Indian Judge to an English Gentlewoman*. These volumes, which spoke to my snobbish young self of Mr Tipping's profound erudition, all bore on their inside pastedown a bookplate showing a field of waving corn in a rather English landscape, in the style of an Ethelbert White wood engraving. Beneath this vignette were the words:

Harold Braithwaite Tipping
His Book

I imagine that Mr Tipping – the first bibliophile in my acquaintance – must have chosen the cornfield in homage to the cereal from which he derived his Krunchies fortune.

Rodney's father had an aloof manner, like his son's, and it was impossible to imagine him doing the things my father did: making breakfast, for example – a task my father had assumed when we were still quite small. Every morning, while Mr Tipping was no doubt perusing *The Age* or *The Argus* over his poached eggs, my father was busy making our breakfasts, squeezing oranges in a nimbus of burnt toast and whistling a chirpy reveille:

Come to the cookhouse door, boys.
Come to the cookhouse door!

We would hear this maddening refrain as he climbed the stairs to my mother's bedroom with her tray. It was the signal for her to sit up in bed, don her pink feather-and-fan-stitched bedjacket and prepare to accept the matinal offering. When it was placed before her, as it was almost every morning for at least twenty-five years, she would look up at my father with a little cry of surprise, as though breakfast in bed was an undreamt of luxury arriving, as she always insisted, just as she was about to get up and prepare it herself!

One Christmas, a holiday when most schoolboys sought small part-time jobs to earn pocket money, Mr Tipping offered his son and me a lucrative chore at the Krunchies factory in the industrial inner suburb of Richmond. It was just a Saturday job and an absurdly easy one. We were driven to the factory and given brooms as tall as ourselves with which we swept enormous drifts of Krunchies – like autumn leaves – into huge mounds on the factory floor. These loose russet flakes, which had somehow not found their way into packets, were then stuffed into hessian sacks and bundled off to an unknown destination. Even then, long before recycling had a name, I suspected that from another part of the factory our day's winnowing, seasoned with a little zesty dust and a few rodent pellets, might yet emerge packaged for the breakfast tables of Melbourne. After all, the gaudy packet told us that Krunchies, thanks to their sealed inner envelope of waxed paper, were 'factory fresh'. It was the age of honest advertising.

Although I often saw Mr Tipping – a preoccupied businessman jumping in and out of his car or hurrying upstairs – I rarely glimpsed his wife. Joy Tipping seemed to spend most of her time in her bedroom and not their large kitchen; indeed the entire home was run by Mrs Neatfoot, the blue-aproned, white-haired housekeeper. She once made Rodney and me some lunch and for the first time in my life I tasted an exotic combination that I supposed was the everyday fare of the rich: sweetcorn on toast. Mrs Neatfoot had opened the tin herself. It was a product never to be found on my mother's prosaic shopping lists.

By the age of ten I had tasted virtually every cake in Mrs Beeton's lexicon, but like most other Australians of my generation I was far less sophisticated in other culinary areas. I was practically a gastronomic virgin. We subsisted on chops, mashed potatoes, rock-hard peas, white bread and cake. My mother made

excellent cakes and steamed puddings but she fell down badly in
the preparation of vegetables, so that I prayed the time would
come when I would never have to eat another watery parsnip or
impenetrable Brussels sprout. Sunday lunch, or 'dinner' as the
midday meal was called, was almost always roast lamb with
mint sauce, for which I picked the mint while my father, straight
home from church and already preoccupied with a tense *sotto
voce* argument with my mother, prepared the gravy by merely
augmenting the dripping from the roast with a spoonful of
Gravox and a brown, viscid splash of Parisian Essence. On
Sunday evenings it was often 'silverside' and salad, mashed
potatoes and tinned peaches and custard.

Despite our severely circumscribed, even bowdlerised
diets, we all grew up to be healthy young Australians with terrible teeth. Of course, we were plied with tonics. A big spoonful
of Hypol Cod Liver Oil was pushed daily between clenched lips,
and Saunders Malt Extract was regularly administered along
with Syrup of Figs or Waterbury's Compound – two disgusting
laxatives – and a soothing beaker of Akta-Vite at bedtime. We
drank enormous amounts of pasteurised milk, in the vague hope
of reducing our risk of contracting that scourge of childhood,
infantile paralysis, as well as tuberculosis. Grazed knees were
anointed with Mercurochrome and faces washed with Faulding's
Solyptol Soap, which, so the small print on its black and green
wrapper informed us, had won a gold medal in the Franco-
British Exhibition of 1908.

In Mr and Mrs Tipping's kitchen there was a panel high on
the wall next to the larder with numbers on it and Mrs Neatfoot

would often glance nervously in its direction. Once, an electric bell shrilled, a number lit up on the panel and the housekeeper shot out the door and up the back stairs. It was a summons from Mrs Tipping. White-faced, Mrs Neatfoot returned and we were neglected as she whipped up a tinned-asparagus sandwich and a cup of tea for her demanding employer.

Albeit, Rodney's mother did emerge at last for the Tippings' great Musical Evening, which was by far the most important social event I had ever attended. There was, to begin with, a printed invitation announcing this *soirée musicale* and the refreshments that would accompany it. Here at last was a chance to wear my new suit from Ball & Welch, its wide lapels a homage to Dick Powell and Ronald Colman and the sartorial modes of the previous decade.

Arriving on the appointed Saturday evening, my hair gummed to my scalp with Potter and Moore's brilliantine, I noticed with pride that I was the only school friend of Rodney's invited to this highbrow adult event. There were a lot of women in furs, smelling of something rich and strange – the perfumery equivalent of sweetcorn on toast – and some of the men smoked cigars as I had only seen Winston Churchill smoke them on the newsreels and calendars. About thirty chairs had been arranged in rows in the library, there were large vases of flesh-pink gladioli and at the far end of the room, in the curved bay window against the beige 'vale of tears' or festoon blinds, a string quartet was tuning up. Mrs Tipping in a long, red dress seated the guests, with Rodney and me at the back.

A waiter with bad BO, in a black tuxedo over – I noticed –

a fawn cardigan, dispensed strange brown drinks with orange and cucumber slices floating in them, which, over half a century later, I can identify as Pimms Number One Cup. This beverage must have been the apogee of sophistication in that far-off place and time, and although it was a surprising choice for an evening cocktail, I now reflect, it was greedily quaffed by the suburban music lovers. Mr Tipping no doubt had harder stuff aside for those who might deem Pimms an inadequate stimulant.

Soon the lights were dimmed, and the quartet began its recital with an arrangement of themes from Sigmund Romberg's operetta *The White Horse Inn*. The small audience listened with rapt attention to the familiar melodies and politely applauded. Next came 'The Blue Danube' and the guests almost purred with pleasure. Many of them may have dreaded this ominous evening of culture, but here was serious music they could almost sing along with. I saw the Tippings exchange a look and a nod. The night was a success.

The music assumed a more solemn note with an abridged version of the *Warsaw Concerto*, but by then everyone was beginning to feel so relaxed and unintimidated by the classical repertoire that whispered conversations began, rising in pitch and volume until the string quartet was barely audible.

Mrs Neatfoot had produced a spectacular buffet, with a number of hot delicacies including her signature dish, creamed sweetcorn, but there was also a tureen of Salmon Mornay, Asparagus Rolls, beetroot-stained salads, and prettily iced 'continental cakes' that you could only buy at the Myer Emporium. In the hubbub of eating and chatting, the poor musicians were soon totally forgotten. But for a brief time they had commanded the undivided attention of the Tippings' friends and had reassured them of their just entitlement to the Finer Things in Life.

Although Mr and Mrs Tipping had barely spoken more than a few words to me in our entire acquaintance, I was beginning to feel that I loved them. I sought every opportunity to visit their splendid house, and Rodney and I used his printing press to design and print bookplates for ourselves. Some of these I have rediscovered inside the covers of once-precious volumes such as *The Story of Living Things and Their Evolution* and *The English Countryside in Pictures*. In imitation of Harold Braithwaite Tipping's ex-libris – and with the addition of my never-used prosaic first name – my book label, in red ink within a decorative border and on pale blue paper, read:

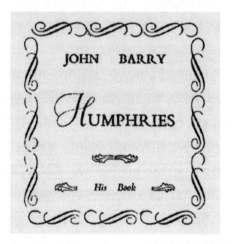

I so admired, hero-worshipped and even adored this aloof, privileged and possibly rather stupid schoolboy, Rodney, that once, as we ate our lunchtime sandwiches (mine, walnut and date; his, creamed sweetcorn) beneath the blooming wisteria arbour in the school garden, intoxicated by the scent of those soft blue chandeliers of blossom overhead, I lurched across and gave him a peck on the cheek. He made no response other than to raise his nose at a slightly haughtier angle in regal acknowledgement of what was after all his due.

One May holiday my family went for a week to the Dandenong Ranges to stay in the Grays' log cabin. My parents asked if I would like to invite a friend to stay, and I chose Rodney.

Herb and Doris Gray were our neighbours across the road and Mrs Gray frequently appeared at our kitchen door with a request for anything from half a cup of sugar to a couple of junket tablets. This borrowing and lending of comestibles amongst suburban neighbours was usually an excuse for a cup of tea and a gossip and it was one of the few activities in which I recall my mother taking a real pleasure, although she would affect dismay and sigh deeply whenever an importunate woman in an apron and bearing a cup or some other culinary receptacle appeared on the back lawn.

Doris Gray always announced her propinquity with a little cry of 'Yoo-hoo!' Naturally she was not the only yoo-hooer in Melbourne, or even Australia. Women were yoo-hooing each other all over the island continent, although I doubt the salutation now exists, having been replaced by the mobile phone.

Doris Gray, having borrowed or not a cup of self-raising flour or a teaspoon of cream of tartar, never left without a cheery 'Bye-bye.' It was the bookend to her earlier 'Yoo-hoo!'

Not as modern a farewell as it would seem to be, 'bye-bye' has been around since the mid-nineteenth century at least; in *Vanity Fair* people are constantly bye-byeing each other.

In later years, when Mrs Gray waved, her 'bye-byes' wobbled. In the vernacular of the Australian housewife, 'bye-byes' are those tender jowls of flesh beneath the triceps of mature women, which quiver in the valedictory gesture.

The Grays' weekend house was at Ferny Creek, an hour's drive from Melbourne, and not far from the bellbird-haunted, boronia-scented, platypus-infested Sherbrooke Forest. When our family did not go for a Sunday 'spin' in the family car to one of the beaches on Port Phillip Bay we sometimes drove up into the Dandenongs, the mountain range that could be seen on the horizon from my parents' upstairs bedroom. As we motored there through farms and open country that has now become a uniform and dispiriting suburban sprawl, those wonderful hills rose slowly before us: a lavender parapet, with here and there a distant roof glint and a blue trickle of woodsmoke – an effect so deftly captured by Arthur Streeton in his painted vistas. I always peered over my father's shoulder through the windscreen, trying to catch the exact moment when those magical hills lost the glamour of distance and became merely a prosaic gum-tree green.

On the steep ascent, around hairpin bends to Ferny Creek and Sassafras (the leaves that whisper in that name!), the boscage changed to tall tree ferns and lofty mountain ash and messmate, dripping with tattered stalactites of sloughed bark. In the back seat I would turn the Bakelite handle and wind down the window to inhale the cold fungal smell of the forest, hoping for a glimpse of a startled lyrebird.

Along the way there were signposts to hamlets with evocative names: Ferntree Gully, Belgrave, Olinda, Kallista and Kalorama, all with their picturesque Devonshire tearooms in the Tudor style, named Devon Dell, Dew Drop Inn or Clovelly. They were cheaply built of whitewashed fibro in the thirties, with painted-on black half-timbering and cottagy leadlight windows. The trim was always cherry red, that ubiquitous colour of the period. Often these cosy teashops wore a picturesque wig of morning glory, or Boston ivy that in May turned to deepest crimson.

The Grays' mountain cabin had been built before the war of rough logs and 'crazy' stonework to give it a rustic look, and it stood at the end of a long driveway lined with chestnuts, which, when we borrowed the house for that distant autumn holiday, were in damp but still golden leaf. There was an exiguous garden with a few random walls of porous Sunbury rock studded with that unlovely yet once-fashionable succulent, pigface.

All went well on the holiday for a couple of days until there was some childish dispute and Rodney became petulant, then tearful. The next minute, it seemed, he was bundled into my father's car and sent home, five days before our holiday was due to end.

'The poor boy was homesick,' said my mother as the car drove off in the rain down the chestnut avenue, under the broad, sallow leaves.

Rodney did not wave. I just caught a glimpse of his huffy profile in the back seat, with my father the chauffeur. I went back indoors and looked around the rather primitive interior of the Grays' shack, with its cobwebs on the cornice, smoking chimney and freezing cold bedrooms. Then I thought of the Tippings' mansion and its electric fires, glowing lamps, quilts and rugs. I had let down the side.

It was not long after this that Rodney was removed from Camberwell Grammar and sent to a remote and illustrious boarding school. Our flagging friendship petered out of its own accord. However, I visited the Tippings' enviable domain one last time. Rodney and I were to have a tennis lesson from a local coach called Lobby Wilson, who had once been quite a star. He had an extremely red face – probably from long exposure to the sun – and I assumed that he was called Lobby because of his resemblance to a lobster, entirely missing the tennis reference. Mr Tipping was home that afternoon, and more than usually preoccupied. Mrs Tipping was nowhere to be seen.

We were both running late for our lesson and Rodney's father told us to jump into the car and he would run us down to the Deepdene tennis courts, where Lobby was the pro. We were just getting into the luxurious, leather-scented Alvis when a strange thing happened. A voice, high-pitched and eldritch, came to us out of the foliage above the driveway. Both Rodney and his father froze. I wound down my window and looked up. The beautiful Mrs Joy Tipping was leaning out of an upper window, her face a contorted mask of malice.

'Harold!' she screeched. 'Come back, Harold, or *I'll scratch your eyes out!*' She was flailing her arms, her fingers like the claws of a harpy.

We drove to the tennis courts in silence and the incident, which still remains vividly with me in all its terrible detail, was never mentioned.

Rodney Tipping, though this is not his real name, is now retired. He rose to spectacular heights in the Australian branch of an international firm of accountants, became a stalwart of the National Trust, collects Georgian silver and is regarded by his inevitably limited range of acquaintances as a notorious bore. His wife reputedly makes embarrassing scenes in public.

I HAD begun to notice how few friends my mother, Louisa, seemed to have. Her closest relationships were with her sisters, Violet, Elsie, Ella and Dorothy (Aunty Billie). Outside this tight family circle there were the other couples at the tennis club, for whose benefit my mother donned her white pleated tennis skirt, white blouse, green sun visor and tennis shoes every Saturday afternoon. Apart from occasional card evenings at home, this was the only social event that seemed to give her pleasure. She remained, however, on good terms with Ada Scott, who lived in the neighbouring suburb of Canterbury, and Jessie Haggert, an old school friend.

Jessie was an unlikely intimate since she was what my mother might otherwise have described as 'countrified' or even 'ordinary'. She looked wildly Caledonian, with unruly reddish hair, snaggled teeth and freckles, spoke loudly and was roughly affectionate with children. Some accident in infancy had caused her to walk with a severe limp, but she came, according to my mother, from 'a very nice family'. It was darkly hinted that Jessie may have married beneath her but, in spite of this, we often made excursions to see her and her aged parents in the seaside town of Frankston. I now believe that my mother kept up with the Haggerts because they had been friends of her parents in the days before her marriage and they were a link to her youth.

Although I was very young, I felt my mother's joy as she saw her friend hobbling down the garden path to greet us, drying a freckled paw on her faded floral apron and brushing a strand of hair out of her eyes with a soapy wrist. There would be warm cakes in the offing and sandwiches freshly cut by Jessie. Before eating, and after a brief Presbyterian grace, Barbara and I and our young brothers, Christopher and Michael, would glance at our mother, who would give us an imperceptible nod. It was the all-clear signal; it meant that in spite of some indications to the contrary, Jessie's food could be consumed with safety. Later in the car my mother might say, 'Some people may not have much of the wherewithal, Barry, but it costs nothing to be spotless.'

In many ways my mother's closest association was with the women who worked for her. When Michael was born, my mother engaged a sixteen-year-old girl from the nearby Salvation Army orphanage as a nanny. Her name was Valmai Grubb and she was a very sweet girl with mottled skin, big green eyes and a lot of curly brown hair, who quickly became devoted to my little brother. She may have been a foster child, not an orphan, because when Barbara and I eagerly asked our mother for details, she spoke sadly of a *very ordinary family*

Sunny Sam

Rosebud with Barry and Barbara

The ice-cream vendor and his clientele

Barbara, Michael, Barry and Christopher

Caricature of Eric Humphries
by the author, 1945

Louisa Humphries in the garden,
author's drawing, 1949

Expressionist self-portrait, 1950

The Corner Shop, Fitzroy, etching by John Shirlow, 1919

Mrs Ellis Bird

By sea to Sydney: Louisa and Barry Humphries on deck, 1950

The artist explaining a 'shoescape' to a group of admirers, 1952

Dr Aaron Azimuth

BRUNO BENINI

The young actor, 1955

The author making up for his first English role, in *Sweeney Todd*
at the Lyric Theatre, Hammersmith, 1959

An inauspicious advertisement, Sydney, 1956

Phillip Street Theatre players on stage, including Brenda (seated left),
B.H. (third left), Max Oldaker (fifth left) and Gordon Chater (second right)

A 1956 Sydney backstage party, with author lurking (right)

The Bunyip, Melbourne, 1958

Mrs Edna Everage apostrophising her acolytes, including Patricia Kennedy (front left), Bambi Shmith (second front) and Mary Hardy (back right), 1958

The author as Fagin in *Oliver!*, Piccadilly Theatre, London, 1967

indeed, who lived, I was thrilled to learn, somewhere in the 'slums'. Fortunately, although rejected by her parents, Valmai had been cared for by the Salvos, who were the only religious organisation outside the Anglican Church for whom my mother had the slightest respect. 'Say what you like about the Salvation Army,' she often declared on Sunday mornings, searching in her purse for 10 shillings – a large sum then – to give to the uniformed captain when he came to the front door to collect money for his brass band, 'they do wonderful work.'

Sometimes we saw Valmai's only sister, Wilma, when she called for her on her days off. My mother was less than enchanted by Wilma, who wore strong scent and too much make-up. Compared with our sweet, shy Valmai, the sister was, in my mother's opinion, 'a totally different kettle of fish'. *Our* fish, it was hoped, was not 'tarred with the same brush'.

Valmai's adoration of my brother was fervently returned, so that it must have been devastating for the child when, after two years, Valmai left. She had asked if she might spend more time with Wilma, whom my mother regarded as a bad influence, and when this permission was not granted she gave her notice. My mother was furious at this abrupt defection, paid her and told her to leave immediately. She also forbade my father to drive the poor girl to the railway station, so in misery we watched Valmai with her small, battered Globite suitcase walk down the driveway, weeping and alone. We never saw her again, although I once glimpsed her snapshot, as will be told later.

This incident made me think of my own early bereavement when Edna, my nanny, left suddenly and, it seemed to me, without warning. It may have been to matrimony that this beloved friend of my infancy fled, and not to the stews of St Kilda or Fitzroy, but for years thereafter I prayed she might some day return and take me in her arms.

My mother found it hard to find 'reliable' help for the house. In desperation she once even considered hiring an English housekeeper. 'Everyone says the English are natural servants,' she said, diplomatically attributing to hearsay an opinion that might have hurt my father's feelings had she claimed the observation as her own. My paternal grandfather, John, was English after all – a Lancashire man who had emigrated to Australia in the eighteen-eighties – as was our vicar, Canon Hopkinson. They were, now I think of it, the only English people we knew.

With few exceptions, my mother got on exceedingly well with the women who helped her in the home. These elderly and often indolent satellites all laughed at her jokes and in later years, when arthritis confined her to a cushioned throne in the sunroom, made her laugh as well. It was with these cleaning ladies, cooks and hairdressers that she seemed to have her most intimate relationships.

When I recently asked my sister for the details of a long-ago transaction of my father's, she replied, 'Fergie would have known all about that. Pity she's dead.' Fergie was Mrs Ferguson, my mother's most trusted housekeeper and one of the few who really worked: buffing the arms of chairs and the tops of tables until the varnish disappeared, and dusting and polishing the rarely visited rooms. Fergie, with her grey, bobbed hair and faded floral apron, was my father's confidante as well and a reliable and diplomatic gauge of my mother's moods.

For years our only housekeeper had been Mrs Shores – or Shores as we always called her – whose husband worked in the furniture removal business and was given to habits of intemperance. According to my mother, she had 'a good heart', which was my mother's way of saying that she was totally incompetent at her job. Shores talked nonstop, frequently when my mother was out of the room. It was as if her voice were some strident reed instrument that she played in ceaseless obbligato to the sonorous accompaniment of washing machine and vacuum cleaner. When my mother found Fergie, a real worker, she had not the heart to dismiss Shores so both women formed a garrulous duet, to my mother's deep amusement.

With these women my mother's sense of humour received its daily exercise, and she was either laughing with them as they busied themselves around her – literally dancing in attendance – or *at* them when they retired.

It intrigued me to learn that my mother had had a brief, very brief, career as a comic performer in amateur theatricals and her sisters recalled that she had been particularly funny in a show surprisingly sponsored by the Holy Trinity Church, Thornbury, in which she appeared with a banjo as a blacked-up minstrel. In this unlikely guise she sang a 'flapper' song from the jazz age of rouged knees:

Roll down your stockings
Roll 'em, girls, roll 'em!

I am often asked how I came upon the character of Dame Edna Everage. This usually happens at dinner parties when a perfectly nice woman on my left or right attempts to initiate a conversation. A terrible weariness descends on me at these moments and I sometimes wish I could just discreetly pass them a booklet or a video-cassette explaining it all. Instead I usually manage to tell Edna's story briefly, or at length, depending on the attractiveness of my interlocutor. Although I could successfully place bets on who is going to ask me this question, I am always astonished and grateful that a character invented for a university revue nearly half a century ago still intrigues people today.

My poor mother has often been press-ganged into the role of Edna's prototype. This theory, encouraged by the speculations of critics and biographers, is hugely attractive to journalists and academic hacks, who have constructed *and deconstructed* impenetrable theses on the subject. Naturally the character has borrowed more than a little of my mother's astringency of phrase, but Edna's garrulity derives from Shores, who would follow us from room to room maintaining a shrill and steady stream of inconsequential verbiage. Aunts, neighbours and radio programmes for housewives also nourished this theatrical invention. But I will only be accused of protesting too much. Since Edna has become a subject of exegesis, writers now and in the future who persist in being pompously analytical will always prefer to see Edna Everage not so much as an act of comedy as an act of revenge. There is no more terrible fate for a comedian than to be taken seriously.

My mother's mentor, three doors down Christowel Street, was Mrs Kendall. Mrs Kendall had taken my mother under her wing after my father had sold the Kendalls their mock-Tudor, tapestry-brick home. It was clear to me from an early age that my mother confided all her problems as a young wife and mother to Mrs Kendall. It was to Mrs Kendall that she had run one day with me in her arms, having found me sitting cheerfully in a bath full of blood. My mother had only been out of the bathroom for a minute to answer the telephone, and in that time I must have slipped and knocked my chin on the edge of the tub. The doctor whom Mrs Kendall summoned stitched me up and told my mother that the scar might only give me a little trouble when I shaved. My mother often said how amazed she had been to imagine the far-off day when her beloved two-year-old son might actually be shaving! None of her young children bathed alone after that.

Mrs Kendall advised my mother on all the obscure rituals of suburban respectability. There were some products one bought, and some that nice people never had in their larders. Not once do I recall seeing my mother carrying a shopping basket or returning with parcels from a day in the city. Everything was delivered: fruit and groceries by way of the designated tradesman's entrance at the side of the house; clothing and other purchases from the big stores in Melbourne by van to the front door, presented by uniformed drivers. Often my mother made a selection of dresses or blouses at Myer's or Buckley & Nunn or Ball & Welch, and these were sent to our house on approval so she could try them on and choose one, or even none, before the rejected garments were collected and an invoice prepared.

My mother always insisted that I never leave for school without shining my shoes with Nugget on the kitchen doorstep. Nugget came in tins just like Kiwi shoe polish, but it was obscurely deemed 'nicer'. Who knows where such absurd class distinctions in bootblack originated? In their tins both products looked and smelt identical, but Kiwi was owned by Melbourne's Ramsay family. Perhaps, one day long ago, Mrs Ramsay had committed some notorious solecism at the Melbourne Cup, or was seen in town at Georges department store without gloves. It would have been enough to make any respectable family switch to Nugget.

Tinned food, with the exception of staples such as Rosella tomato soup and AJC peaches in syrup, was generally considered by my mother's class to be rather common. However, rules about what was and what was not socially acceptable became more relaxed during the war. As a general principle, when people called they must never be given 'bought' food. Cakes should be plentiful and freshly baked at home. (Why else would Jessie have been drying her hands as she ran down the agapanthus-lined path to greet us?) There should be evidence, if someone trespassed in the kitchen, that the cakes had just been made: preferably a warm oven, still-wet icing, or gooey utensils in the sink. A trace of flour on the hostess's hands was not undesirable. This was why the little homemade-cake shops of my childhood flourished, for here, from nice clean ladies like the Misses Longmire, one could buy a sponge with passionfruit icing or butterfly cakes, or even pies and pasties, and serve them up to visitors as 'homemade' without fear of successful contradiction. Jams and jellies and preserved fruit were all made at home, and if one were forced to buy them, then they should be in glass jars like Clegg and Kemp's Apricot Jam rather than large tins like IXL's Plum Jam.

I recall once leaving Ada Scott's home with my mother after a rather lavish morning tea, clearly laid on to impress her.

'That was good,' I said, or some similar phrase of approbation.

My mother smiled. 'Bought,' was all she said.

Everything in the way of food came either from Camberwell Junction or the 'little shops' in Camberwell Road. The little shops were run by little men too.

'Barry, please get out your bike and run down to my little butcher and pick up some nice loin or chump chops, and while you're there, pop into my little chemist for some Vick's for your sister's chest.' Servants and tradespeople were always designated by this diminutive epithet.

There was a traditional covered market at the Junction, where my father occasionally took me when he wanted to buy oysters. The big fish shop had water undulating down the window, as did most fish shops of this period, to give an aqueous illusion of freshness. The marble slabs were covered with gleaming schnapper and flathead garnished with huge bouquets of parsley. The atmosphere here was far more exciting than that of the sedate little shops. It was all noise and bustle at the market, with the strong fishy smells and the sharp flowery odours from buckets of daffodils and carnations, poppies, glads and arum lilies outside the florist's booth. There was a bootmaker too, and a famous pet shop where urchins peered through the glass at the puppies and budgies.

Here at the market one even sometimes heard Greek spoken at the fishmonger's, and Italian at the greengrocer's, whose
shop seemed to be run by two boys not much older than I – the
Della brothers. Their mother, a very fat Calabrian, stood behind
the till. There was no sign of Mr Della Bosca – to give him his
full family name – for the poor fellow, who had left Italy for
Australia long before the rise of Mussolini, was languishing in
an internment camp in some remote part of the state for the
duration of the war.

But markets were for the Poor. 'Different' people went
there, and my mother was unhappy when she learnt of our visits. I overheard our neighbour Mrs Whittle say to her once, 'I
couldn't help seeing Mrs Long going into the market the other
day! She had no *need* to be there!'

There was a similar snobbery in the attitude prevalent
amongst my mother's circle towards married women obliged to
take employment to help support their families. Once I went
to play with a friend and mentioned to my parents afterwards
that his mother was not at home.

'I've heard she *works*,' my mother said. 'Can't you find
some nicer friends, Barry?'

AT THE AGE of eleven I was allowed to ride my bicycle to
Camberwell Grammar, nearly two miles away. It was a splendid
vehicle that had been especially made for me, and the name I had
chosen for my bike, Blue Streak, was hand-painted on the cross-
bar by an old-fashioned sign-writer. I was always late for school

when I went by bicycle, not tram. But apart from knuckles ravaged by winter chilblains, I enjoyed everything about peddling blithely along those suburban streets, especially in autumn under the luteous leaves of the plane trees. Up Prospect Hill Road I would pant, right into Stanhope Grove, across Canterbury Road, looking both ways, and at length up the last steep hill of Rubens Grove to Camberwell Grammar, its playground deserted and its building silent and ghost-like, with Morning Assembly already in progress. There is no silence quite like the silence that greets the tardy pupil.

After some time a back-pedal brake was fitted to my bicycle, and the next Sunday afternoon I decided to test it out by riding down our driveway. My mother stood at the front gate farewelling some friends or relations who had come for afternoon tea, and as I sped down the cement incline towards them I panicked, for having grown used to handbrakes I found myself unable to slow down with the new and untried device. I suppose I could have swerved onto the lawn, but instead I careered towards the group standing by the gate, yelling that I couldn't stop. Ahead lay a rather busy street and the steep hill descending Marlborough Avenue. It was then that my mother, realising my plight, stepped forward into the driveway. I can still see her standing there directly in my path, arms raised in unintelligible semaphore so that she resembled the letter X: St Andrew without the cross. A second later her body, never strong, took the full impact of the bicycle and we were both hurled to the ground as the bike spun away and smashed into the gatepost.

I never rode Blue Streak after that and the injury to my

mother's leg never really healed. From time to time in after years she quietly reminded me of what might have happened had my bicycle sped out of control into the traffic. It was as if she were trying to tell me something else – something more complicated and more personal.

Nice Nights Out

~

I think the whole periodical press takes
a vastly disproportionate view of the
importance of Mountebanks and reviewers

HENRY JAMES

ONCE when we were staying at our Mornington beach house, we went, at my insistence, into the small township for a show. There had been intriguing posters for it beside Boyle & Woiwod's grocery and outside the post office and the shire hall. The poster was distinctly old-fashioned and brightly coloured, and it advertised an attraction simply called 'THE INCOMPARABLE SLOGGETTS'. A man in evening clothes was seen to have successfully decapitated a vivacious young woman in a green spangled dress, and the embellishment of snakes and skulls more than hinted at the macabre. The lithographed billboard promised song, comedy and, above all, magic. The event was for one night only, and with great excitement we all attended.

When the lights abruptly went out – nothing dimmed in the Mornington shire hall – Mr Sloggett appeared, wearing a mildewed tailcoat, and in the wobbly spotlight, before a threadbare red curtain and in an old-fashioned theatrical voice, he extolled the gifts of his wife and daughter and promised his audience a gallimaufry of marvels. It was indeed a touring family show of only three persons. The Sloggetts were not so much on a planned theatrical tour as, like Dickens's Crummles, 'in the course of a wandering speculation'. They must have been wandering for years before we witnessed them, and with the same rudimentary sets and props, although the 'wife' and the 'daughter' may have been subject to replacement.

Even to a child like me there was something risibly seedy about the whole performance. More than once juggled balls fell where they were not intended and were gleefully retrieved by the audience. Mrs Sloggett, if it were indeed she, was no longer young; nor could she sing like Gracie Fields. And the theatrical tradition to which they were all sadly vestigial – the vaudeville magic show – was on its last gasp and alien to the slick American entertainments we enjoyed at the Pictures. There were, however, gasps of admiration when Mr Sloggett, who must have been at least seventy years of age, performed his *pièce de résistance* of juggling eggs with his mouth.

Throughout the venerable tricks, the hoary jokes and the incomprehensible patter, the small audience of Australian holiday-makers laughed and clapped with good-humoured gusto. With growing alarm I realised that they were laughing not at the success of the performers, but at their failure. The show's triumph was that it was so bad. But the Sloggetts slogged it out to the end, with a poignant bravado. Even as they stood at the curtain call in their faded and heavily mended finery, holding hands and bowing extravagantly, the members of the audience were rising, turning their backs and hurrying out to their cars.

We were barely in the car before my mother, with a small smile of satisfaction at life's predictability, made her customary observation after witnessing any superannuated spectacle: 'Isn't it pathetic at his age?'

IN SPITE OF their later resistance to my chosen profession, it was my mother and father who introduced me to what used to be called, in the old days of Melbourne, 'flesh and blood theatre' – although at my parents' preferred entertainments there was little flesh visible and no blood whatsoever. The theatre they liked was strictly for special occasions. It was a Nice Night Out, of furs and perfume, Hillier's chocolates and souvenir programmes.

Thus, with my parents, I saw all the big musical comedies, although rarely a straight play. When the Comedy Theatre staged Eugene O'Neill's *Mourning Becomes Electra*, a title nobody could explain to me, especially those who had attended the performance, I overheard my mother on the phone to one of her sisters wondering why they had put a thing like that in the Comedy. A 'dirge' my mother called it. *Annie Get Your Gun, Oklahoma!* and *South Pacific* were a different matter, and we all came out singing the songs, unlike today when show tunes are so unmemorable that we leave the theatre trying to cheer ourselves up by remembering songs from *other shows*.

The big theatrical event of my youth was the arrival in

town of Laurence Olivier and Vivien Leigh in 1948. This glamorous husband and wife team had received massive advance publicity: intimate photographs of the couple at home affectionately reading scripts together, eating candlelit meals and posing in their rose garden like a sophisticated Darby and Joan had appeared in *Pix*, *The Australasian Post* and *The Australian Women's Weekly*. By the time they had opened in Melbourne in three plays, *Richard III*, *The School for Scandal* and Thornton Wilder's *The Skin of Our Teeth*, the shows were sold out. All Melbourne was talking about 'Sir Oliver Leigh', as the Mayor of Sydney had so deftly elided the names of the actor and his wife, as if into a single, Janus-like being. In those days we had a touching, if fawning reverence for distinguished English visitors, although pity help them if they let us down. When the young Sovereign paid us a visit in 1954, the *Women's Weekly*, that *vade mecum* of Australian culture, ran a popular competition: 'What would you say to the Queen?'

The arrival of Anthony Eden on a brief diplomatic visit at the end of the forties received ridiculously prominent coverage for he personified, in Australian eyes, the suave English gentleman and he was renowned as one of England's 'best-dressed men'. 'But not so!' trumpeted the Melbourne *Argus*, showing a front-page photograph of Eden shaking hands with our own knight-in-waiting Robert Menzies. A circle had been described around the cuff of Anthony Eden's jacket and arrows pointed to – *a missing button*! The press heaped scorn and derision on this hapless dandy who dared to greet our Prime Minister in such a state of disrepair. How good a diplomat was this bastard, anyway? Not up to much most agreed and, as it happened, with prescience.

But wasn't it about time we Australians stopped sucking up to the Brits in sartorial matters when this was the pathetic example they set? There was such a storm in a thimble over Eden's gaffe that he was forced to attend a small press conference to explain why he had come to Australia in rags. In the presence of journalists and photographers, Eden deftly *unbuttoned* the cuffs of his suit – a facility even the best Australian tailors failed to provide – and pointed out that one of his cuff buttons had merely been unfastened. It was definitely one up for England, and yet another deflating reminder to Australians that we were just a bunch of ignorant, ill-dressed hicks.

But when the Oliviers came to Australia we were more generous. They were, after all, theatrical Royalty. Of course nobody particularly wanted to see the plays – or very few – but everyone wanted to see the Oliviers. And didn't the Oliviers adore Australia! Why, they said so at every interview, and Melbourne was one of the finest cities they had ever visited in their lives. Their smiles and their sparkling eyes were all the proof we needed.

Anyone remotely famous visiting Australia was always asked their opinion of the continent minutes after their plane touched down. How they could possibly have formed a favourable opinion – and it had to be a *very* favourable opinion – in so brief a time boggles the imagination. Noël Coward mumbled something about Sydney having 'beautiful rooftops', since that aspect of Australia was all he had glimpsed from the aircraft window before the journalists moved in on him.

Prior to all my Australian tours, I always give a press conference at the airport to drum up business, so I have had my own fair share of airport interrogations. I remember the first time I nervously confronted a large group of Sydney journalists as I stepped off the plane. After the usual advice that I would find Australia greatly changed in the two years I had been away – 'Things don't just stand still in Australia because a few blokes like you reckon far-off fields are greener' – one patently hostile journalist got down to the nitty-gritty.

'How long are you gonna be in Australia this time, Baz?' he inquired with a disarming smile.

'Just a few months for this tour,' I replied. 'I've had a nice offer from the BBC to do a bit of television.'

'Yeah, that figures,' he rejoined. 'I suppose your old mates seem a bit boring now after some of the fancy types you've been hobnobbing with overseas.'

Suitably rebuked, I thought I had better change my tune for the next interviewer.

'G'day, Baz. How long can Australia expect to see ya this trip?'

'Oh, ages,' I gabbled. 'I mean, there's a few jobs on offer in the UK but it's wonderful to be home. I mean, it's just about the most interesting cultural centre in the world and I'm proud to be a part of it. I don't think I'll be leaving for a long time.'

'Yeah, that figures,' replied the scribbler. 'The word's out you're not doing too well over there.'

At another memorable airport press conference a national television interviewer expressed a keen interest in the vocal technique that enabled me to perform Edna show after show. I am sure, nay convinced, that the foreign word he sought to describe the required Edna sound was 'falsetto', but in Australia one foreign word is as good as another.

'Barry,' he began, 'isn't all that fellatio tiring on your vocal cords?'

An incredulous silence fell over the press conference, but undaunted he compounded his error. 'I mean, Baz, how do you keep that fellatio up all night?'

For the Oliviers' tour my father had secured the best dress-circle seats from the Save Time Ticket Service, and he bought a ticket for me to *The Skin of Our Teeth*. My mother felt the other two offerings might have been 'slightly unsuitable'. As it was, the Thornton Wilder play proved slightly unsuitable for my parents, but as we left and my mother settled herself into the passenger seat of the family Buick, she broke the silence with her customary post-theatrical pronouncement, 'Well, at least we can say that we've seen it.' The next morning I overheard her, in a telephone conversation with one of her sisters, summing up the previous night's entertainment as 'slightly uncalled for'.

For me, however, the play was a thrilling epiphany. It was so *modern*, so full of symbolism, which I was sure I understood or at least almost understood; and Vivien Leigh, wearing the briefest of post-nuclear tatters, 'donned to be doffed', was the most alluring creature I had ever seen. I must have been at the perilous threshold of adolescence, for Mrs Olivier moved me in a fashion in which I had not previously been moved. My parents' bafflement at the play only enhanced my excitement and it was yet another intimation that I knew better than they did. At least I could say that I had not only seen it, but *adored* it.

SEVERAL years later, when I was Private Humphries doing part of my compulsory national-service training at the mephitic Puckapunyal military camp in the Victorian hinterland, I attended my first one-man show. 'Entertainments for the boys' on Saturday nights were periodically arranged by Colonel Duffy, and acts were sometimes imported from faraway Melbourne. This was a special occasion because a performer from Paris was to appear on our makeshift stage beneath the stars. He was a French crooner called Jean Sablon, who at the time was in Melbourne on a tour. I was probably one of the few trainees present who had actually heard of Jean Sablon for I possessed a 78 recording of his jaunty 1939 success *Le Fiacre*.

The night sky over Puckapunyal was spectacular. The stars swarmed and pullulated in that immense canopy: it was mildewed with milky ways. There must have been an unexpected breeze for the stench of the camp had been briefly flushed away and displaced by a sweet eucalyptine exhalation from the encircling bush. I remember once complaining to one of the medical orderlies about the pervasive stink, and he looked surprised.

'It's only a faecal odour, Private,' he reassured me, as though I had objected to some totally unacceptable aroma.

A multitude of soldiers, both regulars and conscripts, had hunkered down on the stubble of a sloping hill an hour before

72

the performance, and the small stage constructed on the back of two trucks was flooded with light from lamps rigged in nearby gum trees. At length a drab Master of Ceremonies appeared, to a great hullabaloo of catcalls, to test the microphone.

'One, two, three, four, testing.' His tinny voice echoed around the camp, and there were a lot of piercing, whistling noises caused by some fault in the amplification.

'I'd like you all to put your hands together for a great little artist who's come all the way from Gay Paree . . .'

It is safe to say that none of us had seen a man in a gleaming midnight-blue lamé tuxedo before; or a man with cufflinks that sparkled in the spotlight; or a man, somewhat short, with a black moustache beneath which large white teeth gleamed in the unconvincing semblance of a smile – and who clearly wore a great deal of orange make-up. To expose an audience of uniformed hobbledehoys to a theatrical performer of any kind, let alone that rarified species, the sophisticated French *boulevardier* and *chansonnier*, would have been hazardous at the best of times.

A tide of merriment spread across the khaki throng. Jean Sablon could have been Danny Kaye he was so funny, and all he did was just stand there smiling, blinded by the light and not a little vexed by the large moths that had taken such an interest in him.

A pianist played the introduction to the song for the third time, in the hope of quieting the quaking audience, and Sablon began to sing. From my uncomfortable seat just behind the deckchairs reserved for officers, I could see a twitch of relief cross Sablon's *maquillage*.

Les souvenirs sont là pour m'étouffer.
Des larmes, des fleurs, des baisers.
Oui, je revois les beaux matins d'avril.
Nous vivions sous le toits tout en haut de la ville.

Suddenly, and in the midst of a tender silence before his next ingratiating musical phrase – a pause that the singer had achieved by some miraculous exercise of artistry and sheer force of will – a voice just behind me cut through the night air.

'FROG POOFDAH!'

The last syllables of that terrible interjection echoed around the dark, reboant hillsides.

'. . . og-og ogg Ogg OGGG . . . dah-dah Dah DAH DAAHH!'

Uncomprehending, Sablon frowned and briefly stumbled mid-song. He then resumed, but he need not have done so. Laughter such as I have never heard exploded over the camp. Inaudibly he finished his song, and the next, and the next, and he had bowed and gestured to the pianist, who had also bowed, but the audience was still in some wild trance of hilarity. They stamped, they whistled, they even took to chanting the appalling interjectory phrase – not with malice, but merely as a joyful asseveration of a self-evident fact.

Here, on a balmy evening in the early fifties, at a desolate military camp in the middle of the Australian bush, had indeed ventured a Frog poofdah. He may have thought he was a singer or a world-famous entertainer loved by beautiful women and full of Gallic charm, but it took a young infantryman with a very loud voice to put him in his place.

Dealers and Askers

~

I have always imagined
that Paradise will be a kind of library

Jorge Luis Borges

'Where are my books?'

One day I came home from Camberwell Grammar and found my books gone. I remember standing frozen in my bedroom doorway staring at the empty shelves. My mother was downstairs in the kitchen preparing something grey for our evening meal. (I always thought gravy should have been even greyer than it was, or greyer than its name implied, to match the monochromatic Australian dinner.)

'*Where are my books?*' I breathlessly repeated, racing down the stairs.

My mother in her floral apron, bought as all aprons were at a church bazaar, turned towards me, smiling.

'Oh, those,' she said. 'You'll be pleased to hear I gave them to the nice man from the Army. They'll go to poor Protestant children who haven't got any books.'

I looked up at my mother, or mothers, for the image of

her by the stove had multiplied in a lens of tears. I was now a child without books; even a bookless Protestant. Would the Army be replacing mine, I wondered, or wasn't I poor enough? With the war still in all our minds, I thought at first that they were soldiers who had sequestrated my book collection and had marched off with it, until I realised it was the *Salvation* Army to whom my mother had so gladly donated my small library: those kindly, bespectacled people in Edwardian uniforms of peaked caps and bonnets, whose golden cornets, tubas and trombones serenaded streets such as ours on the Golf Links Estate every Sunday morning with their plangent arrangements of 'Onward Christian Soldiers' and 'What a Friend We Have in Jesus'. Their fat, comforting music wafted down the street and mingled with the Sabbath effluvium of a thousand incipient roasts.

'But they were *my* books,' I blubbered.

I remembered every one of them: the colours of their bindings under the frayed dust jackets, the simulated leatherette spine of William Orpen's *The Outline of Art*, a present from my Uncle Wilf, my *Arabian Nights* with its illustrations by Edmund Dulac, my *Tiger Tim* annuals and all my Wonder Books with inscriptions from the Aunties. There were Sunday school prizes too: *Kidnapped, Bevis, Masterman Ready* and a book that I had read three times about a father who disappears – E. Nesbit's *The Railway Children*.

'But you've read them, Barry,' laughed my mother, as if it were the height of self-indulgence to retain books after a first perusal. She dried my eyes with the corner of a Pyramid handkerchief. 'I hope you're not going to grow up to be a selfish little boy,' she added sternly.

Sadly, I did. I certainly attribute to that early traumatic incident the occasional savage bouts of bibliomania that have afflicted me all my life. It is as though I am forever trying to replace those precious volumes confiscated by the Salvation Army, with my mother's charitable connivance. All those hours in second-hand bookshops, sometimes crouching on the floor, peering at the bottom shelf and scanning the titles of that *second layer* of books often hidden for years, have been part of this never-ending pursuit. For somewhere there is a bookshelf that cannot be sufficiently filled, a library that will never contain enough volumes.

In recent years I have searched – lately with the help of the Internet – for exact replicas of the lost library. How few I have replaced: a tattered copy of *Honey Bear* with its mysterious, even frightening Klimt-like pictures, and *Mother Goose*, an American edition of the traditional nursery rhymes illustrated with photographs of twenties children re-enacting the stories in the blurry, crepuscular style of F. Holland Day. I found this only last year in an Adelaide junk shop, and with a *frisson bibliographique* I turned the pages, remembering each sepia image in precise detail. They seemed to transmit an electric current: a conduit linking me to the distant past.

AFTER a long day at Melbourne Grammar, my secondary school, if it were not protracted by wasted hours in football kit, shivering beside the mirey oval at some compulsory sports 'turn-out', I would leap on a tram outside the school gates and make my way to the nearby city. It was possible to visit a couple of bookshops, and a record store such as John Clements's, Glenn's or the Orchestrelle, and still catch the train home from Flinders Street Station in time for tea. These expeditions were the most exhilarating moments in the week and I would usually come home with a treasure or two in my Gladstone bag – 'Barry's nosebag' as a school friend irritatingly called it, since I always seemed to have my head in it, delving amongst the papers, books and drawings stuffed therein.

Invariably the bookshops I frequented were second-hand ones, although, needless to say, my mother always strongly opposed my visiting such places – or indeed any shop that sold anything that someone else might have owned: antique furniture, old silver, clothing of any kind, but especially books.

'You never know where they've been, Barry,' she would say, flinching slightly at the sight of yet another germ-infested volume entering her spotless home.

However, I sometimes also visited regular bookshops such as the Continental Bookroom in Sonora House, Little Collins Street. It was delectably hard to find and sparingly advertised, and you found it only by travelling up several floors in a small lift and walking down a dim corridor. The bookshop specialised, as its name implied, in European books in the original language and in translation, and it was run by two formidable women with short hair and neckties. They extended little warmth and cordiality to a spotty schoolboy with an interest in Franz Kafka and Rainer Maria Rilke. Only over several years, and after numerous small purchases, did the ladies offer me the bleakest version of a friendly smile. Notwithstanding, I liked the Continental Bookroom with its shelves of Stefan Zweig, Max Brod, Guillaume Apollinaire and my favourite, Kafka. I was sixteen and already beginning to feel slightly foreign.

It is interesting to note that Melbourne's Jewish community had the highest number of Holocaust survivors in the world. The only other community like it was Toronto. Half of Melbourne's Jewish population were survivors of the Holocaust; some came from Central Europe before the Second World War, for the Kristallnacht arrests brought home to those who thought 'it would pass' that it would not, so we had the first wave in late 1938 and 1939. My father built houses and flats for some of these refugees. Then, after the war, before Israel was born in 1948, the survivors left Europe for the furthest and safest destination they could find on the map: Melbourne.

There was a Czech café in Sugden Place, near the Continental Bookroom building, called the Topsy, and underneath the placard at its entrance ran the lilting and *gemütlich* legend, 'It's cosy, it's handy, it's the Topsy!' It sounded better recited in a phony Viennese accent. Inside the Topsy not one word of Australian, or even English, could be heard. Sitting with a school friend at one of the small, round tables, surrounded by clouds of Balkan cigarette smoke, I would devour something amazingly exotic like a wiener schnitzel and sauerkraut or breast of goose with cherries and, for dessert, a delicious, if rather diluted, chestnut purée with lots of cream. I would imagine I was in Central Europe where I belonged, surrounded by my own people, although had I but known it, my fellow diners had gone to enormous trouble to put Central Europe as far behind them as possible only a few years before.

Looking back, I am astonished to observe how many things I *hadn't* eaten until the age of sixteen. I had never tasted broccoli, for example; however, it is an invented vegetable so may not have existed in my youth. I had never tasted pasta, although I once sampled another boy's spaghetti sandwich made with Mr Heinz's tinned variety. Only after school debates, with my friend Rob Maclellan, did I experience the delights of real spaghetti at the San Lina Café in Exhibition Street. The only cheese we ever ate was Kraft Cheddar, with its soapy texture and inclusions of silver foil. My grandfather preferred 'tasty cheese', an appetite that my mother viewed with mild disdain. There were no delicatessens in those days, but instead suburban 'ham and beef shops', which sold a limited range of merchandise that had been even more limited during the war. Here ham and German sausage were shaved and sliced by an impressive machine (for some reason the enemy epithet had not been elided as it would have been during the First World War). There were no olives available at the ham and beef shop, nor were there artichokes, potato salad, pickled herrings, liver pâté, salami or balsamic vinegar. Today we can barely exist without balsamic vinegar, and on my theatrical tours I generally leave behind me a trail of near-empty bottles of this fashionable condiment.

None of these exotic delicacies ever appeared on our table, or on the tables of anyone I knew. My generation of Australians grew up without having tasted garlic, avocado pears (a sixties discovery), duck or game of any variety, veal, ravioli, macadamia nuts, yoghurt (another sixties affectation), snow peas or any Asian food.

John Clements's record shop was one of the more arcane places of pilgrimage on my after-school jaunts to the city. It was not really a shop in the conventional sense, but a small room crammed from floor to ceiling with tiers of crude shelving, groaning with shellac recordings of 'classical' music in worn brown-paper sleeves, crudely ticketed with the scribbled names of composers. The shop was at the end of a tenebrous corridor on the second floor of an old building at 243 Collins Street, and I cannot now recall how I ever heard of it. But it was an Aladdin's cave, a place where rarities could be found, and John Clements, the proprietor, a sardonic, unsmiling curmudgeon, seemed to think his task was to discourage customers from buying anything. Indeed he seemed positively contemptuous of the importunate music lovers who thronged his cramped premises, and he reserved for me – probably his only schoolboy customer – an especially patronising scrutiny.

One day I made a great discovery. It was the three-disc Decca set of William Walton's *Façade*, recorded in 1926 with Edith Sitwell reciting her own verses assisted by Constant Lambert. I had never heard music or words so modern and thrilling.

I had been reading Constant Lambert's *Music Ho!* in the school library, which had a surprisingly good music section. In another reference book I discovered Ernst Křenek's so-called jazz opera *Jonny spielt auf*, and I wondered if I would ever hear this once-celebrated work of the Weimar Republic. Somewhat nervously I asked Mr Clements if he knew the piece, not daring to inquire whether a recording might exist. His long, sallow face regarded me for a moment with something remotely like amusement, then after rummaging through a cardboard box for a few minutes he miraculously produced the old Odeon disc of extracts from the opera, performed by the bass baritone Ludwig Hofmann with the Berlin State Opera Orchestra in 1927.

I bore my fragile prize, with its purple label, home that night, sharpened a 'fibre' needle, which serious record enthusiasts always used to protect the grooves of their shellac discs from wear and tear, and sat down to listen. It was at once an exciting and disappointing experience. The notorious 'jazz influence' consisted largely of a few banjos and saxophones augmenting the orchestra – a little gratuitous syncopation – and a long, lugubrious quote from 'The Swanee River'. It sounded rather like something by a pupil of Mahler played by Paul Whiteman. But the curdled harmonies, the curious dragging rhythms and the air of melancholy that lay behind even the more sprightly episodes captivated me. I thought of all those sad Slavic faces at the Topsy; many of them had probably attended live performances of this forgotten work. It had, after all, been translated into eighteen languages and performed all over Europe, and it had only failed – and failed dismally – at the Metropolitan Opera in New York, where the audience, fresh from productions of *Lady Be Good* and *Oh, Kay!*, knew what a real jazz operetta sounded like. Křenek's music was enervated romanticism crudely spiked with modernistic effects – and yet . . .

Many years later, in 1977, I went to Palm Springs to meet Ernst Křenek and his Norwegian wife, Gladys, to discuss a new production at the Sydney Opera House that I was to direct. He came into the house dripping from his swimming pool: a sturdy, nut-brown septuagenarian, still closely resembling his portrait by Kokoschka on the wall of the living room where I waited. He tended to dismiss *Jonny* as a mere *jeu d'esprit* and was by then much more interested in arranging performances of his recent electronic experiments, a road down which I was unable to follow him. I outlined my ideas for *Jonny*, especially the climactic scene at the railway station when everyone goes off, in the nick of time, to America. It seemed such an obvious, but moving parable of the times: premonitory of the great flight from Nazism in the thirties, an exodus that had swept Křenek himself across the Atlantic to uncertain employment in American institutions.

I planned to have a chorus member in white overalls, his back to the audience, high on a scaffold busily painting an archway of the railway station. At the moment when the valedictory music reached its tumultuous climax, his paint-flecked domino would drop from his shoulders as he turned into the spotlight, revealing that the painter and decorator was Adolf Hitler, twitching into a triumphant salute. Křenek listened to this and other more melodramatic proposals with amused patience, and I went back to Australia with the great composer's blessing.

However, I never did get to direct *Jonny*, a work that I now regard as the most prescient *Zeitoper* of the twentieth century. In Sydney the opera-behind-the-scenes that, throughout the world, is being constantly performed by Chairmen and Boards and Artistic Directors and Divas and Conductors and funding bodies and tone-deaf politicians gave the whole enterprise the thumbs down at the last minute, and I believe the gap in Sydney's operatic calendar was filled by a banal Gilbert and Sullivan revival.

As I recall my adolescent visits to city bookshops and record stores I wonder how I could have afforded such regular purchases. Admittedly second-hand books were then very much cheaper than new ones and not, as they are today, twenty times the price, with the words 'very rare' and 'scarce' scribbled on their flyleaves by enterprising booksellers and 'askers'. (An asker is Australian antique dealers' slang for someone who is unabashed at asking an outrageous price for some trumpery item. The asker often gets it.)

I did not have a particularly generous allowance from my parents, but then I did not spend my money on anything else – not girls, cigarettes, clothes or expensive meals. However, if there was anything I especially wanted, I only had to mention it a few times at dinner and it usually ended up in my possession; a circumstance that, happily, still prevails.

I would play music late at night on the gramophone when my parents had gone to bed. Winter evenings by the fire were the best. The cosiest room in the house, and by far the most popular, was the sunroom, which contained a large walnut-veneered 'radiogram'. This room had been redecorated several times by my mother, and in the fifties, when my father built an extension to the house to accommodate an upstairs flat for me, it was enlarged and refurnished in the carnival style of the period, with slightly too many colours, blondwood furniture and a knotty-pine and duck-egg-blue Laminex breakfast bar giving onto the new galley kitchen. My mother's favourite old cane furniture, brass buddhas and other ornaments, once so fashionable, were banished to the Mornington beach house and, at my suggestion, cream-framed prints of Van Gogh and Cézanne appeared on the tan 'feature' wall of the refurbished apple-green sunroom.

At night, illuminated solely by a crumbling and incandescent mallee root on the hearth and the small ruby pilot light of the gramophone winking across the expanse of mushroom Axminster, the sunroom acquired a congenial harmony. It may have been a cold night outside, where, on the far side of the narrow driveway, my mother's beloved camellias chafed their dark, glossy leaves against each other, but inside it was exquisitely warm as I sat in my armchair with a large beaker of Milo, Akta-Vite or even the recently invented Nescafé, prepared with hot milk, and played my records. Sometimes I would even smoke an exotic Sobranie Cocktail cigarette from a packet given to me for my birthday by my spinster Aunt Elsie, who owned the wool shop in Burke Road, Camberwell, and subscribed to *Vogue*. Smoking was not, for some reason, forbidden by my parents, and although they were both nonsmokers they never objected to my occasional indulgence in this languorous vice. Sobranie Cocktails came in a quilted black box and they were every colour of the rainbow, with gold tips. They seemed to me, then, the height of luxurious decadence. Sometimes I saved up and bought a packet myself from Damman's, the tobacconists in the city, before crossing Swanston Street to Queen's Walk arcade and visiting Henry Buck's men's store, where my father had a long-standing account. Under the glass top of a mahogany counter in the shirting department was displayed an intriguing series of diagrams that I avidly perused, and later practised at home:

How to tie a Windsor knot

Ever and anon I had to haul myself up out of my comfy 'heritage' armchair to change a record or sharpen a fibre needle. Recently when my eighteen-year-old son was repeating himself somewhat tediously, I pointed out that he sounded as if 'the needle had got stuck'. He looked at me blankly. For today's youth the word 'needle' has a sinister connection, and few under the age of forty have ever changed a needle on a gramophone, or heard a musical phrase constantly reiterated when the needle on the pick-up strikes a minute obstruction and repeatedly jumps a groove. Many today would not connect needles with the reproduction of sound, any more than they would know the purpose of blotting paper, or carbon paper, or even string.

The digital generation has little need of these quaint and outmoded accoutrements; nor, incidentally, does it whistle. Who whistles these days? The age of the *siffleur* has passed, yet there used to be many artistes who were famous whistlers: Ronnie Ronalde, Roger Whittaker – even Bing Crosby puckered up on some of his earlier recordings, while Ilse Werner whistled for the Wehrmacht. In my youth it was impossible to stroll in any city street without hearing a trilling errand boy or even a jaunty businessman assibilating some popular air such as 'Whistle While You Work' or 'Give a Little Whistle'. Perhaps today's pop songs are not amenable to cheerful chirruping. If you don't believe me, try whistling Limp Bizkit or Radiohead.

The sunroom, where I sat by winter fires listening to music, was a long way from my parents' bedroom so I could confidently turn up the volume; but not seldom my poor father would appear at the door – a haggard figure in his fawn-check dressing-gown – pleading for some work by Hindemith or Varèse to be turned down 'just a little'.

'If you must play music late at night, Barry,' my mother would admonish me, 'can't you play something Australian?' Or 'Must you play all that continental music, Barry? It wasn't that long ago we were at war with those people.'

When I was eighteen I occasionally invited a few friends around to listen to records. A favourite was Ravel's *L'Enfant et les Sortilèges*, one of the most perfect and beautiful things ever written. Love is its theme and when I think of my youth and try to isolate a joyous moment, I see again our sunroom at night: a few friends sitting around or sprawling in the dim lamplight as we listen to Ravel's magical creation diffusing its rapturous message.

In the early fifties of the old century there was a popular

musical event held throughout the summer in a natural amphitheatre beside Melbourne's Royal Botanic Gardens. It was a *fête champêtre* called Music for the People, and huge crowds flocked to enjoy it – a family outing with music thrown in. A large symphony orchestra mounted on a prefabricated stage – and later accommodated in the Myer Music Bowl, donated to the city by a munificent merchant – was conducted by Hector Crawford. The programmes were lightly classical in the style of the Boston Pops. My spastic cousin, John, adored these concerts and the family usually attended them at his instigation. 'John loves his music,' the Aunties clucked.

On a nice afternoon it was pleasant reclining under the trees with a large picnic rug, a basket of cakes and sandwiches and a Thermos or two. You could chat quite loudly during the music without anyone swivelling around and saying 'Shhhhh!'

There were also vocal interludes when Glenda Raymond, Hector Crawford's charming and accomplished wife, sang excerpts from the light operatic repertoire, or a promising baritone sang 'Trotting to the Fair' or the ever-popular 'Trees'. The concerts always ended with the long version of the National Anthem, at which everybody scrambled to their feet and stood to silent attention: a touching patriotic ritual that would be unimaginable today.

At one of the concerts some older members of my family looked with ill-concealed disapproval at the occupants of a nearby picnic rug, who were ostentatiously drinking wine and talking rather loudly in Italian. The men wore sunglasses, an accoutrement disdained by virile Australian men of that epoch, and they had, moreover, removed their jackets and draped them loosely over their shoulders. Foreigners!

When at length the timpani rolled to announce 'God Save the King', we all struggled to a respectful vertical, except the cheerful party on our right. They continued sipping their exotic beverages and laughing, oblivious it seemed to the enraged and affronted Australians around them. My mother whispered something to my father, to which he responded with a look of extreme anxiety. When the anthem ended, he gingerly walked across the grass and I saw him say something to the Foreigners, to which they reacted with expressions of polite puzzlement.

'See,' said my mother triumphantly. 'They're not going to get away with that. Your father's having a word with them now.'

Once when I was browsing in Mr Clements's record den, I felt myself nudged by a pale, ginger-haired man who had, a moment before, foolishly requested a recording of a particularly nauseating song of the period, 'Nature Boy'. The proprietor of this exclusively classical shop gave him very short shrift. Unabashed, he loitered in the shop, fumbling through a box of discs. I noticed this man's hands: they were unpleasantly freckled, and the nails were bitten to the quick. Walking back down the long, dark corridor to the stairwell, I heard accelerating footsteps behind me, then harsh respiratory noises to my right, which I can now identify as 'heavy breathing'. It was the pale, nailless Nature Boy. I walked faster but he caught up, and bumping against my shoulder, hoarsely muttered something in my ear.

'Hello, son, could you raise a stiffy?'

At least I think that is what he said, but I had fled before he could elaborate. I ran like the wind down two flights of stairs, into Collins Street and right around Damman's Corner, and I didn't stop until, breathless, I had reached Flinders Street Station. It may be that my accoster had received a bigger shock than me for, before I bolted, I had swung my school satchel with a tremendous thwack against his solar plexis, shattering, as I ruefully discovered later, a three-record set of Schoenberg's *Transfigured Night*.

On my forays into the city after school, I often paid a visit to Mrs Ellis Bird's second-hand bookshop at the top of Bourke Street. Sometimes Shirley, her assistant, would be holding the fort, but more often than not the kindly and sapient widow, Mrs Bird herself, would be there, with her wispy, grey bun, old-fashioned blouse and bottle-green cardigan, sipping sherry with a priest behind the counter. Mrs Bird seemed to have innumerable sacerdotal customers and her popish connections gave these visits to her wonderful shop an added, heretical piquancy.

For most of my youth I had been segregated from 'Roman' Catholics, as Australian Protestants persisted in calling them, just as I had been kept away from boys who were rough; or, as my mother preferred to call them, 'ordinary'. Melbourne's 'good' schools catered to the popular Christian denominations; Melbourne Grammar was strictly Church of England, although a handful of Jews were admitted on a rigorous quota system. The top Catholic school was Xavier College – by far the most

impressive school building in Melbourne – which stood impos-
ingly on a hill in the old riverside suburb of Kew. 'They always
pick the best positions,' as my mother, and many others, liked
to say.

Mrs Bird always had a book reserved for me, and as she
fished it out and presented it across the counter she would say,
'Mr Humphries, I think you're ready for *Melmoth the Wanderer*.'
Or Meredith's *The Egoist*, or *Futility* by William Gerhardie, or
The Hill of Dreams, or *Hadrian the Seventh*. All still remain
firm favourites of mine for Mrs Bird instilled a life-long prefer-
ence for the byways of literature. When, in the late fifties, her
shop lost its cast-iron verandah and was usurped by a dry-
cleaning depot with a blue-tiled fascia, I wept. It seemed like the
end of Melbourne.

IN MY rambles around London in search of old books, when I
first lived there in the early sixties, I came upon a little shop in
the Royal Opera Arcade, which even well-versed Londoners
might suppose to exist near Covent Garden. In fact it is the vestigial opera colonnade running behind the old Opera House,
Haymarket, now Her Majesty's Theatre. It was added to the
original building by John Nash and George Repton in 1816–18.
The tiny shop I discovered was the retail outlet of the Richards
Press and browsing there I found a large number of books from
the eighteen-nineties in attractive modern reprints. As a schoolboy I had devoured Holbrook Jackson's monograph on this
period when it first came out in the sky-blue Pelican edition, and

I had then and there decided to collect the minor poets of the English 'decadence' – a task that never ends. (Which of my readers can find me a copy of *Whispers*, verse by Robert Harborough Sherard, published by Rimington & Company, 1894?) There was an ancient man behind the counter who seemed almost old enough to have known Ernest Dowson or Hubert Crackan-thorpe or Theodore Wratislaw or the other half-forgotten writers whose works I had first discovered in Mrs Bird's shop. After several visits and a growing acquaintance, I learnt that he was none other than Martin Secker, publisher of D.H. Lawrence, Compton McKenzie, Norman Douglas, Arthur Machen and later Franz Kafka. In this unfrequented arcade, behind the monstrous box of New Zealand House, one of the great British publishers of the twentieth century, with his Edwardian man-ners, still pottered around in a buff dustcoat.

I enjoyed meeting spry old parties such as Martin Secker. They were links to the past and I could talk to them about many things not easily shared with my own generation. My friend John Rothenstein was one such person. He was the retired director of the Tate Gallery, a fine and liberal art historian who often took me to lunch at the Atheneum amongst the gaiter'd bishops and Men of Letters. I also went to his house in Oxfordshire, which was full of Max Beerbohm caricatures and paintings by his father, Sir William Rothenstein, who had been a friend of Charles Conder, Oscar Wilde and Aubrey Beardsley. John had met Conder once when, as a child, he had gone downstairs to answer the doorbell and admitted the by then drink-ravaged and syphilitic painter of fans and *fêtes gallantes*, whose works I collected.

John had never seen one of my shows but whenever he introduced me to anyone it always amused him deeply to explain what I did for a living. Goodness knows what Chinese whispers had first misinformed him, but he clung tenaciously to the misinformation despite my protests. 'You won't believe this,' he would say to an astonished and invariably distinguished group, 'but when Barry leaves this club, he's going off to some theatre to impersonate a negress!' The notion so tickled him that in the end I stopped refuting it.

A MELBOURNE bookshop so expensive that it was usually only possible for a schoolboy to browse therein was that of N.H. Seward at 457 Bourke Street. It was a shop that dealt mostly in microscopes, although upstairs Miss Eddie managed a small and specialised bookstore patronised by gentlemen with particular tastes. Much of the shop was devoted to volumes on gardening and scientific instruments, but Miss Eddie, if smiled at nicely, might proffer a key that opened the gate to the small staircase leading to the upper gallery lined with books that old-fashioned catalogues used to describe as *livres gallants*. In short, dirty books. By today's standards it was a tame collection, but there were illustrated monographs devoted to erotica and the licentious artists of the late nineteenth century such as Rops and von Bayros.

Occasionally there was another browser beside myself, usually a middle-aged man with febrile fingers: a doctor, perhaps, or a lawyer or even a judge, for Seward's was not far from

Melbourne's legal precinct. We Sewardians never spoke or made eye contact as we leafed covetously through the pages of Aretino or Pierre Louÿs, preserving, had I but known it, the etiquette of the brothel.

To this day I can still sometimes take a book from my shelves and, on opening it, observe fluttering to the floor an old Seward's invoice for one guinea or even 55 shillings, for there were times when I yielded to some extortionately priced temptation. Yet I bought at least one book by Baron Corvo at Seward's that I have never seen since.

Rob Maclellan and I often made an excursion on Saturday mornings to a certain part of Fitzroy, one of the very oldest inner suburbs of Melbourne. Here were rows of small artisans' houses, many of them in bluestone, built from about 1850 and then on the very outskirts of Melbourne and the fringe of the bush. A century later the neighbourhood had declined, so that when I first visited it these were squalid streets indeed, with ragged children playing in the narrow alleyways. Our visit to this working-class purlieu must have been conspicuous, as we sauntered along in our navy-blue double-breasted suits and our caps with their embroidered crest.

In 1958 this picturesque quarter was razed to the ground and replaced with bleakly utilitarian Housing Commission flats. The destruction of old Melbourne by municipal developers was so relentless in this and the succeeding decade that it seemed informed more by malice than by greed. Had this part of Fitzroy survived the creeping blight, these terrace houses would now have been gentrified and reinhabited by same-sex partners, Malaysian students and people 'into' advertising.

At 151 Fitzroy Street, on the corner of Palmer Street, stood the Corner Shop, the premises of John William Duncan. In the early fifties the shingle above his door read exactly as it appears in John Shirlow's etching of 1919:

R. Duncan & Sons
Furniture Brokers

Rob Maclellan's mother was enviably 'artistic'. She knew about antiques and silver and pictures and batiks, and Mr Duncan 'found her things'. My school friend was interested in prints by George Baxter and he already had a small collection of these Victorian chromolithographs, which were then quite inexpensive.

It was on Rob's quest for these that I first accompanied him to Mr Duncan's lair, and it was indeed an astonishing little shop, crammed seemingly with rubbish from floor to ceiling. You had to edge your way down a dark and crooked alley between broken chairs, picture frames, rusty ironwork and piles of grimy books to a small clearing. There, beside a coke fire over which swung a blackened kettle, sat John William Duncan, sunk in a decayed armchair and staring into the embers. His long, pallid face always looked up in surprise, then he would stagger to his carpet-slippered feet and extend an arthritic hand in greeting. In contrast to the exalted squalor of his bower, Mr Duncan was miraculously clean and usually dressed in a white collarless

shirt, layers of much-mended cardigans and a hessian apron. His
voice was a light croak – almost a falsetto – his hair a few white
wisps on his ivory pate, and his large, old man's ears, abundantly
tufted, were as translucent as vellum.

It surprised me at the time that such a small space, choked
with trash of all descriptions, could yield anything of interest to
a suburban connoisseur such as Rob's mother, or even to the
indiscriminate browser amongst Old Wares.

There were in the Melbourne of that time few – but very
few – antique shops. They reeked of varnished mahogany and
were filled with chiffonniers, cheval mirrors, lazy Susans, cruet
sets and silver-plated sugar scuttles. Old things held little interest for the middle classes of the fifties when everything had to
be new; but there were, throughout the city, a handful of dealers in 'left-off effects': the residue of deceased estates. For
ordinary people in search of a bargain, however, this was the age
of the 'opportunity shop'.

Trawling through these shops was a popular pastime, and
the local voluntary helpers in their floral frocks and straw hats
seemed not to mind the peculiar whiff: an aroma compounded of
mothballs, stale scent and another, sourer odour. Browsers
would search for tea-cosies, pretty aprons, musical milk jugs,
popular editions of Pearl Buck and Paul Gallico, or even a practically unworn chenille dressing-gown kindly donated to the
shop by the family of the Recently Deceased and dropped off,
with less saleable prosthetic appliances, on their drive from
nursing home to necropolis.

These highly competitive little charity bazaars thrived in

almost every suburban parade, and they were ostensibly run on behalf of the Church, Rotary, Red Cross or the Blind. Howbeit, more than one canny society matron strove to infiltrate the op-shop committee so that she might discreetly intercept particularly interesting donations of pictures, glass and furniture. Expropriated antiques, given in good faith to charity by gaga widows, became the basis of many private collections in Toorak and South Yarra. No doubt the philanthropic committee ladies felt that an 1874 panorama of Melbourne by Buvelot, or a large Webb cameo vase, would look better in their suburban lounge than at the local op-shop, in the lowly company of chipped Winston Churchill beakers, hand-knitted 'afghan' hot-water bottle covers and abandoned walking frames.

But Mr Duncan's Corner Shop was no such genteel emporium of suburban cast-offs. At first, gazing around his grotto of picturesque junk, I wondered why anyone remotely interested in objects of *virtù* would consider calling upon this dotard rather than visiting the venerable auction rooms of Leonard Joel, or patronising Kozminsky's gallery in the city, which was filled with treasures – and not a few unexpected prizes such as a Fabergé ice bucket, a set of Vienna Secession silverware by Hoffman or a Loetz glass vase. Fragile wrack, washed up by the Second World War on the furthest shores of Australia.

Yet if Mr Duncan's eyes were watery, they were also alert.

'I've got you the Baxter you wanted,' he said to my friend, shuffling off into a dark alcove and returning with a portfolio fastened with a dirty ribbon.

Mr Duncan cleared a space on the rickety table, where a

small and trembling doily of sunlight conveniently lay, and withdrew the print from the portfolio. It was a fine coloured lithograph of Baxter's famous title *News from Australia*. Rob already possessed its companion piece, a lithograph of *News from Home*. It was an exciting collector's moment, which I vicariously enjoyed.

Mr Duncan quoted the modest price, which my friend paid, and I noticed something new about the old man: it was the way he handled the little picture, the way he indicated its merits and expounded on its provenance and rarity in his light, quavering voice that dispelled my hasty and snobbish opinion of him. I later learnt that Melba had been a regular customer, frequently weaving her way between piles of musty books five feet high in search of a rare item, while her Rolls Royce loitered outside.

Rob mentioned that I too was interested in pictures, and to my astonishment Mr Duncan asked me if I liked the work of Jacques Callot. By chance I knew a little about this great seventeenth-century French engraver, but only from books. The idea that some of his prints reposed in an insalubrious Fitzroy junk shop seemed incredible. Mr Duncan produced another portfolio and soon, in that patch of light on a gimcrack table, I was examining print after print of Callot's famous Beggars series. I became a customer.

Over many, many weeks, a few shillings at a time, I paid my beggars off, and in the next few years Mr Duncan offered other temptations from the recesses of his cavern: De Launay's fine engraving after Fragonard's *The Swing*, a haunting female portrait by the Australian impressionist Tom Roberts, a set of Conder lithographs, a small painting on a wood panel by Meissonier, some rare and exquisite woodcuts by Edward Calvert and a Whistler pastel drawing, the sad fate of which I have related elsewhere.

John William Duncan had a brother, Robert George, who was his total opposite. R.G. was short, jovial, ventripotent and given to habits of intemperance. He had a small shop in the old Eastern Market in the city, another demolition casualty of the fifties. Those in the know never rated his expertise as highly as that of his abstemious sibling in Fitzroy.

Beside the Corner Shop, thrusting through the buckled asphalt, there stood a valiant elm – a tree still common in the streets and parks of Melbourne – in whose benign shade successive generations of guttersnipes had played marbles and 'tors'. When the elm was finally extirpated, the local council claimed it was dying anyway from a gas leakage. Next, overnight the gas lamppost outside the front door was whisked away, at an hour when most acts of civic vandalism are performed.

About a year before our last meeting I discovered that Mr Duncan resided in the house next to his shop, and on a few occasions I called upon him there in his more austere domestic surroundings. He offered me many extraordinary pictures, and I have sometimes wished that I had bought them all; but I was only a student with a student's limited means and, in any case, had I possessed them then it is unlikely that I would do so now. They might well have been swept away by one of the financial calamities that overtook me in later years – when I swore to abjure forever the collecting impulse.

BILLO'S BOOK

~

It was a vague pleasant dream he had,
something that was going to happen to him some
day that would be unique and incomparable

F. Scott Fitzgerald

THE BOOKS we were required to study at school were a strange mixture indeed. In my last two years at Melbourne Grammar we were given two plays to read, both by the Georgian poet and dramatist John Drinkwater – 'dull as Drinkwater' in John Betjeman's phrase. We were obliged to study *Loyalties*, which was, I think, concerned with anti-Semitism in Edwardian Clubland, and his American Civil War play, *Robert E. Lee*. These must have been prescribed in the twenties by some enlightened functionary in the Education Department, but their themes held slender interest for an Australian schoolboy in the early fifties. We read very little by Australian authors – no verse by Henry Lawson or 'Banjo' Paterson or C.J. Dennis, just a rather dull volume by Francis Ratcliffe called *Flying Fox and Drifting Sand*, hardly an exciting title. Rather, in a generous concession to the Mother Country, we read books such as *Tess of the D'Urbervilles*.

Hardy's Wessex seemed a much more familiar landscape than Ratcliffe's parched and bat-infested terrain. All Australian literature appeared to be about outback life and its privations, but since at least 75 per cent of us lived in the coastal cities, the outback and even the bush were *terra incognita*. With Peter Dawson on the radio singing 'Glorious Devon' and 'Old Father Thames', and the young Princess Elizabeth soon to be enthroned, we had little or no interest in our vast and inhospitable hinterland. When I left school, I could point to a map of England and show you exactly where Huddersfield and Wolverhampton were, but I hadn't the faintest idea where Alice Springs was, had never heard of Ayer's Rock, and Tasmania was not even on the map until we learnt that Uncle Dick's wife, Beryl, had been born there. The stories of the early explorers all ended in death, madness and despair, convincing us from a very early age that Australia was the one place on earth we must never dream of exploring, and should abandon at the earliest opportunity.

The convict settlements in Australia's early history were only mentioned in whispers by respectable people and, anyway, they applied to Sydney and Hobart, not nice Melbourne. Certainly in all our schooldays we were never taught about Australia's convict origins. It was a shameful piece of our history, which our teachers and textbooks mentioned in passing or carefully elided, and time has barely reversed this odd historical denial.

A friend of mine, a maker of distinguished documentaries, was recently commissioned by the New South Wales government to create a promotional film about Sydney. He duly submitted a script and was at once summoned to a conference with the local-government 'historian' – a lady who looked as if she needed a man like a fish needs a bicycle.

'Must we have this bit about convicts in the script?' she began, in an aggrieved tone. 'Do you realise this film will be seen Overseas?'

My friend was, to say the least, taken aback.

'But, Carmen . . .' he protested, 'that's about all the world knows about Sydney – the convicts. Perhaps, a long way second, they might have heard about the Opera House and the Olympic Games.'

'Exactly,' replied the historian fiercely. 'We want to emphasise the positive things.' Then she softened, if granite could be said to soften. 'If you must show a few convicts, couldn't they be Greek?'

'Greek!' the film-maker exploded. 'The Greeks didn't come to Sydney in any numbers until after the Second World War. There weren't any Greek convicts.'

But the revisionist historian was implacable. She would have been more at home spreading disinformation for the late and unlamented cultural apparatchiks of East Berlin.

'Well,' she persevered, 'if we can't have Greek convicts, how about some Lebanese or Thais or a few Filipinos? We want to draw the world's attention to our multiculturalism.'

WHEN I studied history at school, the word 'multicultural', happily, had not been invented. I had yet to meet an Aborigine, let alone a fugitive from Lebanon or the Philippines. I was good at history and enjoyed it – probably for no better reason than that it was taught by schoolmasters who were comparatively intelligent and fitfully amusing. The subject that gave me the most difficulty was always mathematics and its relations.

For a while, with moderate success, I flirted with geometry, which was almost artistic; it was after all about shapes. But then came algebra and I gave up. I gave up with only the briefest sign of struggle, for I continued to attend classes in this occult subject – I was compelled to do so by the curriculum – but my mind was forever absent.

Even before I was twelve, the problem I had with numbers had been brought to my parents' attention. My preceptors were forever reminding me of the importance of a mathematical grounding, often emphasising my deficiency in this area with physical punishments, so that I truly believed I lacked the most important of what would today be called 'life skills'. I was constantly told that whatever I did in life – and it was feared that I would do something foolish – I would need another skill to 'fall back on'. The image of falling backwards, painfully and inevitably, was impressed on me from an early age.

Tutors were sought outside school hours and I had, over the next few years, a series of them. There was Mr Brauer, a handsome but weary-eyed Austrian Jew who lived with his wife in a noisy little flat at the wrong end of Toorak Road. He would sit glumly beside me as I stared at the meaningless sums and then, with a kind of languorous despair, try to explain where I had gone wrong: where I always went wrong.

I was invariably late for these expensive Saturday morning

classes and the homework he set was rarely done; or if done, done wrong. We had a kind of tacit pact, Mr Brauer and I, for he needed the money my father gave him and so must maintain his unconvincing air of melancholy encouragement. He would sit beside me for that interminable hour every Saturday morning furtively looking at his watch and doing the homework for me on condition that I came back next week with that brown envelope. We pitied each other.

But Mr Brauer was not the first person hired by my parents to raise my mathematical status, if only imperceptibly, from that of imbecile to dunce.

Mr Tipping, the father of my old friend Rodney, had heard of a schoolteacher called Kelynack in need of extra cash. My prospective mathematics coach lived with a slatternly wife and a lot of children in a small, felicitously named coach-house behind Deepdene, a Victorian mansion in the suburb of Hawthorn. In my youth there were many large houses like this, built of cement-rendered brick and bluestone in the Boom period of the 1880s. They were set in extensive gardens with plots of canna lilies, venerable Norfolk Island pines and always a tottering pergola, strangled by grey pythons of wisteria from which, once a year, heavy racemes – the colour of English skies – dropped their fragrance.

Deepdene was surrounded by crinolines of verandahs, with petticoats of iron lace from which arose a high Italianate tower commanding, no doubt, fine views of the silver bay, distended in the distance. Few of these turreted villas remain today, the rest having been demolished in the fifties and sixties to make way for flats and cream-brick 'units' or town houses, if

they were sufficiently hideous and expensive. It may be that Mr
and Mrs Kelynack had rented their small abode from the family
who still shuffled around inside the huge, doomed mansion.

Mrs Kelynack would bundle their yelling kids into
another room after breakfast, and Rodney and I would sit with
our mathematics coach at the greasy and jam-daubed table
while Mr Kelynack brutally attempted to inculcate the incomprehensible. Those mornings in the Kelynacks' kitchen, with its
smell of fried food, burnt toast and cigarettes, and the racket of
caged urchins from the next room, were my first alarming taste
of Irish-Australian family life.

Once when the noise had become overwhelming and a tat-
terdemalion brat, its nose streaming with lettuce-green mucus,
climbed onto our work table, Rodney censured it in his snooti-
est manner. Overhearing this, Mrs Kelynack, her dishevelled
hair held in place with a twisted pencil, and a Turf cigarette in
the corner of her mouth, stormed into the room, snatched up the
child and accused Rodney of being 'truculent'. I was deeply
impressed for I had never heard that word before, although in
retrospect I think Mrs Kelynack meant to say 'arrogant'. She
was clearly at her wits' end, and probably secretly grateful when
we never returned.

MUSICAL appreciation was my favourite subject since all we
really did was listen to recordings down at the music lodge on St
Kilda Road while the school's organist and music master, Albert
Greed, dozed off in a postprandial torpor. His lunch hour visits

to the Botanical Hotel in Domain Road usually guaranteed his mellow mood. A star music pupil was Harold Badger, the son of a famous jockey, who occasionally gave recitals in the Memorial Hall. His choice of music was astonishing, and would not be today in the repertoire of a fourteen-year-old boy: Skryabin, Khachaturian and the Finnish composer Selim Palmgren. Where can I hear more of this 'modern music'? I thought, as I thrilled to Khachaturian's Toccata. It was strange and wonderful and I couldn't get enough of it.

We sometimes attended interschool musical evenings at the ladies' colleges of Melbourne: intimate soirées that encouraged a deeper appreciation of music and of each other. Lively, talented girls, some rather attractive, nestled their cheeks against their

The author's sister, Barbara, practising the piano (by B.H., 1948)

violins, caressed keyboards and pouted into flutes. I was strangely moved when one exclusive young horn player paused during the *Romance* of Saint-Saëns to decant a stream of silver spittle.

Watching these adolescent recitals, with ill-suppressed lesbian rapture, were the girls' tweedy music teachers and choir mistresses. We schoolboys had little or nothing to offer in the way of musical competition. My friend van Senden might give an autumnal account of Sinding's *Rustle of Spring* and Freddie Grimwade could always lower the tone with a vampy rendition of 'Heart and Soul'. On the night we went to Lauriston Girls' School, however, I decided to enliven proceedings and to frog-march my lowbrow school and its oafish and tone-deaf representatives into the avant-garde of musical taste.

Amongst the many private lessons for which my mother secretly paid were my desultory studies in pianoforte with Mrs Bremner. Progress had been slow, but enough to convince me that I, who loved music, was no executant of that art. Not-withstanding, I tried to compose. (Since that time I have written many songs, but my compositions are either picked out with one finger on the keyboard or hummed or warbled to an amanuensis, after which they often sound very impressive: reminiscent, it is true, of other men's work, but if this be a fault it is a fault shared by at least one celebrated composer of contemporary operetta.)

At the interschool recital at Lauriston, when Helen Heatley had finished a devotional song that belied her reputation after school dances, I announced, with moist hands and a pounding heart, that I would play my own composition entitled

Melbourne by Night – A Nocturne. A hush fell on the twitter-
ing audience as I seated myself at the Beale baby grand.

The work began, appropriately enough, with a very, very
long silence of which John Cage would have been proud. Then my
right hand announced an insidious and discordant tunette, which
was repeated insistently several times and at different speeds
before the left hand began to thump the bass notes in arbitrary
fashion. I played very slowly and deliberately, frowning a lot with
concentration to give the impression that I was performing a
written work and not merely improvising. Occasionally I would
recapitulate my early, almost melodic motif to give an illusion of
symmetry and musical progression. The young ladies were
enthralled. Their crop-headed schoolmistresses leant forward,
intently listening. After a dissonant crescendo with a lot of base
pedal, I stopped. There was a silence, then wild applause.

Pam Horowitz, the most senior music teacher present,
stepped forward. 'Mr Humphries,' she said with a sly, triumphant smile, 'we enjoyed that so much. May we hear it again?'
But I was in improvisatory mode.

'Miss Horowitz,' I replied blushing, 'I'm afraid I wasn't
being strictly truthful.' The audience gasped. 'You see,' I continued, 'the piece wasn't written by me at all, but by . . . by Edgard
Varèse, a very modern composer.'

'That's marvellous,' said the canny pedagogue. 'I've heard
of him, but we'd still like to hear it again,' she cooed. 'Wouldn't
we, girls?'

'Ye-e-e-e-s!' they sweetly chorused.

'The truth is,' I heard myself saying, 'I only know the first movement and the music's at home. Next time I'll play the whole work.'

Pamela Horowitz, DipMusEd, looked at me fixedly but did not press her request further. I knew she smelt a rat, but I also knew that I had called her bluff, the ignorant old battleaxe.

Sadly, after that, I could not attend any more of those delightful cultural exchanges for fear that I might be called upon to perform all four fiendishly difficult movements of Varèse's *Melbourne by Night*, a work, strange to say, that is not noted in any edition of Grove's *Dictionary of Music and Musicians*.

A TURNING point in my school reading, as Thornton Wilder's allegory had been in my experience of theatre, was a cheaply printed anthology called *The Modern Muse*. How this excellent little collection of twentieth-century verse ever got onto the syllabus passes my understanding, even though it was a conservative selection concentrating mainly on the later Edwardian and Georgian poets, with a few Americans such as e. e. cummings and Carl Sandberg thrown in. Yet I cannot forget the thrill of discovery when I read for the first time poems by Robert Graves, Walter de la Mare and Edith Sitwell. I had always tried to write poetry, and I envied my sister, Barbara, and her Presbyterian Ladies' College magazine. This was full of passionate girls' poetry, whereas my own school magazine, the dreary *Melburnian*, was mostly about sport and the futile achievements of the school's more notable dullards. To be sure there was a section on hobbies, but verse was conspicuously absent until my contributions began to appear. The influence of *The Modern Muse* is very apparent now as, not without rapturous self-admiration, I reread some of these schoolboy lucubrations. How perfectly, or so I thought at the time, I captured the exact tone and sentiment of Siegfried Sassoon:

> *He stood*
> *Said what he thought he should*
> *To so many boys believing they must die*
> *In order that the lie of war-bought freedom*
> *Might be told once more*
> *Beneath a third dun sky*
> *He knew*
> *That what he said was never true*
> *Nor would be ever,*
> *Two such speeches he had made before*
> *And twice his hearers had been slain by war:*
> *This time, he must be clever.*

Satirical effusions like this were often, at the expense of metre and rhyme, bowdlerised by the anonymous editors of *The Melburnian*, especially when it was obvious that they had been inspired by the annual assembly at the school's War Memorial Hall, when very Sassoonish old generals with knighthoods and scarlet faces delivered patriotic addresses on Anzac Day. The whole of our youth was steeped in legends surrounding this one episode in the First World War: a bloody defeat from which Australians were encouraged to feel they had snatched some kind of glorious victory. We were all brought up on wildly fictionalised versions of the Gallipoli campaign, written with Hibernian relish, in which the British were always depicted as murderous villains. Little has changed. Michael Davie's recent book *Anglo-Australian Attitudes*, which draws attention to these revisionist fables, has been either neglected or dismissed by the Australian press.

I also wrote a book of poems in the manner of W.H. Auden and Stephen Spender called 'The Exact Hills' (now lost), and another poetic influence was the Sitwells. Having read *Façade*, I immediately became the fourth Sitwell, writing endless pastiches in its style:

> *At dawn by Ecuador's tawn shores*
> *The paw paw flaunts its palampores . . .*

I was an autodidact in poetry – and art – as much as I was in music. My paintings were either chocolate-box impressionist or starkly cubist; expressionist self-portraits, full of adolescent angst, or whimsical surrealist collages. In poetry I jumped from style to style, one minute writing *vers libre* in the manner of Ezra Pound, the next Wyndham-Lewis-like polemics or crude anticlerical satires: distant colonial cousins of Osbert Sitwell's contributions to *Wheels*, the Vorticist annual, a set of which I had picked up at a Presbyterian church bazaar.

AT THE same jumble sale I found some American first editions of the romances and short stories of F. Scott Fitzgerald, mint in their dust jackets. This was just before Arthur Mizener's biography and the Fitzgerald revival. The by then forgotten author had been dead for fewer than ten years. I immediately connected with this lyrical writer, who was so much more sympathetic and in tune with my romantic yearnings than Ernest Hemingway, whom I had struggled to read without success. With insufferable priggishness, as I recognise it today, I liked to baffle and one-up my preceptors by larding my school essays with literary references they had no hope of recognising. These effusions, in purple ink, contained little or nothing of critical substance, but endless name-dropping of the *recherché* kind: William Beckford, Monk Lewis, Ronald Firbank, Ernest Dowson and, surely most puzzling of all to those stolid Melbourne Grammar schoolmasters, arch quotations from Fitzgerald's *Flappers and Philosophers*.

I superimposed upon prosaic school dances the sheen, the soft-focus glamour of a Fitzgerald fable in *Redbook* or *The Saturday Evening Post*: a world of bootleg gin, fast debutantes and rich boys from Yale and Princeton. I longed to inhabit some imaginary ballroom – provided, of course, that I didn't have to dance. What a punishment that was; all those 'I'm sorrys' and 'Terribly sorrys' as I regularly ground my partner's slippers into the dance floor. Somehow dancing was always more fun in fiction: in a Fred Astaire film or on some dreamlike dance floor in Waldorf-Australia.

La mer
Qu'on voit danser le long des golfes clairs
A des reflets d'argent...

Jean Sablon might fail to captivate the national-service conscripts at Puckapunyal military camp several years later, but another French *chansonnier*, Charles Trenet, provided the anthem of late adolescent romance. At dances in Ormond Hall and the more urbane Powerhouse lights were dimmed as midnight approached, and to the strains of Trenet's 'La Mer' girls' corsages of maidenhair fern and gardenia were pungently crushed. In the song the poet effusively salutes the sea, with its silver reflections, dancing beside the clear bays. 'The sea is a shepherdess clothed in heavenly blue, and look at all those wet reeds by the lakes,' he sings, 'look at those white birds and russet-roofed houses! The sea has cradled them all, as well as the poet's heart.'

'La Mer' was a salty ballad by no means overtly aphrodisiacal, but this tune was sufficient to bring all those Brians and Gillians, Jeanettes and Geoffreys, Ians and Allisons into erotic collision. Of course, no one ever tried to sing it in French, but the Dennis Farrington Band gave it a suitably Gallic rendition and Ray Noble's 'Goodnight, Sweetheart', which usually followed, never had quite the same electrifying effect on the shuffling and, for the most part, terrified couples. It took a sudden turning up of the lights and a dusty, stomping version of the Mexican Hat Dance to shake off the languors of Trenet's 1948 hit, before we drifted out to the cars and took the girls home, sometimes after a brief detour in 'tail-light alley'. It was an innocent age, when 'safe sex' meant locking the car door.

In my university days, having grown far too sophisticated for innocuous dances, I sometimes lingered in nightclubs. There were two in particular, the Moulin Rouge at Elwood Beach and the Troika. Hardly real nightclubs, these were just small, rosily lit restaurants that closed late and offered live music and, if you were known to the waiter, wine or grappa furtively served in teacups. At the absurdly misnamed Moulin Rouge the music was supplied by an accordionist. He was Leo Rosner who, less than a decade before, had stayed alive in the Lodz ghetto by playing jaunty polkas and mazurkas at SS orgies. His life was saved by Oskar Schindler and he is a key figure in Thomas Keneally's tremendous story.

We were young and green Australian students, hardly touched by death or history, as we sat late at night at the club's tables, with their red-checked cloths, flirting with our girls in the ruddy light. How could we have known or comprehended what canyons of hell Leo had sauntered down to be standing by our table now, with his accordion, benignly smiling as he serenaded the spoilt kids of Melbourne?

Years after school dances and Melbourne nightclubs Rosalind, my second wife, and I spent Christmas at the famous La Mamounia Hotel in Marrakesh. I think we had hoped to avoid

Christmas in London, only to discover that this Moroccan oasis during the festive season was filled with Berber tribesmen, dressed as Santa Claus, galloping wildly around the town brandishing holly-trimmed cutlasses. At the hotel, which Churchill had loved, there was a *grande fête de Noël* on Christmas Eve, and the cabaret performer was to be none other than Charles Trenet. On all the tables, which were draped with pink linen and groaning with Arabian delicacies, stood enormous candelabra and when, towards midnight, the celebrated *chansonnier* was announced, the lights dimmed and Trenet himself, with straw boater, pink cheeks and sparkling eyes, stepped up to the microphone and the orchestra played the first chord of his most celebrated song:

La mer . . .

Above us, small hatches opened in the ceiling, and those of us whose attention had momentarily strayed from the singer observed grinning Berbers pushing hundreds of pink balloons out over the dining room. The rosy globes, no doubt released on a mistaken cue, floated downwards until they touched the candelabra. The rest of 'La Mer', song of my youth, was drowned by a seemingly endless series of explosions. I watched Trenet's face as I had watched his compatriot Jean Sablon's on that ill-fated night at Puckapunyal. But on this Christmas Eve there were no crude homophobic taunts from the sophisticated audience, who in any case were far too busy scrambling to catch these quasi-bombs before they hit the flames. Trenet, no doubt thinking of his fee, soldiered on, miming his repertoire through the stench of burning rubber.

WHENEVER, as a young child, I asked my mother 'difficult' questions she would say, 'One day your father will give you a book.' I could never understand why a book came into it.

I had asked quite specifically how babies were born: how, for example, had I come into being? She did not reply, merely looked evasive and said more firmly, as if she hadn't heard the question, 'I told you, Barry, your father will give you a book like Mrs Kendall gave Billo.'

Billo, the son of my mother's mentor who lived up the street, was a much older boy, almost a young man. He was often upheld to me as a paragon, and so what was good enough for Mrs Kendall's Billo was good enough for me.

When Billo was killed in the early years of the war, I was told the tragic news in only the briefest detail. Perhaps due to wartime security the place and the circumstances of his death were hush-hush, but by then I assumed that it would have been futile for me to inquire anyway. Death, I had come to understand, like babies, was a taboo subject, and in due course I would receive a book about it. I wondered if Mr Kendall had been as forgetful or dilatory as my own father in this regard. Had Billo read the Death Book before actually dying, or had he been given an opportunity to enjoy it prior to being blown up in Tripoli (as I discovered forty years later)?

As it happened, my poor father never got around to telling

me anything, verbally or in literary form. There was never even a hesitant moment of mutual embarrassment as he *tried* to tell me something. In consequence the onset of puberty was an alarming experience, and I assumed that the physical phenomena – the hormonal maelstrom, the pustules, sproutings, stiffenings, surges and ejaculations – were all shamefully exclusive to me. It was a measure of my aloofness from rougher boys of my own age, and perhaps of a congenital loneliness, that I never compared notes.

Ultimately I bought my own books, where the mysteries of sex, if not explained, were at least depicted in the varied panoply of fiction. Clandestinely, in the works of notorious authors, I read of improbable couplings and sexual behaviour that was more often artistically occluded than helpfully described. Alas, the *Tales of D.H. Lawrence* was confiscated from my shelves before I even had a chance to read it, but from my parents' strange looks and manner when I asked for it back, I gathered that by merely possessing this volume I had somehow forfeited my innocence; the part of me my parents had loved. Thus I felt blamed for not knowing; guilty because I was afraid.

When stubble began to appear patchily on my impetiginous chin and elsewhere, I secretly borrowed my father's Gillette safety razor and, carefully guiding it around the pimples, managed to restore my face at least to something like its prepubescent innocence. One day, unannounced, there was another razor – a new one – placed without comment beside my father's on the bathroom shelf.

With such a pact of secrecy, in which I learnt to collude, it was all the more horrifying when one day my parents discovered a drawing in the back pages of my exercise book: a simple academic anatomical study, in Dürer-like detail, of an erect penis. I am uncertain how old I was, perhaps only thirteen, but my self-portrait was clearly intended to be discovered; it was not so much a *cri de coeur* as a *cri de verge*.

The school required all parents to initial their children's homework, and on that fateful day mine was left on the dining-room table just after breakfast for the routine monogram. They only had to turn a few pages beyond some routine essay to behold, in tumescent and explosive detail, the unequivocal phallus making its claim at last; breaking the silence and pre-empting Billo's book, which no doubt contained far less graphic illustrations. I remember my father's words as, reeling from the shock, he charged upstairs.

'What is the meaning of this?' he asked, brandishing my sullied exercise book as I was cleaning my teeth.

Stunned, I made no reply. Had I found the words, I would have said – *should have said* – 'I don't know, you tell me!' But I remained mute and shamefaced, resigning myself to their disappointment. They assumed, I suppose, that a caricature of a disembodied organ meant that I knew far more than I should have known about that which, in reality, I knew nothing.

But they were off the hook. No further need for father–son chats or awkward equivocations or Billo's books. Just years of reproachful silence, until much later, and certainly later than many of my contemporaries had conducted their sticky experiments in parked cars and behind dance halls, I warily and clumsily sought my own erotic information at first-hand – and was once again found out. What they found out I can't remember, and it can hardly have been much, but my father – normally a mild-mannered man and never a swearer, except for a few 'bloodies' in front of the carpenters and brickies – went berserk.

It was my mother, at her chilliest, who provided the prelude to this appalling incident.

'Your father has had a phone call from G's parents,' she announced from the table, not looking at me as I entered the dining room.

A 'fast' girl was named, who could occasionally be induced to expose her breasts after a dance and a few sherries. My father dropped his knife and fork with a clatter on his plate and stood up, white-faced. I attempted an unconvincing denial. A scuffle ensued, followed by an undignified chase around the house. I was too quick for my father, who finally stood, ashen and panting, at the front door as I fled into the garden. I can still see him there under the neo-Georgian fanlight, the back of his head reflected in a round, scallop-edged, peach-coloured mirror.

'I've got a good mind to cut your cock off!' he cried, while my mother, hovering behind him, called out ineffectually, 'Eric, come inside. Do we really want the whole world to hear this?'

She retreated to the neutrality of the sunroom, where, had she but known it, the advent of television would anchor her for thirty years.

Days later, after a long and frozen moratorium, she said to me, 'What a pity, Barry. You used to be so *nice*.'

Sunny Sam, it seemed, had gone forever.

AARON AZIMUTH

~

It may be taken for granted that the avoidance
of ennui, in whatever form that whimsical complaint
makes itself felt, is one of the most instinctive
prepossessions of the human race

ARTHUR CHRISTOPHER BENSON

I ONCE asked Graham Greene what book he was working on at present.

'My address book,' he replied. 'Crossing out the dead!'

Now, several times a year, I perform the same melancholy task. But when I was eighteen, death was an unfamiliar visitor. The only people close to me who had died were my Uncle Wilf and little Roslyn Forbes.

However, at my first military camp, after I finished school, I expected to follow Uncle Wilf and Roslyn. Around me were regiments of the Keen. In that khaki hellhole, Keenness assumed for me the repugnant lineaments of a vice. Keen young recruits were everywhere, and moreover they were armed with lethal weapons such as rifles and grenades.

When the time came for me to enter a narrow trench,

withdraw the pin and hurl my grenade over the parapet at some mythical foe, Sergeant Quee, a foul-mouthed English regular-army bully, snatched the grenade from my hand and threw it himself, with a whispered injunction to 'Never say a fuckin' word about not hav'n' fuckin' thrown it your fuckin' self.'

Sergeant Quee wasn't taking any chances with a butter-fingered, pansy private who looked as if he might easily drop a live grenade.

It was a relief to escape from camp, at the end of my incarceration, to the comparative luxury of that other place of internment, Melbourne University.

WHILE still at school I had bought, by instalments, the art books from which I first learnt of the antics of the Berlin and Zurich Dadaists. Instantly my life changed. There were some boys who wanted to be farmers; others businessmen; and my friend John Levi wanted to be, of all things, a rabbi. I, not without a sense of deep relief, decided then and there to become a Dadaist, starting immediately.

Instinctively, it seemed, I had a gift for that peculiar combination of ferocity and absurdity that marked the authentic Dadaist. Poems, 'works of art' and manifestos in this new style were soon flowing from my pyrogenous imagination.

Now the crowbar is well under her, heave, and after five minutes tugging, the first object to strike the eye is a group of milk-white slugs cuddling snugly together.

Howbeit, there is a curious practice followed by dealers in lobsters, which Azimuth always considered the obvious necessity of using specific carbons, undoubtedly the most important event in the history of mankind.

The Daughter of a Rich Shoe, Azimuth had a lifelong admiration for Jenny Geddes' Stool, which, in Glamorgan, can be grown as an agricultural crop. She loved her parents dearly before turning southward and flowing through the Himalayas in a series of gorgeous mughouse riots. His most precious possession was that curious work, Coryate's 'Crudities,' a kind of erotic dog.

The back of Pope Azimuth's scalp was perfect and had a remarkably fresh appearance, the pores of the skin being more distinct, as they usually are when soaked in moisture. At this time he encountered Herrick's Sappho, whose famous salutation we record once more:

'That wottest thou no clearer than I.
What art thou called thou big man?'

It appears that five houses were brought up alive, and in spite of their instructions for threading the desert, the exiles lost their way, the reobtaining of which is as valuable as that of a group.

Aaron Azimuth, *The Blue Lamington*

The above extract from a novel appeared in the 1953 catalogue of the Second Pan-Australasian Dada Exhibition, held at Melbourne University. It was created, in traditional Dada–surrealist fashion, by opening books at random and transcribing sentences and sometimes whole paragraphs wherever a pencil arbitrarily fell. Many long prose works thus randomly confected were collaborations between John Perry, an old school friend with a natural gift for expressionism, and me, but I was the pseudonymous Aaron Azimuth.

At home, however, I was still Barry, a name I found embarrassingly dull. It was, after all, the masculine counterpart of Shirley; a thirties name without a history except for a minor Thackeray novel, which is certainly not where my parents would have found it. It was not a film star's name either: Barry Fitzgerald only became a star in the late thirties and was too much of a professional Irishman to appeal to my mother. Still, I like to think of my parents sitting in the lounge of the new Rivoli picture theatre in Camberwell, passing the Old Gold Assortment back and forth, back and forth, and trying to decide on a name for their firstborn.

At Melbourne University Dr Aaron Azimuth, Dadaist, was sworn foe of all Barrys and Shirleys; enemy of my parents too, with their suburban certainties and their seemingly effortless ability to live happily without Art. Azimuth in his public appearances resembled a mad doctor from the German expressionist cinema: he was like the eponymous hero of my favourite film, *The Cabinet of Dr Caligari*. He wore a long black coat, and a black homburg emphasising a deathly white make-up and mascara'd eyes. He recited his poems and tirades in a loud staccato voice and extolled madness and violence as the ultimate virtues. It was an exquisitely liberating disguise.

Of course, I was not always able to *look* like Dr Aaron Azimuth; for much of the time I was obliged to resemble any other timid nineteen-year-old arts student: tweed sports coat, crewneck jumper, Viyella shirt and grey slacks. But I was an aspiring fancy-pants. A suburban dandy, I contrived to achieve variations on this traditional uniform – as much a uniform then as blue denim is today. I sported a red paisley bow tie, the only one in the faculty, and tied by me – no common made-up tie or clip-on. Sometimes I wore a yellow jumper with a bright overcheck, for it was important to make an impression, a slight stir. My hair was longer than everyone else's, although certainly not by today's standards: *Can't you tell the barber to give you a proper haircut, Barry?* And I smoked gold-tipped Muratti Aristons – a Turkish blend.

In this dandified get-up I would arrive at lectures, slightly late, with Joan Stanton, my friend and companion of that distant time: a beautiful girl with blue eyes and a honey-coloured page-boy who sometimes wore a svelte blue dress, in striking contrast to all those twin-sets of bottle green and maize, Black Watch tartan skirts, brogues and sockettes sported by the other girls.

The lectures passed like a dream. So boring. Nothing was as stimulating as the inner angry life of Dadaism: my life as Aaron Azimuth, my Mr Hyde. It was a secret life of subversive jokes, of adult-baiting, of *actes gratuits*, quixotic and inexpedient.

The first big Dadaist exhibition of 1952, in my first year at university, established my notoriety, with its provocative sculptures of perishable materials such as cake and offal, juxtaposed with undergraduate blasphemy and the odd insult to the Royal Family. At the Puckapunyal military camp I had found a discarded portrait in oils of King George VI by an artist of moderate competence. The medals the King wore were particularly well executed and I merely had to paint the word 'Dada' meticulously on one of them, sign the picture myself and put it in an elaborate frame for the work to be mine. It may surprise a modern reader to learn that this was the exhibit that gave the greatest offence.

Another surprisingly provocative exhibit was a large 'shoescape' consisting of decayed boots retrieved from a nearby rubbish dump. These were nailed onto a board that was then conventionally framed. I created a number of these footnotes to the history of Australian Dadaism, and a photograph even appeared in the local paper of my young self in natty bow tie and sportscoat earnestly expounding the aesthetics of the shoescape to a group of suitably impressed undergraduettes.

I once possessed a copy of this historic photograph but it was lost long ago. Thinking back on this time in my life, and remembering with affection my fellow student Joan, I decided to try to track her down.

'It's funny we should be speaking again,' she said when we finally made contact, 'because I've just found an old photograph of you with one of your shoescapes, and me in the background.'

Joan's photograph – Joan is the girl second from the right – now illustrates this book. Later she told my editor on the telephone that she once had quite a few letters that I had written to her from military camp.

'I wish I'd kept them,' she said, laughing. 'How was I to know he was going to be famous?'

In second year I was up for election to the student representative council, and my public address as a likely candidate was the opportunity for a Dadaist demonstration in the university's largest lecture theatre – where, incidentally, my future father-in-law Stephen Spender was to give a public address and poetry reading a year or so later.

Before a packed audience of students our little group of Johns (we all possessed the first name John, even me), wearing cretin masks, stood bravely performing our absurd acts of provocation. John Levi presided over an electric toaster in which the toast, to the intense frustration of the audience, was allowed to burn without intervention, filling the large lecture theatre with smoke. John Watson, a friend and Dada conscript, merely poured water from one large vessel into another, and back again. John Perry wrote the word 'poem' in huge letters on a blackboard with his right hand while erasing it with his left, so that the word never completely took form. I displayed a large painting of cows in a landscape by the nineteenth-century Australian artist Jan Hendrik Scheltema, which I had bought from Mr Duncan for comparatively little, although today it would be worth at least $20,000. Announcing that I intended to publicly 'execute a painting', I produced an axe and proceeded to hack this large gold-framed picture to pieces until our audience was in a state of uproar.

When the Dada group performed our revue *Call Me Madman!*, it was in the true ferocious tradition of the old Cabaret Voltaire. One of the more sensational sketches was called 'Indian Famine'. A large table was placed centre stage, piled with food that we had bought that morning at the markets. There was a great deal of raw meat, interspersed with vegetables:

a veritable pyramid of plenty. My colleague Graeme Hughes sat on one side of the table, dressed as a clergyman. I was seated on the other in a woman's long evening gown and wearing a crazed wig.

There was a brief announcement over the loudspeakers: 'We take you to a mission station somewhere in Bengal where the Reverend J. Big and his wife, Mrs Tum, are discussing the day's events.'

> HUGHES (*reading from newspaper*) The Indians are starving again, I see. There's a terrible famine. Millions of the population dying from want of food. There's a picture here of a dying woman being eaten alive by a starving child. Oh, the pity of it. The pity!
>
> HUMPHRIES (*laughing wildly*) I couldn't care less.
>
> HUGHES Helpless children, barren mothers . . .
>
> HUMPHRIES I'm glad, yes glad. I've got plenty of food, lovely food, and THEY'VE GOT NOTHING!

At this point, in the role of the vicar's wife, who was obviously experiencing a major menopausal breakdown, I began to hurl meat, cake and vegetables across the stage at my husband, who ignored these missiles and continued to recite grim details of famine from his newspaper. By then I was shrieking with maniacal laughter, and at the same time bragging about Australia's plentiful supplies of food as I began to throw cabbages, potatoes and even filet mignon directly into the audience. It was too much. The packed theatre of students, who had at first been coerced into sympathy with the starving millions, were now goaded into an irrational frenzy of retaliation. They began to throw the food back at the actors, shouting abuse and attempting to clamber onto the stage. Hughes and I made a bolt for it, but a Dadaist triumph had been achieved. We may have been a rather pathetic thirty-five years too late jumping on the Dada bandwagon, but we were successful neophytes in the art of provocation. Our little revue sketch had been of no consequence; it was the tangential irruption of the audience that had become the Work of Art.

Two of our favourite meeting places, where Dadaist events and outrages were planned, were the Ewing Gallery and Luna Park. The Ewing Gallery was a long room up several flights of narrow stairs over the Union Theatre, where I was to begin my career as an actor a few years later. In the Ewing Gallery was displayed a small collection of Australian paintings, mostly of the pastoral school of the twenties, with one rather large and arresting female nude by Charles Wheeler. The collection had been bequeathed to the university by Samuel Ewing. Being a gallery of art, the Ewing was naturally the least visited place on the campus. There, surrounded by decorous green landscapes, gum trees and romantic representations of the bush, we could hold our subversive meetings in peace.

Then there was Luna Park, Melbourne's famous fun fair by the sea at St Kilda, which you entered through the grinning mouth of an enormous and not wholly benevolent mask. Luna Park was like an Australian version of Il Parco dei Mostri at Bomarzo. The painter Sidney Nolan later told me he spent his happiest times as a child riding on some of Luna Park's perilous attractions. It was the atmosphere of Luna Park that appealed to me and my fellow Dadaists – the peals of insane laughter that issued from loudspeakers outside the Giggle Palace, and the real screams of passengers on the Big Dipper, the Scenic Railway and the Jack and Jill as their rickety trolleys crested the switchback and plunged them, bawling, into the abyss. The place was always thronged with people whom my mother would regard as unequivocally common, all noisily surrendering in various ways to the forces of gravity.

I once saw, displayed outside the While-U-Wait photo booth, a snapshot of my young brother's former nanny, Valmai Grubb, and her sister, Wilma, brashly attired and on the arms of two sailors. The heady climate of Luna Park had obviously coaxed this shy Salvation Army lassie out of her shell.

Aaron Azimuth made some of his most effective public appearances at Luna Park, sometimes tapping with a Nosferatu-like finger on the shoulders of a nervous couple in the seat in front of him as the Big Dipper was about to make its vertiginous descent. The young lovers would glance back to behold a white-faced ghoul with imitation blood leaking from its eyes and mouth, compounding their terror a hundredfold.

WHEN I first began university, my friend Robert Nathan and I often drove around the more prosperous suburbs late at night, after the last tram had departed, and trawled for solitary revellers trudging home or, hopefully, hitchhiking. Robert would slow down and ask if they wanted a lift. This was usually accepted with alacrity, especially by young couples stranded without transport after a dance. Once they were seated in the car, Robert would politely ask where they were going and offer to take them anywhere within reason, provided they had no objection to a brief detour at the Kew psychiatric hospital to drop off a patient. The back-seat passengers would then notice, seated beside the driver, a sombrely attired figure with a black hat, swaying gently and crooning softly to himself.

Robert took care to drive slowly and carefully down dark and deserted streets until the mysterious passenger began to make strange choking and gurgling noises interspersed with harsh laughter.

'Faster, faster!' cried Aaron Azimuth, for it was he.

Robert obediently increased his speed.

'Faster, faster!' screamed the madman in the front seat, and the driver obligingly accelerated.

We always found that our petrified passengers leapt from the car at the first red traffic light and fled fearfully into the night, miles from their destination. Thereafter we liked to imagine that their lives had been indelibly imprinted with an experience of terror, staged as fastidiously as a play or poem.

Robert Nathan and I, between our adventures in the early Dadaist days, occasionally attended spiritualist meetings in the Masonic Hall in Malvern. The congregation consisted mostly of elderly women and there was a strong odour, if not of sanctity, at least of talcum powder, stale perspiration and some other nameless emanation – ectoplasm perhaps.

I am ashamed to confess that sitting in the back row

listening to the service, we were prone to painful spasms of suppressed laughter. Afterwards the more psychic ladies gave private readings at the back of the hall. One had to give them some small personal effect, through which they claimed to receive a transmission from the future. Naturally we viewed all this with hilarious scepticism and it was difficult to keep a straight face, especially when one exceptionally whiffy old duck, clutching my handkerchief and closing her eyes in rapt reverie, told me she could see me on a stage of some kind, surrounded by skyscrapers. She could also see Robert, wearing a white turban. In my case she was certainly not describing Melbourne, for our tallest building was only twelve storeys high. Could she mean New York? I wondered. I had absolutely no intention of ever visiting the United States of America, but the clairvoyant insisted that it would one day be my destination.

Within a number of months, my friend Robert was struck down with Hodgkinson's disease, and when I last saw him in hospital, after surgery to relieve cranial pressure, his head was swathed in white bandages.

GRADUALLY my incarnations as Dr Aaron Azimuth grew fewer and by my mid-twenties I had abjured forever the deathly make-up, the blackened expressionist eyes, the homburg and the wing collar that had been a kind of armour for my young self against the terrors of public performance, and in which disguise I had found the courage to perpetrate my puny acts of sociopathology.

WONDERLAND

~

Love is more pleasant than marriage for the
same reason that novels are more amusing than history
Sébastien Roch Nicolas Chamfort

My academic career was only marginally longer and more successful than my career in the Australian Army. After two years spent mostly in Dadaist pursuits and theatrical diversions, I 'dropped out'. Unfortunately the phrase 'to drop out' had not been invented and an uglier, although perhaps more honest, term was applied to my abandonment of academic life: failure.

My parents were at their wits' end, and at that stage in my life I suppose I should have been grateful that the word 'loser' was also an epithet of the future. All my friends seemed set on their vocational paths; but I, once so full of promise, felt already burnt out and adrift. In order not to bring total disgrace upon the family, I numbly accepted a job that my father had wrangled for me in the wholesale record department of EMI, although I continued to appear in student plays and revues by night. Ultimately these led to my first professional theatrical engagements, and my decision to become a full-time actor. However, all too soon my family would receive the final blow: an event that took even me by surprise – marriage.

I had fallen in love with Brenda, an exquisite young dancer and actress, and the most inconvenient thing about this otherwise delightful liaison was that I still lived at home, and so did she. I had made, in the past, a few desultory attempts at independence but had been lured, and in one case hijacked, back to Christowel Street by my baffled parents, who failed to see why I would prefer some dismal and 'bohemian' lodgings to the sumptuous flat, furnished in the latest fifties mode, that had been created for me at the back of our house. The fact that it possessed no separate entrance, but was only accessible by ascending the main staircase and passing my parent's bedroom, seemed to them not in the least degree inhibitory.

I had disappointed my parents with my academic failure, and I had also acquired a dubious circle of new friends, moving in raffish artistic circles where drink and nicotine exerted their perfidious influence.

Once, when my parents were away for several days, I decided to throw a party in the family home for my new acquaintances. It seemed a pity that no party had ever been held there in living memory and several of the larger rooms, especially the recently extended sunroom, which opened through French windows onto the back terrace, were perfect for entertainment. It was perhaps the Convivial Spirit that was so palpably absent in those large and too-infrequently used apartments.

Surely if I distributed enough ashtrays and got rid of all the empty bottles there would still be a couple of days before my parents' return? By that time I would have opened all forty-five windows and allowed Melbourne's sweet and respectable zephyrs to flush out the miasmic residue of my clandestine soirée.

On the appointed night, and to my alarm, a lot more people turned up than I had expected. It seemed that all the habitués of the saloon bar of the Swanston Family Hotel thought they were invited, even when they were not; moreover they assumed that this tacit invitation included their friends. Never had such a heterogeneous collection of artists, models, alcoholic journalists, small-time actors, suburban potters, hangers-on, gate-crashers and barflies descended upon the quiet decorum of Christowel Street.

Shouting, laughing and singing, my guests debouched from a strange caravanserai of taxis, battered station wagons and ramshackle pick-up trucks and made their way up my parents' sedate driveway. Lights flicked on in neighbours' houses and curtains twitched. Soon every light downstairs in our house was blazing and the radiogram, long accustomed to Ravel and Delius, was blasting forth at full volume that tiresome new musical novelty, rock'n'roll. During the course of an interminable evening the telephone rang several times with complaints from sleepless neighbours as I tried in vain to turn the music down and at the same time prevent intoxicated strangers from wandering upstairs or extinguishing their cigarettes on the mushroom wall-to-wall. At length, between 4 and 5 a.m., the liquor ran out and my guests noisily departed.

No sooner had they gone than I began attacking the

Augean stables that had once been my mother's spotless home. It was as well that I had begun the cleaning-up process rather than passing out, for at 8.30 a.m. there was a telephone call from Geelong announcing that my parents were returning earlier than expected and would be home within an hour or two. I worked furiously, vacuuming every corner, washing plates and glasses and moving furniture to conceal cigarette burns in the carpet.

There remained a distinct reek of stale beer and tobacco smoke hanging in the air, and I frantically tried to dispel this or at least smother it with the sweeter and more distracting odour of eau de cologne, which I splashed around in lavish aspergations. As I lugged the last sackful of empty bottles and stashed it in the boot of my mother's baby Austin, which I was then permitted to drive, I caught a glimpse of Mr and Mrs Tootell, our next-door neighbours, standing on their front lawn staring at me through the shrubbery. Their expression was far worse than disapproval; it was disappointment. That phrase of my mother's, oft repeated, came back to me as I locked away the clinking evidence: *It's hard to believe, Barry, but you used to be such a nice boy.*

I hadn't slept a wink and, although I had been far from sober during the evening, I was sober as, chewing a breath-freshener, I tried to assume an air of nonchalance when the large grey Buick carrying my parents purred up the driveway. The house was almost too clean. The vacuum cleaner that I had plied with such frenzy half an hour before stood incriminatingly in the middle of the front hall. I had forgotten to put it away.

My father, preoccupied as usual with business, seemed not

to notice anything. My mother looked at the vacuum cleaner and the open windows and then at me, but 'I see you've been taking care of the house, Barry' was her only tart comment.

'Would you like a cup of tea?' I asked. However, at that moment my parents' attention was elsewhere. They were looking fixedly up the staircase with an expression on their faces I did not recognise.

Ambling down the carpeted stairs, wearing nothing but one of my father's best Van Heusen shirts, was Pauline, a notorious figure in Melbourne's artistic circles: once model, now dipsomaniac. Despite her harelip, Pauline had been pretty long ago, or was said to have been. Now she was a Toulouse-Lautrec; she was La Goulue. Her dishevelled hair, the colour of hay, was caught up in an unruly topknot, and her rouged cheeks looked as though her face had been the target of a beetroot-throwing contest. The shirt had been rendered shorter by the projection of her large breasts, exposing, as she tottered unsteadily from step to step, a dark delta of pubic curls. She had passed out, as I later discovered, in my parents' bed, and I had never thought to check the upper rooms of the house when I had been so busily exorcising the party.

My mother and father were speechless as Pauline, clinging to the banister and with a certain stateliness that sometimes invests the permanently drunk, croaked, 'Barry darling, is there still a cold one in the fridge?'

The apparition of Pauline and the night of riot that it betrayed were blows to my parents from which they never quite recovered. Incrementally, their disillusionment with me grew.

I had fallen in with 'an older crowd', and a bad lot they were. To some extent, although I never revealed this, I agreed with my parents' assessment, and I hoped I would never see Pauline again. But this other life had its dangerous and heady allure, and I knew that something very terrible and very frightening lay in store for me: the life of an artist.

Not long after this incident I accepted an invitation from the director of the Union Theatre Repertory Company to become a full-time actor with them. We embarked on a tour of *Twelfth Night* and Zoe Caldwell was my co-star. Visiting the small country towns of Victoria in a play by Shakespeare about a group of Arcadians who all fall in love with the wrong people, I realised that a miracle had occurred: I had left home.

It was halfway into the subsequent repertory season that I dropped the final bombshell on my poor parents by announcing my intention to get married. At this distance in time it is difficult to say whether it really was my intention or her intention or anyone's intention, but unlike a new and taxing role in repertory theatre, the role of husband was one that I had to improvise without a script and in the presence of a highly sceptical and unresponsive audience.

Although I enjoyed the season I spent at the Union Theatre itself, I was still far from convinced that acting was my destiny. I always had difficulty learning lines, a task that was not ameliorated by my mid-season excursion into matrimony. In the theatre I generally preferred to improvise. My happiest moments on stage were during the Christmas production in 1955 when we presented a light-hearted revue called *Return*

Fare, for which I wrote a number of songs and sketches. It was the first time Mrs Edna Everage appeared on the stage: a simpering, painfully shy housewife offering accommodation in her lovely home to the foreign athletes who would soon be coming to Melbourne for the 1956 Olympic Games. Mrs Everage spent most of the sketch extolling the felicities of her interior decorations and seemed only willing to billet an athlete if he or she was white, clean and spoke English. Edna was also reluctant to cater to exotic culinary demands. I had once heard a similar Melbourne lady making a fuss in one of the city's better 'continental' restaurants. Having summoned the head waiter, she rose from her chair and pointed to the innocuous plate of ravioli on the table.

'Is it asking too much,' she shrilled, while her husband cowered in the chair beside her, trying to look invisible, 'is it asking too much to get a nice plate of *good, clean Australian food*?'

The angular, censorious and somewhat prissy Edna of lower-middle-class Moonee Ponds might not recognise the grandiloquent and imperious Dame who recently appeared on stage at Buckingham Palace and introduced the Queen herself as 'the Jubilee Girl'. The two Ednas are separated, miraculously, by nearly half a century.

In 1956, without my parents' blessing, I moved to Sydney with my new bride. I had been to that city only once before: as a boy when my parents had decided, one school holidays, to take me on my first excursion outside Victoria. My father thought it might be more amusing if we travelled by sea so we made the two-day journey on that somewhat rusty relic of the Orient Line, HMS *Orontes*. Formerly a fairly luxurious liner, the *Orontes* had served as a hospital ship during the war and was now relegated to short runs around the Australian coastline. My young brothers, Christopher and Michael, whose existence I only rarely contemplated, were absent from this trip. They were probably deemed too young to travel over perilous waters in safety. Approached from the sea, the landfall of Sydney was certainly impressive, and the first sight of the famous Coat-hanger Bridge was a thrilling spectacle, making Melbourne by comparison seem like a big country town even to my adolescent eye.

Now I was back. The big bad capital of New South Wales was to introduce me to many new things, with all their splendours and miseries, terrors and delights. I was in my first year of marriage; I had been invited to join a successful theatrical company at the Phillip Street Theatre, which specialised in intimate revue; and my father and mother were far away on a world cruise.

My wife and I began our life in Sydney in bed-sitting rooms and boarding houses before moving to a proper flat in Wonderland Avenue, Tamarama, near Bondi. Long ago the beach had been the location of a famous seaside fun fair. Ours was not so much a flat as the back half of Hame Lauren, a brick house built in the thirties in a popular but unlovely hybrid style of Californian bungalow, with Tudor embellishments. The house, at the end of a long 'battleaxe' driveway, was perched high on a cliff above a gully that ran steeply down to the surf beach.

I never swam there but it is still considered one of Sydney's most dangerous, with a fearsome rip. There was something wild, bleak and even inimical about the house and its location, particularly since the absent owner had locked off the front of her residence, which faced the Pacific, and we could only peep through her windows to glimpse what a comfortable residence we might have occupied. Every night after the show I would make my way back to Wonderland Avenue, sometimes early, not seldom tardily, on the swaying, rattling Bondi tram.

I RECENTLY found myself once more in Wonderland Avenue. The famous Bondi tram that, years before, had taken me within a few streets of Hame Lauren had long since been consigned to some vehicular knacker's yard. Drawn by curiosity and nostalgia, I rang the bell of that almost unrecognisable abode, and when the door was opened by a bright young 'homemaker' I delivered the classic line 'I lived here once.'

The pleasant young woman gladly admitted me. She occupied the whole house, not just its gloomy and oppressive rear end, and for the first time I looked out at the view: the long gully of Tamarama falling steeply below to the Naples yellow crescent moon of the beach and the curdling surf beyond.

'We completely rebuilt the old kitchen,' she said. 'It was horrible, wasn't it?'

'Yes,' I said, remembering. 'It felt a bit spooky.'

'We found out that in the thirties someone had committed suicide there.'

'I didn't know,' I said.

'And under the house there are some caves that were used by the Aborigines – did you know that?'

'No,' I said.

'Houses built on Aboriginal sites sometimes have a funny atmosphere, but this house feels happy now, doesn't it?'

'It does now,' I said.

SYDNEY without its Opera House was a very different city from today's. Phillip Street, where our little theatre stood, was still largely residential; washing was hung out to dry on the cast-iron balconies of terrace houses and urchins played in the street. The highrise was a thing of the future and there were still at least seven live theatres in the city that no one had yet thought of tearing down.

I discovered Lorenzini's, Sydney's first bistro, in Elizabeth Street, where writers and journalists met for lunch on Fridays. For only a few shillings Hank, the proprietor, would produce a glass of wine and a plate of watery Rigatoni al Pomodoro. More often as an eavesdropper than as a garrulous participant, I would bask in 'literary' conversations on topics such as Kingsley Amis and a new book everyone was talking about called *The Outsider*, by Colin Wilson. Here I met the author Kylie Tennant, and John Douglas Pringle, formerly the editor of the London *Observer* and then editing *The Sydney Morning Herald*. I muttered something to him about my writing and he asked to see a specimen. I think I sent him a fragment of a novel I was working on.

He wrote me in reply what I can best describe as an encouraging letter of rejection.

I also began to visit art galleries around Sydney and befriended Mrs John Young and her daughter Clarice, who had a small art restoration studio in a city building. Mrs Young's husband had founded the famous Macquarie Galleries and his widow occasionally sold me Australian pictures on a generous installment principle. It was from her that I bought a little watercolour of Botany Bay painted in 1888 by the young Charles Conder before he set off for Europe and a brief cosmopolitan celebrity. With its lady on the beach twirling her crimson parasol, it hangs before me now as I write these words.

The tiny box office of the Phillip Street Theatre was often manned by a young Hungarian called Paul Riomfalvy, who was also a director of the theatre. He had not been in Sydney long. Both before and after the revolution of 1956 many of his countrymen had sought refuge in Australia, particularly in Sydney. Traditionally the Poles chose Melbourne.

Unlike several of this theatre's executives who were conspicuously drawn to their own sex, Paul had both a wife and a mistress, who were also Hungarian; and, as most Hungarian women are, they were both ravishingly attractive. Paul's wife would accompany him to backstage parties, while the mistress would often attend performances, always sitting in the centre of the third or fourth row, so I had a clear view of her from the stage. Whenever Szylvia was present I would give my best and what I hoped might be my funniest performance, addressing it to an audience of one. It was a youthful fantasy, but I was convinced that had circumstances been otherwise – *very other-wise* – she would have gladly rejected her compatriot for me. Again I felt the odd, atavistic tug of Central Europe, although what little my family knew of its roots did nothing to confirm the existence of a Magyar ancestor, and the theory of reincarnation always struck me as ridiculous.

Indeed anyone who starts talking about reincarnation invariably finds my attention wandering. Sometimes Dame Edna will ask a surprised woman in the audience whether she believes in it, and if the woman hesitates Edna says reassuringly, 'You look as though you used to be *something*.' Metempsychosis, with astrology, I put high on the list of sexual depressants. When a woman asks me my star sign, however attractive she might be, I experience an instant urge to bolt. Likewise the apologists for reincarnation, who might hitherto have seemed desirable and even intelligent, have the same effect upon me as a letter written in green ink with circles over the i's and a smiley face over the signature. Still, my mother, with her mysterious antecedence, dark eyes and Romany cast, and her un-Australian flashes of intuition, always suggested an exotic genealogy.

Of course, not all Hungarians in Sydney are Hungarians. A number of post-war German and Austrian immigrants to Australia with a dubious political past have preferred to claim citizenship of a nation marginally more sympathetic than their own, although its war record was no less infamous. It was for a different reason, perhaps because I felt so un-Australian, that I whimsically appropriated a Hungarian ancestry. This phenomenon is not so uncommon if, for example, you think of those who have pretended to be Irish: Micheál MacLiammóir, Arnold Bax and Patrick O'Brien – Poms posing as Paddies! And not forgetting that celebrated faux Irishman J.P. Donleavy.

Whenever I am in Budapest, eating goulash and listening to the thrum of the cimbalom and the *zigeuner* fiddlers, I always feel a curious sensation of homecoming. I can find my way around the city without map or guidebook. Moreover I am often greeted like an old friend by perfect strangers at the Gerbeaud coffeehouse or in the lobby of the Gellért Hotel. Disappointingly these usually turn out to be prosperous Hungarians from Double Bay, Sydney, on a brief visit home to show off the money they have made Down Under in restaurants and real estate. Avid theatregoers, they always recognise me.

LIVING in Sydney, liberated geographically from my home town, yet constrained by marital bonds recently and quixotically forged, I began to learn things about my own aspirations and appetites that I was not always pleased to discover. My marriage had been so sudden that my poor parents had not been given an opportunity to adjust to an event they saw as a disaster. My father and Michael were the only family members to attend the ceremony, but six months later, before my parents set off on their long world trip, they relaxed their disapproval and gave us a belated wedding present: a cheque for £500. With this money in a Sydney bank account we might have been able to exist in moderate comfort in that alien city, but I was never a prudent spender.

The theatre was fashionable: it was even what might today be called trendy. The comic roles in the revues presented therein were not altogether worthy of my superior talents – or so I conceitedly felt at the time – but at the age of twenty-two I was being paid as an actor, and my stage antics seemed to divert the audiences of New South Wales as much as they had entertained my Melbourne cronies. Moreover I was surrounded by new and amusing people in a big, raffish, bad-mannered city.

Amongst the stalwarts of the Phillip Street Theatre was an English actor called Gordon Chater, the like of whom I had never met. Over twelve years my senior, Gordon was already a comic star. He had studied medicine at Cambridge, had volunteered for the Royal Navy during the war and in 1946 had found himself demobilised in Sydney. The rest of his life was spent in the theatre and he was an accomplished *farceur*. He wore loud black-and-white hound's-tooth checks and thick horn-rimmed glasses, and seemed always to be chortling with laughter. To my wife and me he was friendly and hospitable from the very first.

When we came to perform *Around the Loop*, a show that ran for fifty-eight weeks, Gordon and I shared a dressing-room with the ageing matinée idol Max Oldaker. It was a show of fast costume changes and we were perpetually running up and down the steep wooden stairs to the stage in various extravagant disguises. Most of Gordon's impersonations seemed to involve black suspenders and fishnet stockings and he had a genius for the grotesque. As we prepared for the show each night in our subterranean dressing-room, Max, patting brown make-up on his bald spot and rouging his earlobes, would reminisce wistfully

145

about the 'old days' of the legitimate theatre in which he had known his greatest success.

'Everything becomes vaudeville in the end, Max,' said Gordon sagely.

Television, that new arrival to Australia, was about to be launched in Melbourne in time for the Olympics. Suburban streets, formerly lined at nightfall with brightly lit bungalows where pianos were tinkled, cards played, books read and suppers convivially scoffed, suddenly fell dark. Instead the dumbstruck families huddled in a back room, entranced by the electrical novelty, television. Soon its bluish grey light flickered like a universal will-o'-the-wisp over the suburban swamp.

Channel Seven's inaugural transmission was to be broadcast live from the stage of the Melbourne Tivoli Theatre, and I was delighted to learn that they had chosen my Mrs Everage Olympic Games sketch for this historic programme. Gordon Chater was to play the Olympic official to whom Edna offers her lovely home, and we were both flown down to Melbourne for the broadcast. It was the first time I had ever travelled by plane. That in itself was enough to give the event prestige in the eyes of my parents, and that I should have proved myself acceptable to the new medium of television not only delighted them, but must also have come as a tremendous surprise. After all, they had been absolutely convinced that my new profession could lead to little but the most dismal failure and now I was to be seen in every house in the land, albeit in the ludicrous disguise of Mrs Everage.

Since my parents were just back from their voyage, they welcomed my return to the family home and extended an invitation to Gordon to stay with us. It was an unprecedented gesture, born perhaps of their recent cosmopolitan experiences, and a marked relaxation of their wary attitude to the theatre. My imminent appearance on television had received much publicity and my father had bought the largest television set on the market: an Astor 21-inch. Alas, no airfare for my young wife had been furnished by the network, but my mother asked solicitous questions of the girl she had never met, relieved no doubt that she could be generous and affectionate about my wife without having to be nice to her face to face.

To my amazement my parents threw a large party in honour of Gordon and me, at which my friend was a huge success, charming everybody. I noticed that in speaking with my father and uncles Gordon assumed a somewhat self-consciously gruff and masculine voice and manner at odds with his fruitier and more outrageous demeanour in far-off Phillip Street. Amazingly Chater and my father were soon on Gordy–Eric terms, although behind my father's back and, strange to say, to my mild irritation, Gordon liked to archly refer to my father's building projects as 'Humphries' humpies'.

Our television début was a success and we returned to Sydney triumphant. However, when I next spoke to my parents, sending warm greetings from Gordon, there was a distinct *froideur* over the phone.

'Oh, your friend,' said my mother dryly. 'Your father has heard a few things at the golf club about him and his kind.'

'What do you mean?' I protested, knowing exactly what she meant. 'I thought you all hit it off very well.'

'If we'd known what we know now,' retorted my mother, 'we would never have had him in the house, let alone staying overnight!'

It was the only reference, albeit oblique, that I ever heard my mother make to the 'taint' of homosexuality.

ONE NIGHT at a Sydney theatrical party I was asked if I had an agent. I did not. I had had an agent a short time before, but no longer. I thought of Ted James, the sly little bloke with an over-polished returned soldier's badge, fawn suit and face to match. I had met him in the back bar of the Criterion Hotel, where he customarily quaffed freezing, specimen-yellow pilsner with Jim Gussey and the ABC Dance Band. Only a few weeks earlier Ted had sent me to a Returned Servicemen's League club in a remote suburb to entertain its members, who spent their Sunday mornings drinking and playing the one-armed bandits. Ten years before, these men, fresh from New Guinea and still skinny and malarial, had exchanged their rifles and other martial hardware for the steel handles of the slot machines, which they now pumped with the relentless savagery of warriors settling an old score.

Every Sunday in that desolate, carbolic-scented club, the ex-soldiers, with their bellies and booze-bitten faces, fronted a phalanx of fruit machines. With one gnarled hand they drank, while with the other they fed coins into the maw of their machines and occasionally pinched the smouldering stub of a Capstan or a Craven A from their chook's-arse lips. They all wore toddlers' clothes: brief little-boys' shirts in lemon and baby blue, and kiddies' shorts. Some were even barefoot. The mechanisms were briefly stilled during the entertainment break; the oranges and cherries and pineapples only stopped revolving when the hired comedian at last appeared on stage. On that fateful day the hired comic was I! Without a conventional act, and in a gesture of professional suicide, I gave the old diggers an expressionist rendition from my Dada days about a mad psychiatrist and an imbecile.

But I failed them on that morning: my act was lousy. It was suicidally misdirected at that audience, who probably thought I was 'slinging off' at them. ('Slinging off' is Australian slang for compressing one nostril with the index finger and expelling the contents of the other in the direction of some object of derision.) I did not deserve the damp fiver that the club secretary contemptuously thrust at me before I skulked home.

After that I never again dared to drink at the Criterion. Ted James would have heard pretty quickly how disastrous had been this first – and last – booking. He would probably look away in disgust when he saw me in the bar: the failure who couldn't even amuse a bunch of drunks. He would turn aside and spit onto the terrazzo floor, already swimming with sputum and dottle.

'No agent?' the chorus girl from *The Ice Follies* was saying. The love-bite on her throat had faded to a smudge of plum and saffron. 'Don't you do radio?'

It was suddenly clear to me that some of the other pleasures that Sydney promised – pleasures of the libidinous sort – might only be available to a radio actor.

'A little,' I lied. 'Mostly serials like *Portia Faces Life* and *When a Girl Marries*.' The pretty young skater looked impressed and helped herself to one of my Rothman's. I prayed she would not ask me which roles I played in these melodramas of the air, but if she should, I was going to say, 'Guess.'

The Central Casting agency in Martin Place signed me up immediately. After all, I was a minor star in the cast of the illustrious Phillip Street Revue. But my radio career was inauspicious. It was not a theatrical form I could master with ease: the dexterous tossing of dialogue from one actor to another in the tense confines of a studio required, like cricket, a special skill and a feeling for team spirit. Some few of us are born centrifugal; the give and take of the playing field, which I had found so antipathetic at school and which is so often a requirement of ensemble acting, baffled me. The experienced radio hacks did little to disguise their impatience when I 'fluffed' my lines or missed cues or even, during one crucial live recording, accidentally dropped my script.

One of the assignments found for me by Central Casting was a cameo role in an Argonauts' Club session, my childhood favourite. Once again I beheld some of my former idols, now much aged, grizzled and irascible, around the microphone. But with what facility they dispatched their silly lines, and with what insouciance they managed to impersonate children and Chinamen, crones and cowboys! Meanwhile they smoked cigarettes copiously and, as they read their scripts, adroitly let the old pages flutter silently to the studio floor.

I met another agent before I eventually left Sydney. Jack

Neary was an amiable Irishman of couperose complexion, who booked acts for the Tivoli variety circuit, and he seemed to entertain a radiant vision of my future, which despite the greatest effort I was unable to share. The first stage in my meteoric ascent to stardom, he insisted, was to obtain a composite photograph illustrating my versatility and desirability. I had very few pictures of myself in any guise, so he did the best he could with a snap from a university production of *The Barretts of Wimpole Street* in which I had played a doddering family doctor. The resulting pastiche, with its absurd captions, its period artwork and the inevitably brief résumé of my career that accompanied it, naturally failed to secure me a single engagement. I discovered it recently between the pages of an old book: a naïve and poignant souvenir from another life.

IN SPITE OF titillating excursions into dangerous places with dangerous companions, I tried to remain true to my beautiful young wife, and yet I felt that my precipitous early marriage had robbed me of youth's right to adventure. We had both been unfairly catapulted from a carefree adolescence into an irksome adulthood, with all its alarming responsibilities and daunting moral obligations. I chafed against them; it seemed too soon to take upon myself the accepted and usual burdens of life.

Sometimes in Sydney I was invited to jolly backstage parties for visiting British stars such as Jessie Mathews, Roger Livesey, Ursula Jeans, Dulcie Gray and Michael Denison, and there were more parties still: riotous shindigs thrown by the casts of other attractions, like the circus, *The Ice Follies* at the Tivoli, and the exotic Katherine Dunham Company, who were creating a sensation in Sydney: theatrical, social and sexual. At that time there were at least twelve live shows running concurrently and within a few blocks of each other. Sadly, amongst all these new professional acquaintances, there seemed to be no one to whom I could express my fears and forebodings, not even my wife, who doubtless had apprehensions of her own.

My discovery, a couple of years before, of the miraculous and inspirational effects of alcohol led me to more perilous experiments with this encouraging and variously flavoured chemical, and often under its influence, combined with the heady atmosphere of bohemian Sydney, I found myself in insalubrious company. More often than not I would miss the last tram home and be obliged to catch an expensive taxi to Wonderland Avenue. In the small hours of the morning, buffeted by the sobering and salty gusts from the Pacific, I would make my way to the dark house on the cliffs. Far below I could hear the crash of the relentless surf, but I was already floundering gracelessly, caught in a sort of amatory undertow of my own.

NEARLY two decades later, in the midst of the Australian tour of *At Least You Can Say You've Seen It*, I was lunching with the Honourable Clyde Packer, as usual at Primo's near King's Cross. We were tucking into their wonderful dressed crab when my friend and then-manager started jingling the small change in his pockets – a sure sign that he was about to make an important pronouncement.

'It's about time you had a decent place to live, old son,' he said. 'In spite of my extortionate commission, you've salted away a few shillings. I know you like living in England, but if you had a *pied-à-terre* in Sydney where would it be? I can have a sniff around while you're in Brisbane.'

I remembered the old Phillip Street Theatre days, in the first year of my short-lived marriage, when sometimes on pay night we would go to a rather grand Italian restaurant in the nearby basement of an exclusive residential building. It seemed grand, at any rate; grand for its time. Minestrone and Spaghetti Bolognaise were house specialities, liberally sprinkled with mousetrap cheese. What made this restaurant particularly posh was the fact that a *different* waiter brought the wine – and in a *glass*, not a teacup as they furtively did at the unlicensed Yugoslavs'.

I mentioned this apartment building to Clyde and he promised to make inquiries. Not long after, he called me in Brisbane to say there was a nice place about to be sold at my pre-ferred location, and we might just manage to acquire it. Over the phone I thought I could hear the change jingling enthusiasti-cally in his Hong Kong pockets. I said okay.

Thus it was that I came to occupy my first flat after many peripatetic years and a second foundered marriage. I had briefly viewed the premises when it was still inhabited by the fragrant old lady who owned it, and then I had had it completely redeco-rated while I continued touring. It was a large, lofty-ceilinged dwelling in the heart of Sydney, high up in an old building with views over gardens to Farm Cove, Rushcutters Bay and the silver, ferry-fretted harbour. In the distance, past Manly, lay the Heads, beyond which stretched the illimitable Pacific. I found an expert cabinet-maker from Tasmania, called Mr Clinch, who built a cosy library for me in the spare bedroom, with sturdy shelves of Western Australian redwood.

Far below my windows ran a broad thoroughfare on which stood Sydney's pink, machicolated Conservatorium of Music, described by D.H. Lawrence in an opening paragraph of his barmy novel *Kangaroo*. It was for the position of musical director at this very institution that Ravel once made an unsuccessful application.

I will never forget that evening at the end of the tour when I came down from Brisbane, collected the keys from Ernie, the caretaker, and let myself into my new home. For several minutes I stood there in the dark watching the dancing, vagrant lights of the harbour through the large windows, and luxuriating in the solitude, *my* solitude. I smelt the untrodden carpet, the new furniture. My bachelor flat had been decorated in a simple, but comfortable style of the period. There were track lights overhead, which would be quaintly dated now, but to me then seemed magical, and as I touched the dimmer switch a soft lambency washed over the pictures hung in the dining room.

In the months to come I would often sit on a banquette in the library window and gaze for hours across the glittering harbour, where the Opera House crouched like a porcelain armadillo. In the purple light of evening I would never tire of watching the jewelled pinwheel lights of Luna Park swirl and coruscate into life beneath the arc of the bridge.

Many years later, in a period of monetary stringency or matrimonial crisis or both, I relinquished this abode; but still from time to time, and with a pang, I miss what I have discovered nowhere else: the spirit of serenity and aloofness which dwelt there.

Not long ago at a charity function in Sydney I was crossing the ballroom to rejoin my friends when a raucous voice assailed me from a crowded table.

'Hey, Bazza!'

I saw a young man in evening dress grinning at me, with a drink in one hand and a cigar in the other. A lawyer, I surmised, since he was loutish enough and rich. Or perhaps he was one of those men of the nineties who described themselves as 'entrepreneurs'.

'Just thought you'd like to know, Bazza, we've got your old apartment.'

I managed a frozen 'Oh?'

'It cost us a bundle to hack all that wood out of the spare room so we could fit in the pool table.' He turned to the smudged woman beside him, who gave a cockatoo laugh. 'He wouldn't recognise it now, would he, Jackie? *He wouldn't fuckin' recognise it!*'

WHEN, in late 1957, I returned home to Melbourne after my eighteen-month exile in Sydney, I returned, except for a few painful and expensive formalities, a single man. Only then did I realise how homesick I had been for the city of my birth and

I threw myself into all manner of artistic enterprises: a production of *Waiting for Godot* – Australia's first – and a revue along Phillip Street lines, but meaner and, for those years, with a more savage satirical bite. Here, encouraged by the director, I expanded the character of Mrs Everage, who was no longer constrained by the format of a revue sketch and had begun to directly harangue the audience.

Yet somehow I knew that if I could save up enough money I would leave Melbourne forever. My assaults on suburbia, mere Lilliputian darts in a slumbering Gulliver, were my only defence against the creeping boredom that Melbourne in the fifties seemed to exude. How could I have been homesick, I wondered, for the city where everyone was so pleased with themselves, so clean, so house-proud, so obsessed by the politics of Niceness?

England had always beckoned, as it did to most Australians of my generation. We all had an English or an Irish member of the family, and not too many generations back either. My own grandfather John, with his strong Lancastrian accent, was still alive. Nice people sometimes still poured their tea from thatched cottage teapots, and hadn't our uncles fought, and sometimes even died, to preserve British culture? Although, come to think of it, 'culture' was not the word they used, or anyone used.

As soon as we could afford it, we all flocked back to the Old Country like salmon flopping upstream to the spawning ground. Most of us came back within a year to marry and settle down, still traumatised by the real England and London in particular, with its size, its filth, its cost and its huge indifference to the quaint little continent of kangaroos and hayseeds with corks

on their hats, which we had formerly thought of as the centre of
the universe.

On New Year's Eve 1958 I met a New Zealand girl called
Rosalind. We were married in April – another ceremony my
parents chose to boycott – and days later we were on the Lloyd
Triestino vessel *Toscana*, which five weeks later berthed at
Venice.

SOME months before I left for England, I had been offered what
seemed like an enormous sum of money by a Melbourne housewife called Babette Large to appear opposite her in a production
of *Lady Windermere's Fan*. I was to play Lord Windermere in
the Oscar Wilde play and the performance was to take place on
two evenings in December, in Mrs Large's front garden in the
bayside suburb of Beaumaris. Babette, who was well known in
amateur circles, was the only real actor in the cast apart from
me. I was fresh from a recent theatrical success as the Bunyip in
a children's play of that name, where I had pranced around the
stage singing and dancing in a fanciful costume painted by
Arthur Boyd.

We rehearsed for some weeks in Babette's lounge, occasionally glimpsing her husband, Keith, a shy Melbourne lawyer
who seemed happy, even relieved, to indulge his flamboyant
wife in her theatrical caprices. I doubt if Babette had ever heard
of Lady Ottoline Morrell, but she resembled a very toned-down,
suburban Australian version of that celebrated Bloomsbury-set
hostess and patron of the arts, and she had turned her detached

two-storey, 1938 mock-Tudor bungalow into a bonsai Gar-
sington.

In the week before opening night, and to our dismay, it
rained almost continuously and unseasonably, and the Larges
frantically searched for some alternative location, or what they
would have called a 'venue' if that silly word, pronounced 'veen-
new' in Australia, had been invented then. Babette in desperation decided that if the rain kept up we would have to perform
in her lounge and dining rooms, with everyone huddled against
a wall or crammed into the hallway. Had this occurred it would
have been an interesting production, rather like Pavilion Opera,
where in grand country houses the audience in evening dress all
but mingle with the cast. As it was, the rain stopped on the very
day we were due to open, the sun shone and there was promise
of a balmy evening.

Keith Large, with the help of a couple of friends, had
rigged lights in the ornamental prunus and the camphor laurel,
and the garden with its port wine magnolia and flowering gums
did form a rather attractive alfresco stage. Quite an excited audience of friends and neighbours, coaxed from their homes out of
curiosity rather than a love for drama, assembled in the house
for drinks and 'savouries'. These latter, in the style of the fifties,
and before the age of 'dips', were mostly pineapple chunks,
gherkins, Kraft Cheddar cheese and salami cubes on toothpicks.
When the play was due to start, the audience traipsed out to a
shadowed section of the front lawn and settled down uncomfortably on the still-damp turf, on rugs, on cushions and, if they
were lucky, on deckchairs.

When the 'stage' lights were turned on, unanticipated problems arose. As if from an orchestral conductor's signal, in this case the downbeat of a membranous wing, the cicadas – those deafening harbingers of Christmas – no doubt grateful for the warmer weather, began their exalted stridulations. Moreover the bright lamps that Keith Large had hired attracted huge swarms of other nocturnal insects, some of a size and ferocity not previously thought to inhabit Melbourne's gentle suburban landscape. Throughout the performance they banged around above us with kamikaze-like fury and sometimes fell dead or exhausted on the heads of the cast.

But there was an even more serious problem that our valiant troupe had not foreseen. The dress rehearsal indoors had gone seamlessly, apart from Mrs Hoskins's inability to accurately memorise her role as my wife, Lady Windermere. It was only when the real show began that we realised our folly in not having rehearsed that afternoon in the actual garden. Babette Large, dressed in hired finery as Mrs Erlynne, swept onto the stage.

PARKER Mrs Erlynne!

Lord Windermere starts. Mrs Erlynne enters, very beautifully dressed and very dignified. Lady Windermere clutches at her fan, then lets it drop on the floor. She bows coldly to Mrs Erlynne, who bows to her sweetly in turn, and sails into the room

LORD DARLINGTON You have dropped your fan, Lady Windermere. (*Picks it up and hands it to her*)

MRS ERLYNNE (C.) How do you do, again, Lord Windermere? How charming your sweet wife looks! Quite a picture!

LORD WINDERMERE (*in a low voice*) It was terribly rash of you to come!

MRS ERLYNNE (*smiling*) The wisest thing I ever did in my life. And, by the way, you must pay me a good deal of attention this evening —

And then in mid-speech Mrs Erlynne stopped dead, as though rooted to the spot. Still delivering her lines, she writhed, she swayed, she performed strange genuflections inharmonious with the play and its period. In fact, she *was* rooted to the spot, as were two other ladies in the cast, all dismayed to find that their high heels had sunk into the sodden lawn and remained there, despite violent efforts to dislodge them.

Babette Large, immobilised by this unexpected catastrophe, was obliged to forfeit her period credibility by kicking her shoes off into a convenient azalea and continuing her performance prosaically barefoot. Laughter, louder than any that might have been precipitated by a Wildean epigram, shook the deckchairs and the huddled spectators as the play became increasingly bogged down. Even I, squelching around in patent-leather shoes at which the grassy stage sucked voraciously, found it difficult not to snort with suppressed laughter. It was indeed a strange episode in Melbourne theatre history, with those witty and urbane speeches, intoned in somewhat la-di-dah fashion by a company of housewives, dentists and solicitors, echoing across the dripping plumbago and red-hot pokers, all but drowned by the inane din of the cicadas and the buzzing death-rattle of incinerated insects.

My parents were not present at this performance, although they might have enjoyed it, for it demonstrated that I was acceptable in some, admittedly raffish, suburban circles. But in the sixties they loyally attended all the first nights of my shows, usually forming a small family party and giving a private dinner at a Melbourne restaurant such as the Latin. However, after the onset of my mother's crippling arthritis, she rarely went out, although my father occasionally made an effort, sometimes buying blocks of tickets for his friends at the golf club. In any case, I believe, she would have felt that to place herself in one of my audiences would have been too cosmically embarrassing, especially if Les Patterson was on the bill.

No longer mobile, and mostly confined to her favourite chair in the sunroom, my mother was content to imagine what my stage shows were like, aided by radio critics whose views of my work were not invariably rhapsodic. After a first night in Melbourne, she usually remained completely silent about my work, unless the neighbour of one of my Aunts had expressed an unfavourable opinion, or a slightly equivocal review had appeared in *The Sun News-Pictorial*. Then she would make a point of saying, 'I see *The Sun* didn't like you last night, Barry.' Apart from her solitary black-face appearance at the church concert in her youth, I doubt if my mother had ever spoken in public in her entire life, and when her son did so she regarded it at best as attention-seeking.

'Do you *have* to draw attention to yourself like that, Barry?'

Do You Know Who
I Mean?

~

If you want to make God laugh,
tell him your plans

Yiddish saw

They say that if you can remember the sixties you were not a part of the sixties. If this be so, then I would certainly qualify as an eager participant, for in the closing years of the psychedelic decade the lacunae widened, the episodes of amnesia multiplied. Yet my denial was robust – although I remained an acute observer of other people's decline.

On some mornings when the British Broadcasting Corporation provided me with a taxi to take me across town to Shepherd's Bush to work – for I was still employable in an institution that then offered an almost benevolent sanctuary for the drunk – I would ask the cab driver to take me first to the Red Lion in Waverton Street, only a few blocks from Mayfair where I maintained an impoverished bed-sitting room. At the Red Lion I could consume a quick, matutinal glass of Fernet-Branca, my preferred *digestivo* of that period. Unpunctual in all other matters, I always managed to get to the pub at precisely the moment when it opened its doors, and I no longer needed to tell the barmaid what I wanted for she would have spotted me already, and the vile black medicine – as much a punishment as a cure – would be standing before me on the bar.

I had acquired a new theatrical agent with an office in a fine Regency house in Mayfair. The building was owned by the extraordinarily rich manager of a successful rock group, and he had extended his empire to include theatre, film and television. The impresario himself was a prodigious drinker and, for all I knew, a lover of other elating substances. These appetites were shared by almost all his employees and a large number of their clients. The chief accountant was a fully paid up, card-carrying alcoholic and my new agent's jolly, pink-cheeked secretary was not jolly and pink-cheeked without chemical assistance. Even my agent, although an enormously nice man, regularly washed down palmfuls of tablets with very large vodka and tonics. An atmosphere of madness pervaded the building. Despite this, large sums of money continued to be made and the rock group that funded the whole enterprise is famous to this day, although it is true that one of their number died tragically of a drug overdose.

Every evening after finishing work on my short-lived BBC series *The Barry Humphries Scandals* I would travel in a black taxi to my Mayfair slum, then visit my agent at the cocktail hour. In that office the cocktail hour extended from eleven in the morning until eleven in the evening, and all drinks, however exotic, were freely available. Promising young starlets of the period called by for refreshment; all of them, I now reflect, are dead, one by her own hand. Strange to say, the impresario, who occupied a luxurious penthouse in the building and continues to drink, in the Australian phrase, 'with both hands', is still alive, although heavily embalmed.

I marvel at the fact that I survived the many hours spent visiting this hospitable office. By then my own alcohol consumption had passed the danger point, but like all alcoholics I thought of booze as something rich and worth pursuing. The results were always catastrophic, yet I kept on drinking just the same because I believed that if I persisted I would one day get it right. Somewhere out there, I knew, there was that unthinkable alternative, abstinence, but in those years at the end of the sixties I could not conceive of having the urge to drink – and not drink.

There were few bars in London that I liked, and few sensitive bartenders. If, when I ordered a drink, the barman had the impertinence to say, 'But, sir, you haven't finished the one you're drinking', I would never go back there again.

Apart from the infamous Colony Room in Soho, I had a favourite bar in Marylebone called John Geare's Wine Lodge. It was small, tucked away and filled like a jackdaw's nest with fancy bottles and glittering objects. Moreover it was open as long as its few customers wished to continue drinking. Jock, the accommodating publican, who had one blue glass eye, gave generous credit and I bought many bottles of the best wine from him. But rare vintages were not advantageously savoured late at night with curry and cigarettes.

When I left London in 1970 for Australia, and soon thereafter hospital to recover my health, I left owing Jock large sums of money. This was always on my conscience, and some years later when I was back in London, sober, doing *Housewife-Superstar!*, my first successful solo performance in the West End, I vowed I would send him a cheque. Jock got in before me by appearing unannounced at the stage door with his wife and daughter. Nervously I admitted them into the dressing-room, ready to make financial amends.

But Jock looked at me rather sheepishly with his one good eye and said, 'I just want you to know the show was great. We loved it.'

'Listen, my old friend,' I interrupted clumsily, 'I left London in a hurry and couldn't come back to the Lodge to settle up and say goodbye.' Feeling guiltier by the minute, I reached for my chequebook. 'I think I might owe you . . .'

Jock, embarrassed in front of his family, brushed the chequebook aside.

'I wouldn't be too sure about that,' he said. 'The truth is, back in the old Wine Lodge days when you were our best customer, we used to charge in . . . well, round figures. When you had had a few too many, we sometimes used our imaginations.' His glass eye twinkled. 'Our prices *varied*, let's put it that way.'

'What are you saying, Jock?' I asked.

'It could just be, Barry, that *we owe you!*'

Cordially we left it at that.

If I had not decided to abjure alcohol at the beginning of the seventies, I would certainly have predeceased most of my old drinking companions, but the journalist and sedentary *boulevardier* Jeffrey Bernard must have made some terrible Faustian pact because he survived to a miraculous age, although, as my Australian car salesman friend would say, 'not in showroom condition'. I visited my old haunts less and less for it is said that when you escape from the lion's den, you are unwise to go back for your hat.

On my rare excursions back to Soho, Jeffrey's once-handsome face, which now resembled in colour and texture a necrotic lung, would loom out at me piteously from some corner of the Groucho Club. By then he had lost a leg, but it was as if he were hacking off his appendages, even gouging out his organs, to fling at the implacable gods. 'Here!' he seemed to be saying. 'Take my limbs, my liver, even my heart, but please let me still have *just the one.*'

SOMETIME in the sixties I had a call from an Australian newspaper office in Fleet Street to inform me that a man called Rupert Henderson wished to meet me. I had never heard of Mr Henderson, although his name struck awe and even fear in the hearts of the Australian journalists I encountered in Fleet Street pubs. He was a big shot apparently and controlled a major Australian television network amongst other things. When we met in his London office, I was surprised to encounter, across the large desk, a rather wizened figure with light brown skin and a rumpled brown suit. To be precise, he was predominantly khaki and the living incarnation of Sandy Stone. His voice was like the scratch of a match, and he wanted to give me a job.

After making a little church and steeple of his long, brown, bony fingers and looking at his office ceiling for many minutes, while I stood there waiting, he said, 'Have you heard of satire, Barry?'

Cautiously I told him I thought I had.

'Let me tell you about satire,' said Rupert Henderson, as though I hadn't spoken. 'Satire is sending things up. Have you heard that expression, Barry?'

'I think so,' I replied.

'I'll give you an example,' said Mr Henderson. 'Now, supposing you want to do a satire on the Prime Minister . . .'

I was listening.

'. . . well, you dress up as the Prime Minister or find a bloke who's the spitting image. He walks up to the camera . . .'

Here Mr Henderson stood up, crossed to the far side of the room, turned around and walked up to me as though my face were a television camera.

'"Good evening, ladies and gentleman. I'm the Prime Minister of Australia and I'm a bloody idiot!"'

We stood there in silence.

'Yes?' I sort of asked.

'Well, don't you see? That's satire!'

'Then again,' he continued, returning to his desk, 'if you want to send up a sporting identity – *not that you would*, not that we do – you'd dress up as a footie star. You'd put the ball on the studio floor, go to kick it, and miss!'

Rupert Henderson beamed at me.

'That, young fella, is satire and it's the latest thing in Australia. Our audiences are lapping it up. We want to do a lot more of this satire type of thing on our channel and someone told me you're pretty good at taking the micky.'

I tried to look surprised.

'Yeah, Barry, if we can do business we'd like you out in Australia next month to do a satire for us, so long as you don't tread on any corns. Are you with me, Barry?'

I was.

We agreed that our representatives would discuss the business implications of this colloquy, and Mr Henderson promised to be in touch, but when the wiry tycoon stood up to shake hands, I saw again how very small he was, and how less than cordial was his upward glance. Did I seem after all *too satirical*, even on first meeting? Had I, after such brief exchanges, taken the micky without knowing it, or trodden accidentally on a corn? I never heard from him again, but I gathered that the 'satire' movement – that subversive bombshell dropped by Peter Cook in the River Thames – had already sent its diminishing ripples to Botany Bay.

I FIRST glimpsed the brilliant comedian, writer and impresario Peter Cook in the saloon bar of the Lamb and Flag, off Floral Street, Covent Garden, in 1961. The cast of Lionel Bart's *Oliver!*, in which I was playing Mr Sowerberry, drank there between matinées and evening shows – or those of us who drank did. Occasionally the players in the concurrent hit at the Fortune Theatre, the topical satire *Beyond the Fringe*, dropped into the pub as well, although it was Dudley Moore we usually saw. Moore's girlfriend, Anna Leroy, was a flower-seller in Bart's operetta.

Peter Cook, who sometimes accompanied Dudley for an abstemious half-pint, was languid to the point of undulation. While he never diffused an aura of vanity, he held his fine features at a haughty tilt as though regarding himself dispassionately in an invisible looking-glass. By then his celebrity was well established and he wore a dark suit of shiny mohair in a modish cut.

There are certain persons one can look at and imagine which parent they resemble. I have always found it an amusing game and I am always proved right. In the case of Peter Cook's physiognomy, however, I felt positive that I knew what his *aunty* looked like.

I did not see Peter again for a year or two. I had done my first, successful Australian one-man show, *A Nice Night's Entertainment*, returned to London and immediately been offered a few months in the United States to help launch *Oliver!* on Broadway. By the time I got to New York, bribed by undreamt-of dollars, *Beyond the Fringe* was already an established success and Peter and Wendy, his wife, with Judy Scott-Fox, their faithful secretary, were living in what seemed to be a sumptuous *ménage à trois* in Greenwich Village. Here and there in the rambling apartment were real Tiffany lamps – only then returning to fashion – and there was an abundance of rich textiles of crimson and mulberry silk and crushed velvet, which created an atmosphere of opulence, or so it seemed to me, living as I did only a few blocks away in an austere coldwater flat above a poodle parlour.

Peter and I, somewhat warily at first, began a friendship that was to last, off and on, until his death in 1995 – if it is possible to speak of friendship with such a curiously inaccessible personage. Peter had, I noticed, Americanised himself. He had exchanged his London winklepickers for sneakers and his suits for jeans and T-shirts, often emblazoned with the slogans of popular baseball teams. On closer acquaintance I was surprised – perhaps even slightly shocked – to find such a brilliant fellow preoccupied with sport and pop music. He did not, as far as I could tell, read anything other than newspapers, and may indeed have spent his entire sojourn in New York without having ever visited the Metropolitan Museum or the Frick Collection.

To a rather self-conscious young highbrow from the provinces like me, Peter Cook's studied philistinism was disconcerting. It seemed anomalous that such an apparently 'aesthetic' personage could enjoy life without books or art or music. It is true that he appreciated some music: we went to Harlem together and heard the Supremes at the famous Apollo Theater, and occasionally went to Village Vanguard when a famous band was playing. But Peter's perpetual, almost compulsive jocosity made intimacy difficult. Unable to discuss sport – his principal interest – or to enjoy rock'n'roll for more than a few consecutive minutes, I felt excluded from the inner court of his friendship.

I had brought with me from Australia a 'microgroove' recording of *A Nice Night's Entertainment* and Peter particularly enjoyed the Sandy Stone monologue. Just before my American contract with *Oliver!* expired, Peter invited me to perform my 'act' at the Establishment, his new London club in Greek Street, Soho. He had already presented there, with great success, the notorious American comedian and drug addict Lenny Bruce, and I secretly feared that my rather anodyne regional monologues, with their multiple Australian references, would be lost on the *beau monde* of Soho. However, Cook was convinced they would work, and offered me the amazing fee of £100 per week.

He never saw the show, fortunately, since he was still working in New York when I opened – and closed. The reaction of audiences and critics confirmed my worst fears, and large cheques on Coutts Bank, signed by Peter in faraway Manhattan, were small consolation to a disgraced comedian. I wondered if I could ever look Peter Cook in the eye again after that, but when he returned to London he never referred to the Establishment Club débâcle, and instead offered me a role in his first film, *Bedazzled*, a modern chronicle of the Seven Deadly Sins. I was cast, somewhat appropriately under the circumstances, as Envy.

Not long after, Peter suggested that I collaborate with the New Zealander Nicholas Garland on a comic strip for *Private Eye*. At the *Eye*'s cluttered office in Greek Street pullulated the Cook coterie: a fan club of real talent, which included the editor Richard Ingrams, the writer John Wells and the cartoonist and comedian William Rushton, diluted with a raggle-taggle bunch of toadies, shameless sycophants and Cook impersonators. Peter seemed to thrive, as most of us do, in this climate of adulation. He viewed with a sublime indifference the wild crushes that he unconsciously and without effort inspired. One of my other monologues on the record I had given him in New York concerned a naïve Australian Anglophobe in Earl's Court called Buster Thompson, whose life was a quest for cold Australian lager. This was the prototype of the Barry McKenzie script that ran, off and on, in *Private Eye* for the rest of the sixties. Cook furnished the name of the character, which derived from my own, and Nick Garland contributed the 'look'.

Inspired by Chesty Bond, a cartoon figure in a white singlet in an Australian advertisement for underwear, Barry McKenzie personified the Antipodean innocent abroad, warily treading the social and sexual quicksands of the sixties and dodging the dastardly Pom. He took a while to catch on. I think Richard Ingrams was less enthusiastic than his proprietor in the early days, but as Nick and I slowly developed a coherent and offensive style Ingrams supported us also. As the decade drew to a close, the adventures of Bazza had been banned in Australia and achieved cult status in Britain.

Peter's marriage ended some time in the seventies and he formed a long liaison with a blonde actress who had the face of a sprite. Her previous partner had been Sean Kenny, the famous designer of *Oliver!* and the Establishment Club, whose premature death was certainly not attributable to the rigours of abstinence. Peter and I saw each other only occasionally in these years, and I heard in the early eighties that he had sought professional help in conquering an addiction to alcohol. There were stories of his splendid resurrections and equally spectacular relapses. Meanwhile his art suffered; or, rather, his public suffered for the lack of it. There was a sudden renaissance when he and his old partner, Dudley Moore, impersonating two cronies called Derek and Clive, collaborated on a scabrous series of gramophone records. These obsessive dialogues of transcendental lewdness – mostly improvised, one surmised, under the influence of various popular stimulants – are amongst the funniest of Cook and Moore's virtuoso turns.

In spite of sporadic appearances on talk shows, through which he nonchalantly sauntered, Peter Cook in his last years devoted most of his time to golf and occasional inspirational visits to the offices of *Private Eye*. His shape had changed rather startlingly, but his appetite for vodka and cigarettes seemed undiminished. I often visited him in his untidy loft in Perrin's Walk, Hampstead, where he sat like a beanbag lady surrounded by old newspapers, congealed Chinese takeaway and an ashtray that was a miniature Pearl Harbor of wrecked cigarettes. He was always available for his friends, and performed many private acts of kindness without getting found out. At a dark time in my own life when I had received an ominous letter from Australia that I dreaded opening, he sweetly performed that office, perused the letter and delivered a hilarious précis of its contents.

Some years ago he came to my birthday party at the Garrick Club. You knew he was present by the gales of laughter emanating from the large group in a corner of the room. We talked for a while before he and Lin, his wife, went home, and I shook hands for the last time with this most original, most generous of men.

WHEN Peter Cook died it would have been impossible to foresee that Dudley Moore would follow him less than a decade later. Alas, he was struck by a debilitating illness and by the time he received the MBE in November 2001, this once ebullient, even antic pianist and comedian was not able to walk unsupported or speak. The brainless bimbo of Hollywood had pressed him too tenaciously to her silicon bosom; he had spent so long amongst those with nothing to say that at length he had become speechless.

The dear people who cared for Dudley in New Jersey brought him to London and installed him with a male nurse in a small 'bijou' hotel. I visited him with the virtuoso Steven Isserlis, who brought along his Stradivarius cello, and there followed the most moving and intimate musical recital I have ever attended. Dudley, a stricken figure, tottered out of his bedroom assisted by his nurse. He sat in a chair in the small hotel room, slack-mouthed and inarticulate – indeed barely recognisable and in a state of distress and agitation – until Steven began to play. The improvised programme commenced with the sarabande from the Bach Suite No. 5, followed by the bourrée of No. 3 and then extracts from the Elgar concerto. All of the pain and suffering that afflicted Dudley seemed to ebb away as he listened to the marvellous music. Finally Steven played Saint-Saëns's 'The Swan', a work that they had both performed and recorded. We were all close to tears as the time came for farewells.

I made a lame joke about low hotel ceilings, especially those of the 'cottage cheese' variety. Perhaps, I whimsically conjectured, they were designed like that to enable commercial travellers to file their toenails on them while in bed. Suddenly the face of the Dudley Moore I remembered briefly returned as he threw back his head and laughed in the old way. It was John Betjeman's 'bonus of laughter'.

We embraced. It was the last time.

JOHN WELLS, another good friend from the sixties 'satire' days, was a former Eton schoolmaster, actor, writer and brilliant mimic as well as a stalwart of *Private Eye* magazine. When I first knew him, he lived in comfortable chintz and mahogany bachelor lodgings in Cadogan Gardens, and we would often meet there for writing sessions and satirical brainstorming when the conditions at our BBC office became oppressive. John always had pretty girlfriends of the Sloane Ranger type, before the invention of that epithet, and in his flat I would frequently encounter Carolines and Vanessas, Harriets and Susannas, all in their Jaeger headscarves, Biba minis and Neatawear hose.

John also boasted an enviable social life and was something of a celebrity collector – so much so that I privately christened him 'John Do-You-Know-Who-I-Mean-By Wells'. He had a name-dropping formula that he employed with ironic humour when teasing those of us who barely knew anybody of importance.

He once diffidently mentioned an illustrious dinner party of the night before. 'Who was there?' I asked obediently.

Wells replied, as though to a hayseed colonial, 'Do you know who I mean by Princess Margaret?'

John's tragic death from cancer in 1998 was a great loss to his family and friends, and I suppose it is a measure of his uniqueness and the value of his friendship that I often hear something risible or absurd and think regretfully, *Wouldn't Wells have enjoyed that?* I visited him shortly before his death; two events he expected and confronted with extraordinary courage. He told me how enraged he was at having to forfeit the last fifteen years of his life when he had planned to fulfil so many hoarded hopes and to realise so many postponed ambitions.

'And those women that I have hurt – I regret that very much,' he said.

I was tickled pink to notice the number of luminaries who came to mourn him and to celebrate him at his memorial service in St Paul's, Covent Garden. Do you know who I mean by the Prince of Wales, Jerry Hall and the Archbishop of Canterbury?

In my very early days as a comic actor in Sydney, so many people told me how funny and brilliant Spike Milligan was that I began to form a somewhat strong resistance to the man and his work. 'You mean you haven't heard *The Goon Show?*' my friends would cry in chorus. 'It's right up your street!'

Still I resisted. A show of funny voices, surreal situations, unbridled sound effects? Admittedly I had adored the Marx Brothers from the start, although such is my nature I might have enjoyed them less if they had been as effusively recommended to me as were these BBC Goons.

It may be difficult for the present generation to imagine the power of radio in those far-off fifties of last century. We were Listeners; today's audiences are Watchers. For those who could not enjoy comedy in the live theatre, the wireless was once the only source of performed humour, and in Australia and distant, almost mythical England it was the radio that provided employment for comics young and old. I had listened to comedy programmes since childhood and was familiar with most of the famous music hall turns that cheered up the Empire during and after the war. Now here was a new kind of radio humour, which mocked all the old patriotic conventions and yet somehow, despite its eccentricity, seemed an insouciant extension of the British comic tradition. Not surprisingly perhaps, its *deus ex machina* was an Irishman.

When I performed *A Nice Night's Entertainment* in Sydney in 1962, I was told one evening, just before I went on stage, that Spike Milligan was in the audience. I was understandably nervous, indeed petrified, and when he came backstage afterwards I was surprised to meet such an affable, sane and astonishingly youthful man.

A year or so later in London, during my brief and poorly received season at Peter Cook's Establishment Club, I was told by a famous astrologer that I would soon be getting good news in a telegram. Within days the telegram arrived. It was from Spike Milligan inviting me to join the cast of *The Bedsitting Room*, the stage play by Milligan and John Antrobus, which had already opened successfully at the Mermaid and was transferring to the West End. I was offered the leading role of Captain Bules Martin.

Spike was forty-six years old when I joined *The Bedsitting Room* cast and already somewhat grizzled. He had grown a beard for his role but he never allowed it to fully develop, so that one might say he was a pioneer of designer stubble.

Working with Spike was one of the strangest and most exhilarating experiences of my career. If he had been funny on the air, he was even funnier on stage, and one could never be sure what would happen from night to night. Given to wild caprices, Spike left the theatre during one performance, never to return that evening.

Spike was always magnanimous towards me. However, there was an actor in the cast with a serious gambling problem who was forever borrowing money, and quite often, in the middle of a scene in which this actor was present, Spike would stop the show and warn the audience against lending him money. At curtain call, when the artistes took their bows, he was also given to pointing out their personal frailties to the audience. Valentine Dyall, whom Spike regularly engaged on radio and in the theatre to impersonate absurdly destitute upper-class Englishmen, was one of Spike's favourite victims, and his private matrimonial torments were communicated to the audience with malicious glee.

Spike was prey to serious bouts of depression and self-doubt. It was his belief, so he told me, that he had been working as a comedian all his life with scant financial reward, and that his present success in the live theatre had come too late. He seemed unaware of the fact that, because of *The Goon Show*, he was already a figure of legend.

His best performance must surely have been as Ben Gunn in Bernard Miles's production of *Treasure Island* at the Mermaid Theatre in 1968. William Rushton and I were also in the cast, Willie as Squire Trelawney and I as Long John Silver, with one leg and a carnivorous parrot on my shoulder. Spike stole the show every night in a make-up that took at least an hour to apply. However, as the season wore on his make-up became more perfunctory, so that in our last week he merely hooked a false beard over his ears as he ran from his car to the stage.

Spike's appearance on stage always brought a roar of delight from the kids in the audience, and he had soon left the text far behind as he went off into a riff of sublime absurdity. In what was meant to be a climactic confrontation, Spike's Ben Gunn drew his pistol and fired it vehemently at the marauding pirates. There was a loud bang and his pistol extruded a limp daisy. When the cheers and laughter from the audience had subsided, Spike, the master of bathos, cast a conspiratorial glance at the stalls and said, very topically for the age of the hippie, 'See – flower-power!'

Spike maintained a large office in Bayswater, which was shared by other comedians and writers such as Frankie Howerd, Eric Sykes, Ray Galton and Alan Simpson. He sometimes slept at the office, and at times would visit me at my house in Little Venice, where we would talk, drink wine and listen to music. Knowing he was often at my house, Paddy, his wife, once telephoned me to ask if he was there. Since I knew that Spike had impetuously departed for Australia a couple of days before,

I was surprised by his wife's inquiry and obliged to tell the poor woman the truth. His mother lived for many years in the euphonious and Goon-sounding district of Woy Woy in New South Wales, and Spike was a frequent and dutiful visitor: so much so that he is thought by many people on the continent to be an Australian, a misconception Spike never discouraged.

He drove a turquoise-blue mini (turquoise was a very sixties colour), and together we often visited derelict houses in London in search of salvageable bric-à-brac. His office boasted a few rather good paintings that he had rescued in this way, although Bill Kerr, his old Australian colleague from *The Goon Show* days, was more enterprising, scouring London with a ladder and a small truck in search of valuable trove such as banisters, large furniture and roofing lead.

At the end of the sixties Spike, who indulged in many philanthropic gestures, decided to personally undertake the restoration of the Elfin Oak, an ugly tree stump in the Royal Kensington Gardens, near his office, upon which some whimsical soul had once carved a host of gnomes, pixies and assorted sub-Arthur-Rackham homunculi, and I was briefly his assistant in this thankless enterprise. Spike's keen instinct for publicity ensured that it received full media coverage.

Spike's flair for publicity also meant he rarely dropped out of the correspondence columns of *The Times* and *The Daily Telegraph*. As well, he corresponded, I believe, with the Duke of Edinburgh, of all people, and befriended the expatriate poet Robert Graves, who by then was somewhat gaga and may not have fully comprehended the identity of his importunate fan.

Spike generously involved me in most of the things he did at this time, including a radio programme, *The Omar Khayyam Show*, on which I was notoriously inept. I tended to slow things down by dropping scripts and missing cues, whereas Spike's radio style was fast and furious. This long-forgotten Milligan creation, including my pathetic performance, may still exist somewhere in the archives of the BBC.

On the evening of the day on which the Prime Minister of Australia, the Right Honourable Harold Holt, vanished on a wild beach off the coast of Victoria, Spike and I happened to be doing a joint BBC radio interview interspersed with jolly recordings. Spike had brought to the studio in Portland Place a bottle of vin rosé, his favourite tipple of the period, and between sips and songs and comic banter, which Spike naturally dominated, we seemed to be going along swimmingly. The programme was live to air and suddenly without warning to the veteran BBC man who was conducting our interview – although the interview element had long been lost sight of – Spike introduced the subject of Harold Holt's tragic disappearance in the form of a cod news flash.

'We're interrupting the programme, folks. Australian sources have just revealed that their Prime Minister was eaten by an *opposition shark!*'

Although I had known and liked Harold Holt for the simple and perhaps rather base reason that he came to all my shows, we all laughed – well, all except the veteran BBC interviewer. As the next record was played, two burly uniformed BBC commissionaires of the old school entered the studio, picked us up and practically frog-marched us down labyrinthine corridors and out of the building. For a joke in execrable taste, and in mid-interview, we had been bounced.

Spike stood outside the BBC shaking his fist at the large Eric Gill sculpture that straddles the art deco entrance.

'You've pinched our bottle of wine, you lousy British bastard!'

It was not until the early eighties that I re-entered the building.

For those unfamiliar with Spike as a stage and radio comedian, his war memoirs, his novel, *Puckoon*, and his children's books attest to his genius. What a fortunate man I am to have known Spike Milligan.

A Conder fan, foreground and background, 1965

Salvador Dalí and B.H., New York, 1963

Sixties satirists: B.H., John Wells and John Bird at the BBC, London

Peter Cook, B.H. and Dudley Moore, 1971

Treasure Island, Mermaid Theatre, London, 1968:
Spike Milligan, B.H. and William Rushton

The Honourable Clyde Packer in conference with the author, 1974

B.H. and Bruce Beresford in Tasmania, 1973

Colin 'The Frog' Lucas (Dick Bentley) and Barry McKenzie (Barry Crocker)
in Paris, 1974

With Sidney Nolan

Patrick White, B.H. and Manoly Lascaris, Sydney, 1976

On a Melbourne tram with Malcolm Muggeridge

NERMAN

Above The apotheosis of Edna, Apollo Theatre, London, 1976, drawing by Einar Nerman

Left Dame Edna on Broadway, 1999, drawing by Al Hirschfeld

In the ossuary at Sedlec, Prague, 1973

With Jiří Mucha, Prague, 1973

Lizzie Spender and W.H. Auden

B.H. dictates to Frances Kroll Ring, Los Angeles, 2002

B.H. with John Betjeman

The author at Salamis, 1969

A Melbourne lunch with Australia's much-loved artists
Michael Leunig and John Clarke

Tessa (top) and Emily

Rupert (top) and Oscar

On the set of *Les Patterson Saves the World* with Oscar, 1987

SHIPS IN BOTTLES

~

All people's pasts are painful.
You have to lose the past sometimes
in order to find it

RICHARD HEULSENBECK

THROUGH the back window of my departing taxi, I watched the diminishing figures of little Tessa and Emily as they waved goodbye. Today Tessa is a talented actress, and Emily a successful painter; but then I thought I might never see them again, for as the sixties drew to a close so, sadly, did my marriage to Rosalind.

With my Australian tour of *Just a Show* over, I boarded a plane alone, bound ultimately for England. In San Francisco I lingered for a while. In a rundown psychedelic rooming-house in the notorious Haight-Ashbury district, where slouched the once-colourful and liberated remnants of hippiedom, the days and nights merged incoherently as my drinking accelerated. Just in time I retreated from the brink of the abyss.

On a whim I took off for Lisbon, where I met up with a beautiful Australian named Ros, a girl who made Julie Christie look almost plain. It was Ros who nursed me through a frightening alcoholic crisis at the Lisbon Ritz Hotel. In those desolate hours of insomnia I began to wonder not *who* I was, or *what* I was, but who did I once *think* I was.

The doctor, summoned in the middle of the night, checked me over and then took Ros aside for a brief consultation, which I could not overhear.

'What did he say?' I later asked, feebly. 'Will I live?'

'Well, if you really want to know,' she said matter-of-factly, 'he just asked me what a pretty young woman like me was doing with a wreck like you.'

St Dymphna is the patron saint of the mad. Nearly half a lifetime ago I resided in a hospital ward discouragingly named after her. It was a dismal sojourn and one that my family and friends hoped might convince me to change my ways. The St Dymphna ward and the private room I occupied were in the psychiatric wing of St Vincent's, a large Melbourne hospital. Elsewhere in the hospital, in another, shabbier wing that I could see from my window, was the alcoholic ward, where derelicts resided. There they were, shuffling around, smoking, playing ping-pong and cards or sitting in discussion groups of some kind. Poor devils, I thought. I pitied them. I was smugly conscious that I had been consigned to the superior realm of the merely mad.

'Liquid refreshments' had played a role in my decline, it was true, but I rationalised that I had been unlucky. I see now that I suffered from the drunk's fatal delusion that next time things would be different. The alcoholic has only to have one transcendental drinking experience in his youth, when his depression lifts, the world briefly comes into focus and he has an experience that counterfeits spiritual ecstasy. Thereafter he will search for a repetition of the same quasi-epiphany for the rest of his life: if necessary to the gates of hell and beyond. In my case, even though I was disappointed thousands of times, I believed that the *next time*, after the next drink, it would be different: I would be in control at last and the old, long-sought euphoria would return. But if insanity is doing the same thing and expecting different results, then I truly was insane and not out of place in the cold embrace of St Dymphna.

As it happened, I was tipped off by friends in the know and escaped from that hospital just before Dr Gerard Sheedy, the resident shrink, hoping no doubt for the Nobel Prize for curing drunks, was about to administer massive doses of LSD in order to help me find out what, in childhood, had triggered my addiction. If he had been allowed to conduct his experiments, I might still be alive but in a locked institution somewhere believing myself to be a cornflake.

My Los Angeles friend Frances Kroll Ring, secretary to F. Scott Fitzgerald in the last two years of his life, recently told me how he had woven something she said into one of his brilliant Pat Hobby stories. One day, having furtively dumped a couple of hessian sacks of her employer's empty gin bottles into Sepulveda Canyon (long before the San Diego Freeway), Frances had gone back and told Scott he would probably be punished in the afterlife by having to fill all those bottles with little sailing ships . . .

WHEN, on the thirty-first of December 1971, with the love and support of others, I finally discovered to my surprise that life was much more stimulating without stimulants, I was living in Delmont, a private nursing home on Warrigal Road in Melbourne. 'Warrigal', I learn, is an Aboriginal word for outlawed Aborigines and dingoes. By then I was certainly a pariah, and with justification my wife served divorce papers on me in hospital. I remember the thump of the heavy envelope of legal documents hitting the end of my bed. I knew I stood – or lay slumped – on the threshold of a new and daunting existence. I no longer had a home; henceforward my children could be visited only by arrangement. My career in England, which had seemed so promising for more than a decade, had petered out and the last show I had been commissioned to do for the BBC had been cancelled. I felt that I had behaved despicably to everyone I cared for, and they agreed.

In hospital I had been writing copiously and getting my lucubrations and cartoons published in an irreverent periodical called *Nation Review*. Considering that everything I wrote during this convalescent period was arch and prolix drivel, I am amazed the magazine ran them – probably it was on the strength of my reputation as a former wag and front-page drunk.

Slowly my emerging self stumbled, blinking, out of the penumbra of illness and began to look around, and even to make

SAME AGAIN SIR?

Liquid refreshments (*Nation Review*, 1970)

plans. They had to be modest ones. I was, after all, starting life anew.

My friend Clyde Packer kindly interceded with a touchy Sydney impresario whom I had deeply offended not long before. The Sydney impresario had a habit, probably learnt on some half-baked Dale Carnegie course, of standing very close and adjusting your necktie as he talked to you, then dusting your shoulders and plucking lint off your jacket, enforcing an unwelcome intimacy. Yet he was very good at his job and possessed of an undeniable charm, and I thought that if I was to work again in the theatre, if only sweeping the stage, he was to be 'schmoozed'. I grovelled, and Packer achieved the necessary rapprochement with a few emollient words and a convivial and, for me, wineless lunch at Beppi's famous Italian restaurant in Darlinghurst.

Inebriates experience, often with a shudder, graphic reminders of their delinquencies long after they get sober. A brandy bottle concealed behind books, incoherent words scrawled in a diary and never-to-be-repaired friendships. Beppi's was a favourite haunt of mine during both periods of my life – the Conscious and the Unconscious – and there was a nice middle-aged lady at the reception desk called Roma. Although I continued to patronise this restaurant for many years, she invariably regarded me with a look of stony contempt. I once approached her and asked if, in the past, I had ever insulted her or done something despicable in her purview; had I, for example, fondled her breasts, exposed myself or vomited discreetly at the table? In which case, I explained, I had been very sick and she had my abject apologies. But nothing softened Roma's heart; she remained tight-lipped, with eyes averted, and replied not. I never discovered my offence.

THERE followed many months of touring all over Australia, the slow recuperation of my health and fortunes, and two visits to London to produce, with Bruce Beresford, the then-outrageous Barry McKenzie films.

When the Honourable Clyde Packer took over the management of my affairs, it caused a temporary rift with the man whom we had so strenuously wooed. Clyde, the son of a newspaper tycoon, was a remarkable person, whose recent death in Santa Barbara grieved many old friends. He was a big man – over six feet tall and bulky when I first knew him – and he lived in a fine modern home in Woollahra, an Aboriginal word meaning 'lookout'. It was one of the best of the older districts of Sydney and was subsequently favoured by lawyers, 'radio personalities', prime ministers and other parvenus. Like Michael Arlen, Clyde sought the respect of his friends and family, but the love of head waiters.

Over the next few years of our partnership I tasted a novel prosperity and I acquired several new and salutary vices. Clyde lived with a beautiful model and artist called Lyndall and he threw lavish dinners and parties, but one knew that he was, despite his taste for the orgiastic, a man of feeling and intellect.

On the twenty-first of November 1975 I noticed Clyde was wearing a black armband.

'Here's one for you too, Barry,' he said, presenting me

with a substantial loop of black satin. 'Someone in this town should be in mourning for General Franco.'

At that time, when everyone in Sydney was walking around in a sanctimonious and somewhat humourless pink cloud, a respectful gesture to the late Spanish dictator was exquisitely subversive.

Clyde was never less than generous. The only gorgeous young woman who has ever knocked on my hotel bedroom door wearing nothing but a full-length mink presented me with an inscribed card:

With the Compliments of the Honourable R.C. Packer

Together Clyde and I visited exotic places and enjoyed bizarre adventures in Hong Kong, Amsterdam, and the Lebanon of the good old days. His ashes are interred at Santa Barbara, but at least a decent pinch of them might appropriately have been sprinkled on the site of the Crazy Horse in Beirut.

When not in Sydney or touring, I lived for long periods at the Windsor, a hotel built in the opulent coffee-palace style of the eighteen-seventies and eighteen-eighties: the years of the gold boom. It was the only grand Victorian hotel left in the town since most of the others had been demolished just before the Olympic Games in Melbourne, when their spacious accommodations might have proved useful. With provincial prudery, however, the city council had decided that it was better to have no hotels than embarrassingly unmodish ones, which might lead international visitors to think we were behind the times and not, in the quaint catchphrase of the time, 'as modern as tomorrow'.

In later years the Windsor was brutally refurbished – veneered with period detail and suffocated with historically authentic carpets and National-Trust-approved wallpapers. When I stayed there, it was still in its own juice, with an old-fashioned dignity, its appointments unselfconsciously dull. In the large panelled coffee room, as palm-fronded as Polynesia, amongst big leather couches and armchairs, the cadaverous Johan, an aged but spry waiter, dispensed wafer-thin chicken sandwiches and petits fours from tiered cake trays to the theatre crowds who thronged there after a night at the Prinnie or the Maj (the Princess and Her Majesty's theatres). At the Blüchner baby grand, embowered in potted palms, a woman in black maladroitly tinkled – between Du Maurier cigarettes – medleys from *South Pacific* and *My Fair Lady*. Why is it that even first-class hotels do not merely tolerate incompetent cocktail pianists, but encourage them?

The Irish management, who had probably run pubs for generations, stood at the mahogany reception desk and watched everyone who arrived. Miss O'Keefe, in particular, would always fix me with a beady eye as I entered the foyer late in the evening after one of my own attractions, particularly if I had a female companion. Her basilisk stare of disapproval seemed to follow us up several floors in that large and creaking cage lift. I was then in love with Rhoze, as she called herself – a raven-haired and patchouli-scented hippie – and the nocturnal appearance of this exotic interloper in the sedate lobby of the Windsor attracted

Miss O'Keefe's most disdainful scrutiny – especially when the manageress glimpsed, beneath the diaphanous pink and turquoise habiliments of Nepal, a pair of nude feet provocatively roughed with asphalt.

My girlfriend, like many other young Australians who sought freedom and intensity in places like Goa and Katmandu – indeed wherever the *I Ching* led them – had recently been stranded without money in a large Asian city and had sought assistance from the Australian Ambassador, a former left-wing Melbourne book reviewer and a political appointee of the reigning Labor Prime Minister. The Ambassador and his wife generously offered the voluptuous young indigent accommodation in a remote wing of their palatial residence until funds arrived from Australia and she could resume her discalceate wanderings. She was not alone in her room for long, however, for in the early hours of the morning she was disturbed by the sound of heavy breathing and a twitching at her mosquito net as His Excellency himself, pouring with sweat and in a state of furtive excitement, paid her a strictly unofficial visit. Diplomatic hospitality, like most things, is never without its price.

HEATHER and Wendy and Lola and Harold and Dot and Alan and Iris and Irene and Victy and Andrew and Phil and Wayne and Laurie . . . All have been my pianists at one time or another. On long runs or long tours they have been my closest companions, for very often the show is just me on stage with a pianist accompanying the songs and filling in during quick changes, before the rousing gladioli chorus at the end. Sometimes, more ambitiously, as with *An Evening's Intercourse with the Well-known Barry Humphries* of 1984, I augmented the single grand piano with other instruments: violin, cello and percussion. In that show the all-girl band were dressed rather mannishly in black and called the Sisterhood of Sound. But I still prefer a single accompanist: a master of the art such as Laurie Holloway, George Stiles, Andrew Ross or Wayne Barker. A good pianist will often know the show better than the artiste himself, and there are still those who remember my offerings of the mid-seventies in which sometimes, after a brief caesura when I realised I had lost my thread, I would turn to the extraordinary lady tourniqueted with feather boas at the keyboard and hiss, 'Where was I, Iris?' She always knew.

Iris Mason was a natural star. I found her in Sydney when I was rehearsing *At Least You Can Say You've Seen It*. Recently widowed, she was a classically trained pianist from New Zealand who had at one stage studied with the great Percy Grainger. When I met her first, she lived alone in a tiny flat in Elizabeth Bay, crammed with innumerable coloured objects, and with full ashtrays on every surface. She was extremely small and obviously once pretty, but now in a picturesque disarray to which nicotine and alcohol had added their characteristic inflections. Iris wore a wig, which she carelessly donned every morning like a hat. Rarely did I glimpse the sparse white wisps that lay beneath this brown bouffant bird's nest. She applied her make-up with the same impatient bravura, slapping on a livid Lautrec-like mask: rouging her cheeks with cyclamen, jabbing at her eyelids with blue or green pigment, and affixing her false eyelashes with little care as to which belonged to upper or lower lid – sometimes with the unfortunate result that when she blinked these long, mascara-clotted extensions locked like Venus flytraps.

When we first met, Iris regarded me with a look of profound suspicion, surpassed only by the scrutiny I received many years later from my future mother-in-law. However, we sang a few songs together around the keyboard of her Yamaha upright, and the ice melted. Iris, like Renaldo Hahn and Hoagy Carmichael, loved to smoke as she played the piano and she enjoyed a drink at those moments as well. This latter proclivity I decided to incorporate into our act when she finally agreed to work for me. She would sail onto the stage, extraordinarily bedizened – choked with ropes of pearls and gaudy scarves, her make-up an expressionist inflation of her everyday *maquillage* – and on reaching the piano she would commence to slowly remove the many rings from her delicate fingers, dropping them noisily into a receptacle beside the keyboard. With the same deliberation, she would reach for a large brandy balloon set on a small table beside the piano and pour into it about three inches of crème de menthe, topping up the drink with a sulphurous dash of advocaat. Having stirred this stomach-turning cocktail, Iris took a long swig, sometimes emptying the glass to groans of revulsion from the audience. She then, with brilliant technical skill, played her introductory medley, culminating in a few bars of the National Anthem: a song that at that far-off time still had the power to bring older and more patriotic members of the audience to their feet.

Was it a joke? Was it real? Should we or shouldn't we?

A spotlight swung from Iris to the curtain at the opposite side of the stage and Edna's pink-Lurex-gloved wrist extended towards the audience, the fingers flexing imperiously upwards. The command was unequivocal; and as Iris played 'God Save the Queen' the audience stood.

I have often lamented the loss of this useful curtain-raiser. A large group of strangers from many differing walks of life have travelled, sometimes at great inconvenience and expense, to assemble in the auditorium of a theatre. But they are not an audience; they are a heterogeneous mob of strangers and for a show to work, especially if it is a comedy, they must become one animal. They must be mesmerised. They must act in unison, obedient solely to the will of the author and performer. How helpful it is, then, to dim the lights before the show and play them a simple tune to which they will all jump to attention and then resume their seats, emotionally joined at the hip.

Today, in this unpatriotic age, the essential coalescence of an audience only takes place when the first exclamation of laughter unites it and the 'bonding' happens. My friend and collaborator Ian Davidson, seated once in a box at Drury Lane, noticed that an audience changes colour with a shutter-like effect when it laughs: pink, brown, pink, as the patrons turn briefly, instinctively to each other as if to say *Did you get it? How is it for you?*

Apart from always knowing what I was going to say next, Iris Mason was an astute critic and observer of my work. When I once complained to her that a sure-fire laugh wasn't happening any more, she merely said, 'Try smiling when you say it, darling.' What a simple, yet important, directive this is to any comic actor who is not of the deadpan school. I followed her advice, and the laughs came flocking back like the swallows coming back to Capistrano.

We were in Perth, Western Australia, once, Iris and I, and on our first Wednesday afternoon we went to the pictures together to see *The Towering Inferno*. Appropriately it was rather hot in the cinema and we dozed off a few times in the less exciting bits until a strange thought crept into my head: Wasn't there a Wednesday matinée? Slowly, and with growing panic, I remembered that there probably was, and if this indeed were the case, we were already very late. Waking Iris was no easy task. In fact she had fallen asleep with her head thrown so far back that her wig had fallen into the lap of the man seated behind her. Ultimately we struggled out of the cinema into the blinding light of day and hailed a cab. Iris was still in a daze and seemed to be under the impression that she was evacuating a burning building in the arms of Steve McQueen.

Fifteen minutes later, as our cab swung around a corner and the Playhouse Theatre came into view, I saw that my worst fears had been justified. A large crowd of people were milling around in the street, some of whom looked exceedingly cross. However, the arrival of our taxi elicited a general cheer, and as we ran into the theatre – Iris with her hair on back to front – we promised our public a show within ten minutes. Although nearly an hour late, it was one of the best shows we ever did.

Iris Mason was a star in London. I doubt that *Housewife-Superstar!* would have been so successful without her presence.

With my companion, and soon-to-be wife, Diane Millstead, this was a joyous time for me. I was performing my own show, sober, in a beautiful theatre on Shaftsbury Avenue and even earning a little money, or such small coin as accidentally fell out of my producer's pockets. (Although it was then that I received an airmail letter from Australia with the desolate news that my wild Rhoze had died alone in Nepal.)

In 1977, when we took *Housewife-Superstar!* for a brief season to New York, Iris was also a considerable hit. Brian Thomson, the designer, had placed her piano on a kind of grassy knoll on the stage, studded with fairy lights and plaster pixies.

But it was in Hong Kong that Iris had enjoyed her greatest social success. In 1974 the Mandarin Hotel was considered one of the best hotels in the world. It towered above most of the other buildings in that island city, although today it is probably one of Hong Kong's smallest structures. Peter Stafford was its gifted manager and he bravely invited me to do a two-week cabaret season in the hotel's nightclub, the Harbour Room. Iris and I were provided with luxurious suites and there were flattering photographs of us, advertising our engagement, in the lifts, lobbies and restaurants as if we were a real cabaret act.

Les Patterson had just been invented, and having appointed him Australian Cultural Attaché to the Far East, I decided it best if he opened our Hong Kong show by coming through the audience to the stage and interrupting Iris's overture with a few drunken words about the colony: remarks that the New Puritanism of today would unquestionably deem 'racist'.

197

After a quick change Edna would appear, bent on a duty-free shopping spree.

On the first night, disguised as Les, I hovered near the entrance to the nightclub, hearing with relief the laughter and applause that greeted Iris Mason's entrance. It was a very smart audience indeed of bankers, stockbrokers and English executives from Swire and Jardine Matheson, stalwarts of the Hong Kong Club. Their pretty young wives, as they sat amongst the Hooray Henrys, glanced petulantly at their brand-new Cartier watches. Most of them had been until recently miniskirted dolly birds on the King's Road on the lookout for a rich catch; now, having caught him and been hijacked to the Far East, they were already missing the discos and boutiques of London and the Hampshire house parties.

That night Iris was obliged to play her overture for much longer than she expected, for where was Sir Les? Shouldn't he have interrupted the music by now? But I was still outside the club, remonstrating with a Chinese maître d'.

'You can't come here. You dlunk!'

'I'm the show!' I tried without success to interject, but by then he had called for assistance.

'YOU DLUNK!'

There was a scuffle, shouts, hoarse imprecations. Gradually, in the warmth of the Harbour Room at linen-topped tables and on plush banquettes, Englishmen in shirts by Mee-Yee and Ascot Chang, and fine lounge suits by A-Man Hing Cheong, turned and beheld a fat, red-faced man in heavily stained, powder-blue seersucker, holding a whisky bottle and struggling with two formidable Oriental bouncers in black tie, built, as the Americans would coyly prefer to say, like brick bathrooms. It was only the intervention of a real diplomat, the manager, Peter Stafford, that finally permitted Les Patterson, none the worse for a little roughing-up, to mount the stage at last to drunken cheers. The show was a hit.

Iris and I were taken up by a charming circle of English expatriates, most of whom lived on the other side of the island at Shek O in white, modernistic thirties villas. Their books came from Hayward Hill, their wine from Berry Brothers and their children – during the holidays – from Eton and Roedean. They were wonderfully hospitable and took us out for day trips on their pleasure junks and gin palaces, moored in Aberdeen Harbour. Or we went swimming on the unspoilt beaches of Lantau, or to lunches at Repulse Bay or picnics on Lamma Island, or sailing from the Royal Hong Kong Yacht Club, or to more informal evenings at the Hebe Haven Yacht Club, in the days before that charming polymath David Tang became modern Cathay's unofficial master of ceremonies.

The beauty and romance of Hong Kong is still to be found there, although so much is gone forever. In the old days, before many fine colonial buildings were demolished, I loved to jump on the Kennedy Road tram and wander off the beaten track, away from the neon-lit arcades, with their interminable shirt makers, camera shops and vendors of transistor radios, to dark and narrow alleys to hear the racket of mah-jong down murky stairs, to catch the reek of stewed offal and to feel, every now and then, dripping down on my new suit by Sam of the

Burlington Arcade, Kowloon, the drooling syrup of a clapped-out air conditioner.

Everything was in Hong Kong, and everything could be had. Enterprising Australian girls turned up there too. One I had known from Melbourne looked transformed and rather glamorous as we had lunch together at Gaddi's in the old Peninsula Hotel.

'What do you do these days, Meredith?' I asked her foolishly.

'I work with men,' she replied laughing, as though no further explanation of her profession were required.

Naïvely I tried to think what jobs with men a nice Melbourne girl could pursue. Some form of nursing in a men's ward perhaps? Or working at a task like bus driving or building construction, which were formerly male preserves? Only in her suite after lunch did I learn, on the house, what form of hard labour she actually performed.

Reasonable Access

~

After a time, in married life, it becomes
the other partner's fault that they have married one,
but the only child, or, as chance may have it,
the many children, have no choices, they are ours,
and this is what fixes the guilt on us

HENRY GREEN

ONCE, in the early forties, on an interminable drive with my parents in the Oldsmobile (Why old? I wondered at the time – it was new!), I overheard them discussing my Uncle Brackston and his wife, Dorothy. This was a popular and volatile subject with my mother, who had often excoriated her brother for marrying a Roman Catholic. To me Dorothy had always seemed a particularly nice woman, but she was rarely invited to the big family get-togethers; and when she was, she was conspicuously snubbed by all but my nicer relations. Unfortunately my mother's youngest sister was also called Dorothy. She was so mortified by a Popish namesake in the family that she adopted the soubriquet 'Billie', which, happily, she retains to this day.

Poor Uncle Brack, the only brother, having chosen to

marry into the enemy camp, must have suffered terrible reproaches from his five sisters, not to mention his forbidding mother. Little wonder that he was inclined to enjoy, in the euphemistic vernacular of his period, 'the odd glass'.

My father regularly lent money to his brother-in-law, and this was accidentally discovered – with hell to pay – when poor Aunt Dorothy put her foot in it by ingenuously telephoning her gratitude to my mother, not realising that my father's more munificent benefactions were performed in secret. Much later I learnt that there were other family members to whom he lent surreptitious financial support and for whom he actually built houses on a pay-whatever-you-like whenever-you-can basis. Indeed I once got into hot water when I mentioned to my mother that I had seen Uncle Tom furtively slipping my father a brown-paper envelope at a family tea party.

On the journey to Mount Eliza that I am now recalling, my parents were discussing the popular subject of Brackston and Dorothy in one of those harsh whispers not meant to be overheard, yet more audible to children than the most strident exchange. The row was progressing as we climbed Oliver's Hill when, from the back seat, I ventured a suggestion.

'Why don't Uncle Brack and Aunty Dorothy get divorced?'

The car nearly went off the road. My father swerved dangerously onto the gravel verge and jammed on the brakes. Both parents glowered at me over the front seat, which in those days was a grey-upholstered banquette and not two armchairs.

'Where did you learn that word?' my mother asked angrily.

'On the wireless,' I answered truthfully.

I was a regular listener to *Martin's Corner*, a radio serial broadcast every evening on 3DB at 6.30, just before dinner. Such programmes, often mysteriously called 'sessions' – *Barry is listening to his session* – were all 'brought to us' by the manufacturers of everything from chewing gum to soap, and *Martin's Corner*, the saga of a suburban grocery shop and the family who owned it, was 'brought to us' by Kellogg's, whose tawny cereals rustled into the breakfast bowls of the nation. Indeed one of their products was advertised as an aid to regularity, but this was never explained so I somehow got the idea that regularity meant punctuality. I consumed large helpings of this sawdust-tasting fibre every morning and was *still* late for school – often later than usual due to the insidious laxative properties of my breakfast.

One evening after the 'snap, crackle and pop' Kellogg's commercial and the familiar theme music from Offenbach's *Orpheus in the Underworld* overture, a crisis engulfed *Martin's Corner*. Mrs Ludlow, the town gossip and busybody (she had a fake English accent), reported to the genial proprietors of the shop, Rose and Philip, that their daughter-in-law, Betty, wife of their beloved son, Alan, was secretly seeing another man, the local roué, Archie Taylor. Of course, Alan Martin found out, and in one of the most sensational cliffhangers in the history of Australian radio he announced to his parents, 'Betty and I are getting a divorce.'

In a subsequent episode the benign intervention of kind old Granny Martin saved the situation and Betty's innocence was vindicated, so the couple were reconciled. However, this may well have been the first time the D-word was ever uttered on an Australian broadcast.

It was a long time before my father restarted the car and we drove on in tearful silence while my parents grimly reflected on the pernicious influence of radio. My father seemed badly shaken by that forbidden word, which had struck him with an unpredictable force. Was it, I wonder now, the thought that for people on the radio and in films, at least, there was an escape from the ardours and endurances of marriage, which those of my parents' class and upbringing dared not even contemplate without a violent moral spasm?

'Never use that word again,' my mother had admonished me, 'or your father will wash your mouth out with soap and water.'

If there was ever an unpleasant cautionary task to perform, it always fell to Eric. It was at moments like these that he became 'your father' and, for the time being, no longer her husband. Had my parents but known it, they were often having these quasi-divorces. Not that I ever used the heretical word again, and when my first marriage, and even my second, ended in that unutterable state it was never spoken of.

Divorce is now a sad commonplace, and amongst my readers there must be many who have experienced this calamity; some, like me, more than once or twice. But in the distant period of which I am writing, the 'single-parent family', if not brought about by a respectable event such as death, was a disreputable curiosity.

There was a boy at Camberwell Grammar School who, it

was whispered, *had no father*! Neale was a boisterous and wiry little kid who would today be described as 'hyperactive'. His schoolyard language was incessantly scatological and his favourite trick was to sidle up behind older boys and suddenly grab their balls.

Neale lived in a leafy crescent with his pretty but sad-faced mother, and I often cycled past their semidetached house. Once or twice I glimpsed a lonely figure by the front gate. Somehow I guessed that the man in the grey suit and hat was Neale's missing father, palely loitering just out of view of his ex-wife *sans merci*. He may have been waiting for a glimpse of his son after school, or keeping an appointment for an awkward hour or two in the park or a suburban teashop. There was something touching, even inconsolable in his demeanour, as though he had spruced himself up – and perhaps even sobered himself up – for these brief reunions. The image of that man with the drooping ginger moustache, waiting by the gate, has always personified for me what the law calls 'visitation rights' and 'reasonable access'.

Many years later I encountered Neale again, a robust and bearded young civil engineer living with a middle-aged gay actor.

It is a commonplace of divorce that, in these often acrimonious sunderings, mutual possessions are arbitrarily divided, rarely with respect for justice or equity. Not seldom an angry husband sequestrates treasures his wife owned long before their union, and vice versa. The histories of these inanimate objects – household detritus such as books, pictures and furniture – are imaginatively rewritten by both antagonists. Who owned what and when, how purchased and with whose money, is the bread, butter and caviar of the divorce lawyer. The courts can never truly adjudicate in these painful matters when couples, no longer able to tolerate the melodrama of their lives together, squabble bitterly over the *mise en scène*.

So it was that once, many years ago, I contemplated a shameful act. At a desolate time in my life I found myself, uncannily like Neale's grey ghost of a father, hovering one damp autumn day outside the home of my ex-wife. Perhaps I was not exactly loitering on foot but, rather, disconsolately smoking behind the wheel of a Budget Rent-A-Car and waiting for my daughters to appear at the gate. They were late. Should I ring the doorbell?

It was strange pushing open the gate and walking for the first time in over a year up the leaf-strewn path towards the house to which I had once possessed a key. A warm effulgence shone through the Edwardian leadlight panels of the front door: an Australian botanical motif in crimson and olive green – gum-nut nouveau.

An enchanting child – my daughter – opened the door. There were apologies as she ran to the back of the house to fetch her sister and a coat. I stood for a moment alone on the doorstep.

There were such a lot of familiar things in the hallway: a Victorian *vitrine* full of books, and wasn't that my old copy of Marinetti's futurist manifesto, inscribed flamboyantly by the author and bought for the huge sum of £5 from Seward's book-shop? And there was the Rosenthal porcelain figurine of a flapper playing the banjo, which I had once picked up in Prague.

I recognised, amongst other objects on a small table, a brown, cylindrical, papier-mâché box encrusted with white and ruby rhinestones. It was the snuffbox of the great nineteenth-century English actor Charles Macready, friend of Dickens and dedicatee of *Nicholas Nickleby*, which he would open with an arresting squeak on the stage of Drury Lane, artfully tilting it to catch the light and bring all eyes to him. I had bought it jointly with a friend from the collection of Walter MacQueen-Pope, the theatrical historian, and had paid it off over many weeks, a few shillings at a time.

Hanging low on my left, near the door, was a small symbolist watercolour by Thomas Cooper Gotch, given to me as a birthday present in Cornwall by his granddaughter Deirdre, the last mistress of 'the Great Beast', Aleister Crowley, poet and satanist. How beautiful that picture is, I thought. Then, with less nobility, How portable.

It is possible for a man intoxicated by avidity and nostalgia to believe that his children's cultural legacy is as safe beneath his roof as that of his former spouse, especially if he can persuade himself – and I did so with ease – that having acquired these objects in the first place, he has a better acquaintance with their history and value. Accordingly, having repulsed the idea many times, I finally decided upon an appalling scheme to correct, as I saw it, a simple error of provenance.

I was occupying a drab and rambling apartment at the

Windsor Hotel, wonderfully unlike a hotel suite of today. There were faded armchairs, glass-fronted cabinets full of trumpery knick-knacks, candlewick bedspreads of an unpleasant squashed-caterpillar green, and open fireplaces in which real mallee roots, regularly stoked by a baize-aproned porter, glowed and crumbled. It was rather like a suburban vicarage embedded in a grand hotel.

Just around the corner from my born-again bachelor dwelling at the Windsor was the dry-cleaning shop of Mr Jablonski. Mr Jablonski and I had become friends, since he did all my cleaning and pressing; and being also a tailor, he regularly repaired my threadbare wardrobe. Somehow he had learnt that I understood a little German, and whenever I called in at the shop he would break into that language, although with a strong Polish accent. I once asked him how he happened to be so fluent, and it was then that he made his small joke.

'I learnt my German at the best university in Europe – Auschwitz.' With an almost mischievous smile, he rolled up his sleeve to expose the faded, tattooed numerals on his wrist.

A few days after I had stood like a tradesman on my ex-wife's doorstep, I entered the small dry-cleaning shop and placed an overcoat on the counter.

'Mr Jablonski,' I began, not without some circumspection in which there may even have been a hint of suppressed shame, 'I have a special task for you, which I cannot fully explain.' I broke off in embarrassment as another customer entered the shop, and only resumed when she had left.

'I need some pockets in the lining of this coat . . . a few of them actually, and not in the usual places. It's . . . it's rather a secret so please don't mention this to anyone . . .' I broke off in confusion.

Mr Jablonski peered at me with a kindly interest; almost a twinkle.

'You don't have to explain,' he said, raising his hand. 'I know exactly what you want. Say no more, Mr Barry. It will be my pleasure.'

'But Mr Jablonski,' I persisted, 'I just have to give you some dimensions and that kind of thing.'

However, the tailor would hear no more, and there were now two more customers waiting.

'I understand exactly,' he said. 'You don't have to tell me nothing. The coat will be ready on Friday.'

I returned to my hotel with a light step. I did not have a clear tactic for the following weekend, when it had been arranged that I would next see my daughters; indeed I could not be sure that I would be alone long enough to unobtrusively liberate a few old friends from that richly furbished hallway, but at least I would be prepared with my voluminous overcoat and its secret accommodations.

At length Friday came, and not without a certain morbid excitement I presented myself at the dry-cleaning shop. Jablonski seemed oddly elated.

'She's done. She's beautiful,' he declared, flinging my overcoat on the counter.

Quickly I examined the lining.

'You see,' said the tailor triumphantly. 'I done it exactly like you want it.'

The inside of my coat was covered with pockets – at least twenty pockets – none more than four inches square. I stared at Jablonski's handiwork.

'You see, Mr Barry . . .' he repeated. 'I do it just how you want. Nice, eh?'

I thought of the picture, a book or two, the porcelain figurine, even a substantial chunk of rhinestone-studded papier mâché.

'But Mr Jablonski,' I exclaimed, 'the pockets – they are so *small.*'

'I tell you, Mr Barry, it's perfect. The pockets are just right. I've done it so many times. I know what I'm doing.'

He had leant across the counter and was holding up the garment proudly.

'You've done it before?' I said. 'You put pockets in a coat like this before? When, Mr Jablonski? Why?'

'In Buchenwald where they sent me after Auschwitz, I was in the tailor's shop. I did this job many times, but the coats were not from Mr Burberry,' he laughed.

'But what were the pockets *for*, Mr Jablonski?'

Again he leant across the counter and squeezed my hands. I saw the shadowy numbers on his wrist.

'Potatoes,' he laughed. 'They fit per . . . fect!'

I paid him what he asked, took the now repugnant coat, and crept back to my hotel.

It was a warm evening when I collected my children soon after. An overcoat would have been superfluous anyway, but I have since often wondered if cupidity was ever so cruelly rebuked?

Alone at Last!

~

Easy is unhappiness, difficult is joy

A.E. COPPARD

PETER COOK had a variety of medical advisers in the sixties, some of whom he shared with Dudley Moore. One in particular, a successful show-business psychiatrist whom we may call Dr Seymour Lovegood, was a comedians' groupie and principal dispenser of uppers and downers to the theatrical profession. He liked to give large parties at his substantial Wimbledon mock-Tudor mansion, and one night in convivial company there I became, after large quantities of wine and spirits, extremely 'tired and emotional'. I woke up in the small hours of the morning on a sofa after all the guests had long since departed, and was staggering to my feet in search of the lavatory when my host appeared in a dressing-gown and suggested that I see him professionally at his Harley Street office the following day for the medical help I so patently needed.

Accordingly, drenched in cologne and with a thunderous hangover, I presented myself at Lovegood's practice. My headache was exacerbated by a nasty bruise on my temple caused by a blow from a low wooden beam when I stumbled down the doctor's wine-cellar steps the night before, hoping to sample unobserved some of his rare vintages.

As I sat on the other side of his desk, trying to suppress nausea and still my tremulous hands, the shrink regarded me with an amused compassion.

'How do you feel?' he asked, with an oleaginous smile.

'Well . . .' I began huskily, 'I may have had a bit too much to drink at your place last night. Actually I think I am inclined to drink a bit too much as a general rule . . .' I trailed off, longing for a cigarette, although if I lit one now the doctor might observe my shaky hand.

'I don't think the grog is your problem,' he said silkily, 'and anyway we've got pills for that, as Peter Cook will tell you. Wasn't he in good form last night, by the way!'

To this doctor anyone was in 'good form' who was not convulsing, bleeding from every orifice and being rushed to hospital.

He leant towards me over the desk. 'What you have to come to terms with, Barry, is that you are a cross-dresser, and there's nothing whatsoever wrong with that. Once you stop feeling guilty about your cross-dressing, you'll be able to drink like a gentleman.'

I stared at him blankly. In spite of my hangover I didn't think I was as mad as all that. What did this fellow mean? And what was a 'kraws drisser', for God's sake? Dr Lovegood's thick Sithifrican accent had become incomprehensible. I could only guess what he was driving at. Dr 'Call Me Seymour' was already scribbling a prescription for some 'harmless' amphetamine and suggesting that I make a series of appointments to discuss my obscure proclivities, whatever they might be.

'I don't come cheap, Barry,' he announced, 'but wouldn't you pay anything just to learn *what you really are?*'

He then mentioned a huge fee, and after a brisk handshake I found myself in Devonshire Place and heading swiftly for that discreet pub, the Weymouth Arms, for a restorative aperitif. Or two.

I have only recently recalled this sinister interview, and I am eternally grateful that I never cashed in his prescription or I might not have lived to tell the tale – and there were those who did not. I subsequently found out what a kraws drisser was, and I can only assume that the doctor, having seen a couple of Edna's early television appearances, must have inferred with simplistic solemnity that I was 'into' ladies' clothes.

Only when I returned to the United States in the late seventies did I discover that Dr Lovegood was not the only person who took a pathological view of this venerable British music hall tradition. Americans, at least until recently, recoiled from a comedian in a frock as from an Anthrax envelope. Even *Dame Edna Everage and the Rise of Western Civilization*, John Lahr's monograph about my act, bears upon its original, University of California Press cover the following subject heading: Film & Theater/*Gender Studies* (italics mine). Presumably the same academic dweeb who made this classification would also catalogue Shakespeare's *Othello* under Theater/Racist Studies, or *The Merchant of Venice* under Theater/Holocaust Studies.

Years ago, during a season at the Regal Theatre in Perth, Western Australia, before that theatre's magnificent refurbishment, my dressing-room was separated from the ladies' lavatory by a thin partition. One evening at intermission as I was changing costumes and refreshing my make-up, I overheard one of my female patrons say very loudly to her friend, 'I dunno about you, Jean, but I liked her better as a man.'

I realised that she was speaking about Edna, whom she clearly believed to be a real person who occasionally, but not often enough, attempted male impersonations during my show. It is interesting for me to reflect upon this strange person that I have invented and in whose reality so many people prefer to believe. A woman told me once that her twelve-year-old daughter came home from school in tears because a cruel friend had told her that Dame Edna was really a man.

'Does your daughter believe in Santa Claus?' I inquired.

'Heavens above, no!' laughed the lady. 'She stopped believing in that years ago.'

The process by which Edna has slowly evolved from housewife to superstar to megastar to guru and even, in her own fantasy, to sainthood, is a curious one to chart. She moved first from the dowdy habiliments in cotton, seersucker and Orlon of a young mother in the fifties, to an aspiring actress in newly fashionable Thai silk in the sixties, to Crimplene and denim, and now to finery more expensive and resplendent than that of the best-dressed women in most of her audiences. Edna also embarked on a chromatic journey from burgundy, through oyster, aqua, cyclamen, peacock, salmon, avocado and tangerine, to taupe, écru and beige.

Acting the part of Edna is the perfect Method acting exercise, for the Method actor, when contemplating a new role, must fabricate his character's history. He must invent its memories, relationships, previous existences, tastes and obsessions. Edna is a character I have known so well for nearly half a century that, once on stage or in a television studio, I can instantly assume her persona. She is not an alter ego as some might like to suggest for I have absolutely nothing in common with this woman, except perhaps my legs.

I have a similar relationship with some of my other stage inventions, notably Sandy Stone and Les Patterson. They all have elaborate lives outside the theatre and I try to give the impression in my shows that they have, as it were, accidentally *strayed* onto the stage, so that what we see and hear in the theatre is a fragment of their total existence: the tip of the iceberg.

WHEN I came back to London in 1972, after a long interlude in Australia, it was to make a film version of the Barry McKenzie comic strip with my friend Bruce Beresford. Peter Cook's midwifery at Bazza's birth in *Private Eye* was appropriately acknowledged in the screen credits of *The Adventures of Barry McKenzie*, and he even played a minor role in the film in his habitual languid manner. He wasn't really an actor and he did everything with a half-smile and a curiously writhing movement of the head and shoulders, so that one watched his performance more than anyone else's.

The Adventures of Barry McKenzie, the first film financed

by the Australian Film Development Corporation, was an immense popular success, even though it was excoriated predictably by everyone who called themselves a critic, from disc jockeys to the cinema-scribblers of the Australian press. It was not so much that they were affronted by the portrayal of Australians as vulgar and incontinent (McKenzie vomited and urinated copiously throughout the film), but that audiences in that intimidating place called 'Overseas' might judge us all by Barry.

By the early seventies the adman had come into his own – indeed the first McKenzie film had been produced by an advertising executive – and the jargon of the advertising industry was creeping into everyday usage. People had fallen in love with the word 'image' and Australia's international image became a matter of national concern. We wanted to be perceived as a rather refined and cultivated nation with superlative skills in sport, armed conflict and even macramé. This popular handicraft was then shaggily dominating the lobbies of hotels, the vestibules of insurance companies and even private homes. Where are they now, those multicoloured merkins of matted wool? There will be some amongst my readers who, happily, have never seen macramé; never had a brush with it, so to speak. Imagine, then, the inflated head of Sir Ian McKellen in *The Lord of the Rings*, dyed burnt orange, harvest gold and brown of an unmentionable hue, its dreadlocks and dundrearies snagged with beads and driftwood and pullulating with dust mites.

Beresford and I, undeterred by the Caliban-like howls of a few journalists and disc jockeys that had greeted our first film, and with the blessings and the money of a munificent soap opera tsar, Reg Grundy, and his wife, Mrs Grundy, went to Tasmania to write the sequel, *Barry McKenzie Holds His Own*.

As with the first film, where friends such as Peter Cook and Spike Milligan had played cameo roles, we cast as many traditional British comedians, young and old, as we could when we made the second one in 1974. These included Roy Kinnear, Arthur English, 'Monsewer' Eddie Gray and Tommy 'You Lucky People' Trinder – the first real comedian I had ever seen as a child, at Melbourne's Tivoli Theatre. Once again Dick Bentley was induced to come out of retirement to join our cast.

Dick Bentley was undoubtedly the most successful Australian comedian outside Australia. He had gone to London in the late thirties, appeared on stage and radio with some success, and only returned at the outbreak of the Second World War. After the war he went back to England and by the fifties he was a famous name on the BBC. In the radio show *Take It from Here* he invented a hapless character called Ron whose comic dialogues with 'Eth' brought laughter to millions.

When I met Dick in the late sixties, he was living in genteel retirement in St John's Wood. He still drove a magnificent cream Bentley automobile and wore venerable suits by Kilgour & French of Savile Row, which he had regularly adapted to contemporary fashion. When wide lapels came back into vogue in the early seventies, Dick was particularly upset because he had had the lapels on his forties suits expensively *narrowed* to conform to the style of the fifties. Since it was now impossible to widen them, he railed against what he called 'the hotel commissionaire look'.

217

'It won't last,' he predicted bitterly, and with wishful thinking. Dick's shoes, probably from Lobb or Tricker, were the shiniest in London, and he always wore a Lock's fedora tilted at a jaunty angle. His thinning hair was an 'assisted' golden brown and his mischievous countenance, like that of an amiable Australian bookmaker or a drawing by Phil May, always wore a discreet *maquillage* beneath which the spider veins and the depredations of age dimly pulsated.

Dick was full of stories about Australian expatriates in London on the eve of the Second World War. Unlike Bentley, a few were later stranded in the beleaguered city. There was one story in particular, concerning a rather precious Sydney actor who staggered into the subterranean cocktail bar in Swallow Street, by Piccadilly Circus, one night during the blitz. There had just been a reverberant explosion nearby that had rattled not a few glasses in this gay rendezvous, and the actor was white-faced and visibly shaken as he ordered his gin and lemon.

'That was close, Trevor,' said one of the queens at the bar.

'Close?' said the Australian actor. 'It was that close it blew a chip off me mallee root pendant!'

A mallee root, it should be noted, is a heavy, nodular hunk of wood deracinated from the soil of arid regions, such as the Victorian Mallee, and burnt as fuel. It is the last thing you would dream of suspending around your neck on a fine chain.

Elsewhere in London during the late thirties lived Patrick White in a flat decorated by Francis Bacon, the 'in' interior decorator, who was yet to paint fat nude businessmen gorily coupling on billiard tables. Patrick's extraordinary late novel *The*

Twyborn Affair gives a vivid picture of the epicene goings-on in prewar London when White was a regular stage-door johnny and Bea Lillie groupie.

When I knew him, Dick and his wife, Petronella (Peta), had a repertoire of hair-raisingly filthy stories, but Dick was oddly circumspect when our McKenzie film script required him to 'talk dirty'. We had cast him in the role of an Australian expatriate in France called Colin 'The Frog' Lucas, who had become more French than the French and was never without a beret and baguette. Much of the film was shot in Paris, and in Dick's big scene he and Barry McKenzie are strolling by the Seine in a mood of romantic reminiscence. However, there was one particular line at which Bentley baulked.

> BARRY (*indicating Notre Dame and the Palais du Louvre*) Don't let this clapped-out culture grab you, sport. Back in Australia we got culture up to our arseholes.
>
> COLIN (*sadly*) It's no good, Baz, wild *chevals* wouldn't drag me back to Oz now. It's a long *histoire*, but I was once shook on a sheila in Melbourne. We was gonna be married. 'Col,' she said, 'I'd bend over backwards for yer.' Then I found out she was bending over backwards for a lot of other blokes as well, including one of me best mates, so I came to the old Gay Paree to forget. *Mon dieu*! I tell you, Baz, I'd have crawled half a mile over broken glass to hear that little sheila piss into an empty jam tin.

At first poor Dick refused to deliver this speech. I tried to explain to him that it was far more innocent than the stories he told us in private, and that its mildly scatological character was surely mitigated by its, well . . . poignancy. Anyway, I protested, his was not the laugh line. The big laugh would follow Barry McKenzie's response.

> BARRY (*moved*) Gee, mate, did youse ever tell her you felt that way about her?

In the end, and through clenched teeth, Bentley did as he was bidden and indeed this short scene was one of the funniest in the film.

Barry McKenzie Holds His Own, like its predecessor, contained a number of 'firsts', and rereading the scripts today I note an early appearance in the language of that delectable Australian slang word 'shirtlifter' to describe a homosexual. Its first-ever appearance in print had been in the Barry McKenzie comic strip. I had learnt the term from a Sydney friend, 'Shearer Bill', who had spent most of his life in the outback shearing sheep and collecting arcane vernacular. The word, with its half-rhyme with 'poofdah', imaginatively evokes a rather decorous, yet necessary, preamble to buggery. I had decided in the sixties to rehabilitate this rare and charming epithet, and also the Melbourne public-school expression 'chunder', meaning to vomit, and I am delighted that both words are now respectably accommodated in the dictionary. 'Pillow-biter', a McKenzie neologism for a catamite, continues to gain ground in popular usage.

Both the Barry McKenzie films still seem hilarious today, at least to me; original also, for they spawned many imitators.

Sadly the negatives of these great epics of the Australian comic cinema – shot by the Oscar-deserving cinematographer Donald McAlpine – have been mislaid. Today video versions of these films can only be seen in washed-out, truncated 'pan and scan' versions.

IF Barry McKenzie was deemed by the prudish to be the Ugly Australian, there was an even uglier Australian waiting in the wings, whose vocabulary would have made even Barry blush. Barry McKenzie had been invented as a two-dimensional, non-naturalistic comic-strip character, who enjoyed a brief afterlife in Barry Crocker's sympathetic film performances. Leslie Colin Patterson, in his original incarnation as Entertainments Officer at a Sydney football club, was intended to convince his audience of his working-class authenticity. But as the character developed, in the years after his London stage début in *Housewife-Superstar!*, and gained international status as Australia's Cultural Attaché to the Court of St James's, it became apparent to me that he would be perpetually relevant. Composing and singing his songs such as 'Never Trust a Man Who Doesn't Drink', 'Chardonnay' and 'Pissing in the Wind' is one of the most satisfying and liberating of all my stage experiences. The fact that most healthy women are sexually attracted to Sir Les contributes in no small measure to my pleasure in inhabiting him. A cautionary figure, as well as a comic one, Les Patterson is that part of me that didn't stop drinking.

The eighties saw the apotheosis and the disgrace of Sir Les.

It was always wonderful and exhilarating to walk into my dressing-room at the theatre and slip into a vast and clammy 'fat suit', obscenely and priapically padded, then to don a deeply stained powder-blue Hong Kong suit, 'kipper' tie and finally a pair of two-toned, Cuban-heeled shoes of a monstrous design, fashionable in the early seventies. A boozy make-up swiftly applied and a clip-on denture of crooked, nicotine-stained teeth completed the transformation. Audiences adored this genial and foul-mouthed figure, and he even wrote a book called *The Traveller's Tool*, a manual needless to say, and one that is now somewhat rare. A new edition, *The Enlarged and Extended Tool*, is surely called for.

In 1987 it seemed a good idea to create a feature film starring this unlikely yet charismatic Australian antihero. The

THERE'S SOMETHING
THAT IS BOUND TO PLEASE
— A LONG SNIFF OF
AN AUSSIE CHEESE!

Les
Patterson

success of *Crocodile Dundee,* a sanitised version of Barry McKenzie, had so enriched investors in the local film industry that they were eager to put their profits into another gilt-edged project. *Les Patterson Saves the World* seemed just such a project. The setting was to be an imaginary Middle Eastern country run by a Gaddafi-like warlord. Patterson had been posted there in disgrace after farting in the General Assembly of the United Nations: a spectacular flatulence that was accidentally ignited, setting fire to a fundamentalist Arab. I will not tax the reader with further details of this gratuitously offensive fable except to say that Patterson stumbles upon a primitive terrorist plot to infect the lavatory seats of the Pentagon, and other seats of Western power, with a deadly virus called HELP (Herpetic Encephalitis of the Lymphatic Polyp), so called because that is what most people scream when they know they've got it. On screen we actually saw NATO generals staggering out of the men's room, their faces inflating and suppurating with the ravages of this sinister weapon. The film ended with a revolving restaurant spinning out of control as a result of a rogue koala interfering with its mechanism.

An entire Middle Eastern town, Abu Nivea, was constructed in a suburb of Sydney. Desert sequences were shot on the sand dunes of Botany Bay, and the final scene in the White House, with Joan Rivers playing the first female president, was filmed in Los Angeles.

But in spite of the gifted players, the skills of the production designer, director and cinematographer and the enormous budget, this film met with universal obloquy. To be sure there were serious flaws in the story, but its doom was sealed by an Australian health awareness campaign launched at the exact time of our première. It was a multimedia, government-sponsored message about the ravages of AIDS – 'the grim reaper' – and the resemblance between HELP and this frightening new scourge escaped no one. If *Les Patterson Saves the World* was meant to be an AIDS metaphor (which it was not), it was in execrable taste, as was the preposterous suggestion that some small Middle Eastern country might be planning an act of biological terrorism.

Emasculated in the cutting room before general release, and not even quite bad enough to become a cult movie, this foolhardy project died a swift, expensive and deserved death. Even the presence on the screen of Dame Edna and a cuddly marsupial failed to redeem it.

A phone rings.

'Barry?'

'Yes?'

'Hey, Barry, how you doing?'

Not American. A friend? No – too friendly to be a friend.

'Cliff here. Cliff Hotchkiss. *Daily Post.*' It was a paper that specialised in ill-natured gossip.

'Who gave you this num—?'

'We're running a big story, Baz, about the break-up. Sorry to hear about it, by the way. Just wanted to check a few facts so we could get your side of the picture. Is it true that . . . ?'

Quietly I put the phone down without returning it to its

cradle. Soon, off its hook, it would start wailing, but I was not going to be tricked, blackmailed into some vulgar public disculpation by a practising alcoholic.

Oppressed by matrimonial woes, I found 1988 a desolate enough time without being stalked by media snakes-in-the-grass. And I had a big show, *Back with a Vengeance*, to do every night at the Theatre Royal, Drury Lane. My public life was going so well, while my private life was painful and chaotic. Every evening I would rush into the theatre as though into some sanctuary of calm and certainty. I had briefly forgotten that John Lahr would be lying in wait for me in my dressing-room. As I entered, the son of Bert Lahr, the famous clown, the Cowardly Lion in *The Wizard of Oz*, half rose from a chintzy sofa in polite greeting. I noticed that the red light on his tape recorder was already winking. Inwardly I groaned as my mother's voice came back to me. 'No rest for the wicked,' she would have said with a small, complacent smile.

I had agreed some months before to let Mr Lahr do a series of interviews backstage, since he had secured a commission from *The New Yorker* to write about my act. The interviews, however, seemed interminable and I began to think he proposed to expand one article into several closely printed volumes. The hour before a performance is a precious period of quiet and reflection and I regretted the intrusion, cordial and well intentioned though it was. Accordingly, as I made up, applying the ruddy, booze-bitten complexion of Les Patterson and subsequently the padded powder-blue suit with its Aristophanic pelvic extension, I was jabbering on over my shoulder into my biographer's insatiable machine, and answering – or dodging – his probing questions. This grew increasingly difficult as John and I became friends. Ultimately the interviews became *Dame Edna Everage and the Rise of Western Civilization*, a book filled, it is true, with enough quotes from the show to entitle me to a generous royalty, but it was brilliantly and fairly written by the best and most sympathetic theatre writer living.

During these sessions the stage management would make routine visits, and I would want to know, for example, whether the gladioli had arrived in full bloom, whether or not we had a full house and, often, were there any interesting-looking people in the stalls with whom Edna might have some fun. Even if they discovered a few likely victims by peering through a hole in the curtain, I invariably chose someone else when the moment came.

With all this going on, and with that dim but persistent ache in my heart, it was always with infinite relief – even joy – that I finally leapt on stage to the roar of the crowd and said to myself, 'Alone at last!'

At this time in my life the telephone was a constant source of irritation; nothing it transmitted, except the voices of my children, brought me comfort. But at the height of the success of *Back with a Vengeance*, with the final performance looming, there came an unusual request. It was from Francesca, the wife of a senior Australian diplomat, our former ambassador to, let us say, Ruritania – an Italian countess who had once invited me to dinner. Her manner on the phone was warm, even gushing, yet importunate.

'Barry dear, is Saturday really your last night?'

Politely I confirmed her surmise.

'My God, thank goodness. His Excellency and I will be in London just for two days at our place in Belgravia. We must see your last show.'

I explained that this might be difficult. The show had been so well received that tickets to the last performance had been unobtainable for weeks. Scalpers were charging a fortune for them. I was terribly sorry.

'But, Barry darling, you can't mean it. What about house seats? You see I know about those,' wheedled the Countess, with a trilling European laugh.

'I'll certainly try,' said I, weakening.

'Call me back, dear, like an angel. Oh, and before I forget, in the orchestra stalls, please!'

It took me the best part of half an hour to reach Nigel, the box office manager at the Theatre Royal. He confirmed the show was sold out, and the 'house tickets' were already bespoke, pledged long ago to close friends. I was about to call the Countess with this desolate news when Nigel rang me back. Eureka! He had done some dexterous fiddling and produced two excellent seats, centre stalls. I thanked him and phoned the lady at her European number, but instead of a torrent of gratitude, she took the wind out of my sails.

'Darling, are they on the aisle? His Excellency *has to be* on the aisle.'

I was so irritated, especially by this 'Excellency' nonsense from the wife of a notorious international bore, that I heard myself saying that I would see what I could do.

Nigel was less than charmed by this new demand on his patience and ingenuity, and it had taken me a very long time to reach him.

'On the aisle! What's the matter with him? Broken leg or something?'

I had not asked, although I should have.

'Must be a good reason, Nigel,' I said, 'but if there's anything you can do . . .'

After a long wait Nigel performed a miracle.

'I've moved a few bods around who won't like it one bit, but your ambassador is the luckiest man in London. Two fantastic seats on the aisle. Will it be cash or credit card?'

I hadn't thought of that. Contrary to popular belief, not even stars get complimentary tickets unless the show is a flop, so grudgingly I gave Nigel my own credit card number as a guarantee.

'His Excellency will be over ze moon!' gushed the Countess. 'He adores you, you know.'

But I could not resist a question. 'Now that you have those tickets, Francesca, please tell me why they absolutely had to be on the aisle. Is there something wrong, a leg problem perhaps?'

Laughter tinkled down the phone. 'Nothing like zat, darling, but you see, we're only in London for one night and we've got fabulous tickets to see *Cats*. His Excellency loves *Cats*.'

'But,' I stammered, 'I've just moved heaven and earth to get you aisle seats for my last night. Is it the *Cats* matinée you're planning to see?'

'No, darling, you silly thing. We're going to *Cats* first.

They assure me it finishes at 10.25 on the dot. We have the government Bentley waiting outside the theatre, and Kevin can get us to Drury Lane in five minutes . . .'

I was not sure that I could believe my ears as the Countess resumed. 'I've done my homework, darling, and they say your show finishes at a quarter to eleven, so we can slip into those beautiful seats you've got us on the aisle in time for that funny thing you do at the end with the daffodils. Break a leg, darling.' And she rang off.

I was speechless, immobilised with rage and disbelief. Never again would I arrange tickets for anybody, or feel the least confidence in the future of Australia's international diplomacy. Why hadn't more people declared war on us?

There was a big crowd of friends in my dressing-room after the performance, and my dresser was busy distributing glasses of wine.

'Have we any champagne?' she said. I didn't think so, but I asked why.

'Oh, there's a vile woman over in the corner who said to me "His Excellency only drinks champagne." Who the hell are they?'

IN THE late eighties television seemed an alluring possibility, and following the success of *Back with a Vengeance* I was able to persuade London Weekend Television to produce an Edna talk show in which the Dame 'interviewed' celebrated personages on a luxurious set that was meant to represent the interior of her penthouse. The novelty of this show, *The Dame Edna Experience*, was that the guests, however famous, were rarely granted an opportunity to say more than a few words, in fulfilment of Dame Edna's infamous definition of a talk show as 'a monologue occasionally interrupted by total strangers'.

Since the journey from her 'front door' to the interview couch was so long, Edna could actually change her mind about the desirability of her guests as they proceeded towards her, and she could abort them at whim. For example, a series of booby traps on the set, not unlike Sweeney Todd's barber's chair, enabled her to dispatch Kurt Waldheim, Larry Hagman and Zsa Zsa Gabor to oblivion, or so it seemed. Charlton Heston, with the aid of a stunt double, appeared to be precipitated in a wheelchair down a steep staircase, and politicians, pop idols and movie stars were subjected to violent indignities at the touch of a button on Dame Edna's armrest. This series and similar interview shows that followed in the US as well as England were a huge success and have since been widely imitated, if never excelled.

There was one guest whom we strenuously courted for this show who resisted our entreaties with equal vigour. It was Her Royal Highness the Princess Michael of Kent. She had been to school in Sydney for some years before her marriage, living at Double Bay, remotest outpost of the Austro-Hungarian Empire. She had a deep, pleasant voice, the Australian accent of which long residence in Royal circles had not perceptibly modified. She was a tall, friendly girl and her husband, Prince Michael of Kent, was the most charming and courteous of men. Diane and I had both slightly known the Princess socially, and although

I was never on intimate terms with Her Royal Highness, she once kindly recommended to me her Baker Street acupuncturist. However, our small son Oscar sometimes played with her daughter, Princess Gabriella. Thus on the strength of this acquaintance I decided to make one last personal appeal to her to join the show as Edna's guest.

It may indeed have been a breach of protocol, but in writing to her I addressed her by the name she was always called in Australia, Marie-Christine, and I explained to her that she would have a full list of questions and a right of veto should there be anything in the interview to which she objected. I received in reply a letter from Her Royal Highness's 'secretary', although the handwriting bore an extraordinary resemblance to Princess Michael's. The secretary pointed out that if Prince Charles wrote a letter to his dustman, he would always sign his letter 'Charles', but that would not mean the Royal Dustman could so address him. Similarly Her Royal Highness, although she always subscribed her letters with her Christian name, must be appropriately addressed by her formal title. And the answer was no.

Somewhat rashly I decided that if we could not get the real thing on Dame Edna's show we should get a look-alike, and after auditioning several statuesque stunt girls we found the perfect double. On the next show Edna announced an exciting Royal guest, and after a fanfare the studio audience were enchanted to behold at the top of the staircase, in the traditional dirndl of a peasant in a Viennese operetta, the spitting image of Princess Michael of Kent.

Suddenly, however, Dame Edna appeared to panic. It seemed that she had forgotten to disarm her elaborate security system, installed to protect the studio from unwelcome intruders. But it was too late. While Edna fumbled for the abort switch, her guest had begun a stately descent to the studio, accidentally stepping into a horrific booby trap. A noose closed around her ankles, whipping her off her feet, and within seconds she was dangling upside down above the set, her dress now over her head, revealing long frilly bloomers of Austro-Hungarian design. Sadly Princess Michael has not spoken to me since, although I believe she is still on good terms with her dustman.

Edna had for many years spoken of her New Zealand bridesmaid Madge Allsop, a widow whose husband, Doug, had perished under gruesome circumstances on their honeymoon at the boiling mud springs of Rotorua. His tandoori'd remains were found weeks later, and to console the grieving widow Edna had taken Madge 'under her wing'.

Audiences, however, had never seen Madge. She was an offstage presence until an Australian actress impersonated her in the Les Patterson film; so when the time came to film the London talk show, I decided to find the definitive Madge, who could sit mutely at the end of the couch, the butt of Edna's jokes. We auditioned many elderly actresses, all of whom tried far too hard. Some were whimsical, some camp, but most were far too over the top to resemble an oppressed, inarticulate New Zealand spinster whom life had passed by.

Emily Perry had begun her professional career before the

Second World War in *Kitty Denton's Juveniles* at the Theatre Royal, Birmingham, and thereafter toured England as a soubrette and dancer in various concert parties and music halls. Then for twelve years she played Susan in *The Desert Song*, followed by the role of Sister Kitty in *The Belle of New York* and numerous leads in traditional pantomime. During the war she entertained the troops for ENSA (the Entertainment of the National Services Association), until she decided to open a very successful children's dancing school called the Patricia Perry Academy of Dancing (she thought 'Patricia' sounded more euphonious than 'Emily') in Crystal Palace, South London, which she ran for twenty-five years.

Since she was registered with an extras agent, Miss Perry occasionally found modest employment on films and television but she was already semi-retired when the agent called her with a suggestion that she audition for a new show at London Weekend Television. As soon as she entered the room, the director, the producer, my chief researcher and I knew we had found Madge Allsop.

Miss Perry had the rare gift of being able to do nothing in the face of overwhelming provocation. Soon she was to become the star of the series, meeting most members of the Royal Family, being photographed for 'senior' fashion spreads in colour supplements and even having a New Zealand armoured tank named after her. Silent on the screen, she is in real life talkative, informed and amusing. She can do twenty-five press-ups on one hand every morning. Once, on a subsequent stage tour, as we checked into a large hotel in Leeds together, Miss Perry was offered the spare key to my room on the mistaken assumption that this diminutive old lady was my wife.

In 1956 I wrote a short story about an elderly, childless Melbourne man called Alexander Horace 'Sandy' Stone. It was really a satire on the dreary life of the suburbs. The prototype of the character was our Christowel Street neighbour Mr Whittle, whom I sometimes encountered as I ran for the 8.30 a.m. train to the city, although later in Sydney I incorporated the vocal mannerisms of an old codger I met one day on the beach. Mr Whittle epitomised decency and, to my young priggish self, dullness. He did everything in an orderly fashion; indeed his life seemed frighteningly predictable. I wondered if, by writing about a man with such an obsession for domestic details, I could make the reader laugh out of sheer boredom. I submitted my short story to a progressive journal and it was instantly rejected. A year later, in a revue in one of Melbourne's smallest theatres, I performed this story on stage, in pyjamas and dressing-gown and clutching a hot-water bottle. Wearing pallid make-up more reminiscent of the German expressionist cinema than the leafy suburbs of Melbourne, I croaked the rambling interior monologue with the intention of driving the audience mad with fatigue.

Some months later a small production company asked if they might record an Edna Everage sketch with Sandy Stone on the other side of the record. *Wild Life in Suburbia* (soon followed by Volume II) was first issued in 1958 and became surprisingly popular, earning me a dubious reputation as a savage local satirist. The material sounds absurdly tame now, but in those days some critics accused me of being cruel and un-Australian, and the popular epithet of the period, 'sick', was frequently hurled at me. Any joke or work of literature that faintly reflected real life was always condemned as 'Siiiiiiiiiiick!'

I learnt that my fellow countrymen in far-flung Australian ghettos such as Earl's Court, London, played this record and its sequel as a prophylactic against returning home! I also heard that the expatriate Sidney Nolan had a copy.

It was not until I was living in London in 1959 that I made a third recording, this time with a Sandy monologue of excruciating tedium, called *Sandy Agonistes*. It was a thirty-minute improvised litany of product names, radio serial titles, suburban railway stations, jingles and forgotten songs spoken into a friend's tape recorder. I approached Sidney Nolan to design the record sleeve and he kindly agreed, producing a fanciful drawing of Sandy's haggard visage metamorphosing from a vase of flowers.

In 1971 I presented a modest anthology show in Sydney called *A Load of Olde Stuffe*. It included a monologue on the death of Sandy Stone, which I delivered from a bed on stage – Sandy's marital bed, his wife, Beryl, represented by a large hump beneath the quilt. Sandy wakes with great relief from a nightmare in which he imagines his demise. Only the audience knows that the dream is true.

It was the first time that I had lived in Sydney for any length of time since the Phillip Street Theatre days, and I had yet to have a home there so the producer had found me a rented flat on the eighteenth floor of a gimcrack tower block at Darling Point. During the sixties and seventies ruthless laissez-faire developers moved in on Sydney's most beautiful harbourside suburbs, demolishing the elegant stone houses and erecting such jerry-built monstrosities in their stead. The building I inhabited was so badly out of alignment that the lift regularly broke down, and on one such occasion, after a panting ascent of all those flights of stairs, I discovered that I had mislaid the key to my apartment. Having trudged back down the interminable stairway, I eventually found a cab and returned to the theatre. The stage doorman might still be there and I could search my tiny dressing-room for the key. As luck had it, Eddie was just leaving but he let me in on a promise that I would lock up when I departed. Alone in the theatre I searched my dressing-room, but in vain.

Assailed by waves of fatigue and despair, I decided to sleep in Sandy's bed on stage. It was a restless night, listening to the scampering rats and gazing down over the bedcovers at the ghostly stalls lit by a single green Exit light, like the light at the end of the jetty that beckoned Gatsby. Next morning I was woken by the snarl of a solitary vacuum cleaner. An ancient Italian lady was hoovering the aisles of the theatre.

'Hello,' I called from my makeshift cocoon on stage. 'Could you please tell me the time?'

The woman took one look at the wraith-like figure rising up from its shrouded bed, screamed and fled from the theatre. Like Sandy, I had really become a ghost.

Old Sandy Stone has attracted a number of distinguished

fans over the years. John Betjeman loved him and Alec Guinness even wanted to play him. Sir Alec did not much care for gladioli and he deemed Sir Les Patterson 'ghastly', but he generously wrote of Sandy, 'He beguiles and moves me from the other side of the grave and enlarges our sympathy for humankind.'

Alec shared my interest in Charles Conder, certainly an acquired taste, and I once suggested that we lunch together at the Ivy restaurant. On the appointed day I was terribly, agonisingly late. The taxi didn't turn up, all efforts to hail one in the Finchley Road failed, until at last, when it was already 1 o'clock, the time of our rendezvous, a black cab took pity on me. I pictured the great actor sitting alone, looking at his watch. I knew he was bound to be punctual. The traffic was gridlocked. By the time we had inched into Bloomsbury, I was already half an hour late. It was before the age of mobile phones, but the car was so often stationary that I was able to leap out and use a public telephone in a pub.

'He's waiting all right, and not too happy,' said Jeremy at the Ivy. 'I've offered him a drink and something to nibble but he declines.'

'Christ!' I said. 'Please explain I'm coming. It's a nightmare in this traffic. I'll be there soon.'

It wasn't quite as soon as I had hoped. When finally I rushed sweating into the restaurant, forty minutes late, I could see Alec sitting white-faced and unsmiling, like an archdeacon, at the most visible table. Gushing with apologies, ringing my hands and practically pouring ashes on my head, I tried to melt what was, if not ice, a chilly encrustation.

'But, Alec, why did you not have something to eat or drink while you were waiting?'

He looked at me gloomily. 'I never eat at the Ivy,' he said.

'But why didn't you tell me that? I could have taken you somewhere else.'

'I was once very, very sick in this restaurant,' said the great knight of the theatre.

'But it's improved. It's transformed since Chris and Jeremy took it over!'

Later I persuaded my guest to take a little nourishment and his good humour slowly returned. By the end of the meal I was forgiven my earlier discourtesy and even the Ivy was exonerated.

Arm in arm we went for a stroll down St Martin's Lane, and he asked if I would send him a Sandy Stone script, which he would endeavour to learn. I promised to provide the dressing-gown and the hot-water bottle. It was the last time I saw him.

When the first volume of Alec's diaries, *My Name Escapes Me*, appeared in the bookshops, I nervously scanned the index. Sure enough, there was my name: Humphries, Barry. I froze. Here for eternity and in cold print was surely the record of my unpunctuality. But the diary entry was merciful:

To the table-hopping Ivy where Barry Humphries gave me lunch. He had pinched Melvyn Bragg's corner. Enjoyed his company immensely. Nowhere in his nature do I detect Dame Edna. Like most comedians he dresses formally but with a give-away Aussie-type hat.

One of Sandy's monologues in later times was inspired by a particularly touching true story concerning a friend of our family, Dot Swift (not her real name). Dot had spent her childhood in one of the big, turreted Victorian houses in Camberwell. When she was elderly and had begun to exhibit signs of senility, her daughter-in-law – there is a running joke about daughters-in-law, whom I have found to be a rich vein of comedy – consigned her to a Twilight Home, which by a grim twist of fate turned out to be her old family residence, now carved up into a terminary for the aged. Dot found herself in one of several beds in what had once been her nursery. As she entered her second childhood she was in precisely the same room that she had occupied during her first. It was a sad but delectable anecdote, which Sandy was able to extend into a forty-minute monologue. A stage character who once needed a great deal of ageing make-up now barely requires any.

SOME of my more durable stage inventions have expanded, or in Les Patterson's case tumesced, to a point where they can no longer share the same bill. Fans of Dame Edna can't stand the increasingly repulsive Sir Les, with his fondlings and expectorations, and devotees of the Australian Cultural Attaché to Washington frankly find the meditations of Sandy Stone boring. In the nineties, therefore, these three personages each had their own show, and the one that gave me most pleasure, although it was the hardest to learn, was *The Life and Death of Sandy Stone*, an entire evening with the desiccated sage of Glen Iris.

CROCODILLOS

~

Every time I have opened a door without knocking,
I have discovered something repulsive

ANATOLE FRANCE

I WAS staying at the Windsor Hotel in the seventies when the phone rang. The man on the other end of the line apologised for disturbing me and wondered if, by a lucky chance, I might be free to join him for dinner that evening at a nearby restaurant. He explained that he was a publisher's man and that one of his firm's authors, the distinguished American essayist and novelist Gore Vidal, was on a brief visit to Melbourne and the dinner was to be in his honour. The Publisher's Representative mentioned that the only other persons present, apart from Vidal, would be his wife and a well-known feminist journalist, an acolyte of the Australian thinker my friend Germaine Greer. Since I had nothing else on that evening, I eagerly accepted in order to meet across the table the notorious and lapidary author of *Myra Breckinridge*.

The restaurant our host had selected was one of the more old fashioned in an old-fashioned city. It had been one of the

240

first Italian establishments before the war, long before Melbourne boasted some of the best Italian restaurants outside Italy. It served one kind of spaghetti – Bolognese – and although minestrone was unavailable, there was Ministrone Soup on the menu. Indeed there were traces of Ministrone Soup on the flock wallpaper as well. The atmosphere was very quiet. Elderly wait-ers shuffled around bearing dishes that had lost all hint of their Italian accent. Except for the watery spaghetti, they were mostly hearty Australian meals Italianised with a liberal garnish of tomato sauce and grated cheese. For some obscure reason – per-haps the proximity of St Patrick's Cathedral – this restaurant attracted Men of the Cloth and the occasional nun, and as I entered that night and scanned the tables for a sight of the famous author, a priest looked up from his ravioli and chips while a mother superior and her chaste female companions peered curiously at me over their T-bones Parmigiana.

A small, rather nervous man in a navy-blue double-breasted suit sprang towards me. It was the Publisher's Representative and he was clearly relieved to see me. I was led to a seat and introduced to his little wife, the scowling feminist and finally Mr Vidal himself. The future biographer of Lincoln possessed a proud, even presidential mien, albeit tonight slightly blurred by wine. His was the face of a louche statesman, which a more generous nation would have proudly published on its postage stamps. It was apparent that the jet-lagged author had been the recipient of much generous hospitality during the day and he lay slumped in his chair, occasionally gulping from a large glass of mahogany-coloured fluid. However, the Publisher's

Representative was clearly determined that his author enjoy a truly cosmopolitan meal with two key members of the Australian intelligentsia.

It seemed that my host and his wife had been coping with the heavy pontifications of the illustrious writer all day, treating him to tram rides and showing him the sights of Melbourne: the lovely originals in the National Gallery of Victoria, the Royal Botanic Gardens and Phar Lap, the most prodigious racehorse in the history of the Australian turf, whose awesome form may still be viewed in the city's new museum, thanks to the cunning of a local taxidermist. I felt sure that the Publisher's Representative and his wife had also shown Mr Vidal 'the Paris end' of Collins Street, where a few wind-blasted tables had been set out experimentally on the pavement in the hope that they might impart a cosmopolitan flavour.

The task of entertaining this famous author cannot have been easy, particularly since it soon became apparent that his local hosts were totally unfamiliar with Mr Vidal's oeuvre. A waiter wearing a shiny dinner jacket over his maroon cardigan appeared, proffering a ragout-flecked menu, and Gore, briefly roused from a jet-lagged swoon, apostrophised him in very loud Italian. Unfortunately none of the waiters in this famous Italian restaurant spoke that language, although one of them was Greek. However, throughout the evening the guest of honour was reluctant to accept this linguistic fact and continued to address the bewildered staff in an incomprehensible tongue, inquiring about their wives and families, details of their private lives and, more regrettably, their sexual vocations.

All would have been well if the distinguished and cosmopolitan man of letters had totally avoided the English language throughout the evening, but alas, seized by a mischievous impulse to goad the lady journalist at our table, he proceeded to discuss at the top of his voice and in vernacular English certain ingenious practices then in vogue in some of New York's more liberated Turkish baths. I looked anxiously across the table at the pale, bird-like wife of the Publisher's Representative and observed that she had decided rather wisely to pretend that none of this was happening. She and her husband proceeded to order large drinks, and as the meal progressed they both slid very slowly and with tremendous dignity under the table. The Melbourne feminist had started to cry, but Gore was beginning to enjoy himself. As his Roast Lamb alla Marinara congealed on his plate, he began indelicately accosting some of the other diners, and it was not long before the manager himself was politely urging us to resume our literary discussions in another locale. The feminist had left anyway, noisily; our host and his wife were on another plane, barely reachable even by embarrassment; but the guest of honour was incensed. As we reached the door and had our hats and coats thrown at us by an exasperated staff, he turned and, addressing the entire restaurant, shouted, 'Don't fuck with old Gore', then swivelled on his heel and was gone.

I have read his subsequent *causeries*, but have discovered no reference to this visit to my home town. Perhaps he didn't remember it, or perhaps he deemed the occasion undeserving of the merest footnote; but it was certainly a footnote in the literary history of Melbourne and at least five waiters, four nuns and I will never forget it.

WHEN Patrick White first came to lunch in my Sydney flat in the seventies, his cold blue eye immediately fell on a drawing by the Dutch artist Jan Toorop.

'We are surrounded by works of art,' he exclaimed, with his characteristic dowager-like look, as over an invisible lorgnette. His 'we' was hortatory and was addressed to me alone.

Then, lapsing into camp Cockney, the Nobel novelist observed, 'I see you got a pitcher of oewer Joannie on the wall!' Inexplicably Patrick was always inveighing against the great Australian soprano Joan Sutherland, and it is true that one of the ladies in the Toorop possessed a slight prognathism reminiscent of the diva.

On another occasion I found myself scrabbling around in the dark with Patrick in a derelict garden in Rushcutters Bay. He had wanted to show me Lulworth, a large house where he had spent part of his childhood. The mansion was now an old folks' home, obscured by an ugly block of flats. All that remained of the garden was a forlorn remnant: a tangle of sour shrubbery, littered with excrement and the detritus of sex.

Of all complicated men, White was the most complicated. He was at one stage a generous friend, and he continued to support me after my divorce from Rosalind, in spite of his deep admiration for her. This was rare. Patrick generally dropped his friends when their marriages ended, and by the time he shrivelled up and died there were few friends – save a handful of old dykes and pansies – to whom he spoke. He, who so often railed against the vitiating effects of flattery upon the artist, was himself the most susceptible to sycophancy. He became naïvely political and surrounded himself with a circle of lisping crawlers and brownnosers.

When the writer Sumner Locke Elliott, visiting from New York, dined at White's house sometime in the early eighties, he was dispirited by the table talk, which consisted of provincial Sydney bitchery and character assassination. Aware of a certain *froideur* and increasingly excluded from the conversation, Elliott, pleading jet lag, thanked his host and left early. As he crossed the lawn and was opening the gate, he was startled by the sound of Patrick's voice booming down at him from the front door of the house.

'Come back, come back!' cried the Nobel Laureate in tones of passionate entreaty.

Somewhat moved, Elliott turned at the gate and called back to his host, 'Thank you, Patrick, but only for a few minutes if I may.'

'Not you, you fool, *the dogs*. Come back!'

Two repulsive pugs, which Sumner's exit had inadvertently released from domestic captivity, scuttled back up the lawn towards their master and the front door slammed shut.

Curmudgeonly behaviour like this marked a sad degradation from former days, but White remains, next to Martin Boyd, Australia's greatest writer and the vagaries of his character can never detract from masterpieces such as *Voss* and *Riders in the Chariot*. Occasionally, when our friendship was in bloom, he could be positively sunny, but he was never more elated than when communicating a piece of malicious gossip.

Once he came to my flat for lunch with Manoly Lascaris, his companion, and they gossiped gleefully about a Sydney hostess I knew, married to a seriously unlikely candidate whose pederastic enthusiasms were legendary. Pursing his lips, lowering his chin and blinking mischievously, Patrick claimed he knew from the girl herself that, although her new husband had forsaken the sex that formerly gave him pleasure, he had not abandoned his customary path to it.

Patrick had a particular aversion for Thomas Keneally, who by then was a popular and prolific novelist. On one occasion I mentioned to him that a new Keneally novel had just been published and had received some critical acclaim. White grimaced.

'Ugh!' he exclaimed scornfully. 'So he's at it again: squeezing his pustules at us in public!'

Patrick adored Cynthia Reed, the wife of Sidney Nolan and the sister of John Reed, a saurian Tasmanian lawyer and art groupie nicknamed in Melbourne 'The Broken Reed'. The late Sir Kenneth Clark said to Stephen Spender that Cynthia was the one woman on earth of whom he was mortally afraid. She certainly radiated a strange and formidable aura. In spite of this I rather liked her, although I declined to accept her at her own exalted estimation of herself.

Cynthia was very kind to Rosalind before the birth of our

daughter Tessa in England. This may not have been disinterested benevolence, however; perhaps she thought I was a rising star worth knowing. But Cynthia was quixotic in her attachments and fond of dropping and cutting people for obscure reasons. This is often the way inadequate persons attempt to exert their power over others, and no one is more powerless than the wife of an artist – particularly an artist prone to bouts of alcoholism. Significantly Cynthia had been a nurse, although I would hate to wake up in hospital and see that sallow and baleful countenance gazing down upon me. She was so eager to assist Nolan's advancement that she befriended all kinds of improbable people whom she supposed to be in the social and intellectual vanguard. Certain howlers resulted. For example, she cultivated C.P. Snow and his wife, Pamela Hansford Johnson, when the former was enjoying a brief vogue as the author of *The Corridors of Power*. Perhaps it was the word 'power' that caught her attention.

When I knew them best, in the sixties, and was in favour with the gorgon Cynthia, the Nolans lived on the river at Putney in a house that had some pre-Raphaelite connection. I recall that on my first visit the walls were decorated with marvellous hand-printed William Morris papers in perfect condition. On the next visit I was appalled to see that they had been replaced by some horrible vinyl-based wallpaper of alternating coloured squares veneered with gold and silver. As I looked aghast at the desecrated rooms Cynthia, whom Patrick White described in his autobiography as having 'unfailing taste', mistook my expression for one of admiration.

'Yes, isn't it beautiful,' she exclaimed. 'Siddy and I found that wallpaper in Japan. It's real gold leaf and costs a fortune, but it's better than that horrible old floral stuff!' I realised Nurse Nolan had never heard of William Morris.

Cynthia's final act was a terminal bid for power; a desperate attempt to have the last word. On the twenty-fourth of November 1976 she sent her husband a telegram that cryptically read, 'Off to the Orkneys in small stages'; then, without telling him, she checked into the Regent Palace Hotel under a pseudonym, with a lethal pharmacopoeia in her handbag. Distraught, the artist scoured the hotels of London, until about two days later Cynthia was discovered dead in her hotel room, having taken a massive dose of sleeping tablets.

When Nolan remarried a year or so later, Patrick White reacted with extraordinary sanctimony and a bitter enmity arose between the two men, which lasted until their death. I believe White identified strongly with Cynthia Nolan, whom he idealised to an absurd degree. He even wrote of 'the Cynthia in myself' for he was compelled, as are we all, ever to remain on the tantalising periphery of self-knowledge. Cynthia was a Patrick White character, rather like one of those *jolies laides* and saturnine spinsters who drift at dusk through the pages of his 'period' novels, their long dresses catching the fragrance of herbaceous borders. I sometimes felt that if Patrick were ever invited to a drag ball he would go as Cynthia.

Another favourite of Patrick's was Zoe Caldwell, whom I had played opposite so long before, when we were both with the Union Theatre Repertory Company. He visited her in New York, where she was already a Broadway star, and wrote her many letters, but he told me he had decided to give up on her since she never replied and he felt as if he was merely 'posting letters down the lavatory'. He must have felt much the same about me for I have always been a dilatory correspondent and 'keeping up', try as I might, has never been one of my virtues.

Once, before White and Manoly went to Europe, he let his house in Centennial Park to a young woman from a respectable family. On returning he discovered that his bedroom had been used for the sexual recreations of his tenant.

'What is so reprehensible about that?' I asked him.

'I found a pair of women's panties in the bottom of my bed! And pubic hairs on the blanket!' he thundered.

The young orgiast later told me that she had discovered, in Patrick's bedroom cupboard, an outsized lady's brassiere of venerable design. The presence of such a garment in the closet of a Nobel-Prize-winning bachelor remains open to conjecture.

Patrick once said that parents were destined to disappoint their children, as children inevitably disappoint their parents. Sadly it is one of life's inexorable reciprocities. I certainly disappointed White, who adopted a queenly attitude of disapproval towards my new marriage, my political allegiances – such as they were – and my perseverance with the character of Edna, whom he believed to be a spent force. He had always assumed an absurdly magisterial role in the lives of his friends, and when they behaved in a manner contrary to his tastes or wishes his wrath knew no bounds. By the time he died in 1990 he had stopped speaking to almost all the men and women who had formerly numbered amongst his dearest friends. One way and another we had all failed to meet his expectations. The artists Lawrence Daws, Brett Whiteley and Sidney Nolan, the poet and writer Geoffrey Dutton, and Bruce Beresford, whose friendship I owed to Patrick's introduction: we were all replaced by a little claque of toadies.

After Patrick's and my estrangement Geoffrey Dutton tried to arrange a reconciliatory lunch.

'I don't think I'll be able to get my act together to see him!' White declared, with a flounce.

By then Patrick had absorbed the mannerisms and quasi-theatrical locutions of Sydney Camp: a particularly virulent strain of international poofery. Dutton himself was subsequently dropped.

Patrick White was *un homme très difficile* and yet a novelist of extraordinary power and nobility.

SIDNEY NOLAN was a fifth generation Irish Australian and he always talked entertainingly about his family and his working-class origins in the Melbourne suburb of St Kilda, home of Luna Park.

Not surprisingly my mother had occasionally made a pejorative reference to this seaside suburb, which, although increasingly gentrified, has always had a reputation for drunks, whores and general riffraff.

Once as we sat sedately under an umbrella on our semi-private beach at Mornington, sipping raspberry vinegar out of

Bakelite beakers, a rowdy group assembled within earshot. They were what *The Sun News-Pictorial* used to call 'youths': in other words, working-class juveniles prone to delinquency. No nice person was a 'youth'. My mother became increasingly distressed by this unwelcome rabble, who had begun flicking their companions with towels and, with strident cries, splashing each other in the shallows.

'Who are they?' I asked her.

'St Kilda types,' she said frostily. 'If your father was here, I'd get him to have a word with them.' I was relieved he wasn't.

Nolan often spoke of the uncle who lived with them in St Kilda and was always coming home drunk. The family were perpetually on the verge of casting him out, but Sid's mother, Dora, in spite of great provocation could never bring herself to evict her brother. Her great dream in life was to own a pair of crocodile-skin shoes; it was the ultimate and unattainable luxury, and when things got rough he always promised her that one day he would buy her a pair.

One night in the early thirties one of Melbourne's most celebrated commercial landmarks caught fire. It was the firm of Ezywalkin, the city's famous shoe store, and in the wake of the holocaust (or pedicaust?) ill-shod looters descended on the smouldering ruins, scavenging for unscorched footwear. Sid's uncle came home drunker than usual and triumphantly dumped the contents of a large hessian sack on the kitchen table. There was a strong, fumid odour.

'Well, Dora, here's yer crocodillos. Fourteen bloody pair of them!'

Mrs Nolan gazed incredulously at the cairn of beautiful shoes, then with tears in her eyes she began sorting through them for her size.

'I toldja I'd getcha some, Dora, and I bloody did. Gi's us a hug . . .' but Mrs Nolan was weeping more copiously than before, and giving her brother one terrible push so that he collapsed onto the kitchen floor, she fled sobbing to the bedroom. Crocodile shoes they indeed were, and of the finest quality – but, alas, all left-footed.

GREEN WALLS, BLACK SAND

~

The only things one
never regrets are one's mistakes
OSCAR WILDE

SOMETIME in the seventies, at the suggestion of a beautiful and persuasive girl, I consulted a celebrated Sydney astrologer called Mrs Liszt. She lived in a never-to-become-fashionable southern suburb, and I remember little of the woman's appearance except that it conformed to my expectations of an elderly clairvoyant with a name such as Mrs Liszt. Apart from several large pediculated moles on her chin, she bore no resemblance to the composer of *Mephisto*. Perhaps my recollection of her appearance has been occluded by her predictions, which conjured up two compelling images.

After the usual ingratiating remarks about my extraordinary gifts and dazzling future, Mrs Liszt seemed to submerge herself to a deeper level of psychic sensitivity. Her eyes rolled back in her head alarmingly, and with a minatory croak she told me to avoid, at all costs, *black sand*. I was also warned against some terrible place with *high green walls*. Mrs Liszt seemed to be describing a long, an extraordinarily long, hospital corridor, or was it a penitentiary or a lunatic asylum? Quite unnecessarily, I felt at the time, she explained that when I found myself in such a doleful precinct, I would experience intense anxiety and depression but that all would finally be well.

Since, only a few years before, I had spent the best part of nine months in various infirmaries, and indeed terminaries, psychiatric hospital green was by no means an unfamiliar hue. The visit to Mrs Liszt, who surprisingly accepted Diners Card, naturally left me with feelings of apprehension. Was I to expect some serious relapse? I fretted, on the long drive back to central Sydney. Quickly, however, I forgot these absurd prognostications; that is, until they came true.

Almost a year to the day after my interview with the Sibyl of Sylvania Waters I had finished a long theatrical engagement in *At Least You Can Say You've Seen It*, and decided that I badly needed a vacation. Clyde Packer recommended a secluded sandy beach on the coast of northern Queensland in the cane-growing region, where the Australian Prime Minister and his wife had recently enjoyed a private holiday. Coconut Cove was not really a resort; it was a large bungalow by the sea run by a retired colonel of the Australian Army and his wife, and the brochure extolled its 'luxurious accommodation and superlative cuisine'. Australian restaurants were just entering upon their pretentious phase and any fare, good or bad, was thereafter called 'quee-zeen', as fish was upgraded to 'seafood'.

The flight from Sydney was delayed and the journey long, so I was relieved to find myself met at the airport by Bryce, the

Colonel's son, a bronzed youth in the comic Australian uniform of the period: shorts and long white socks. He loaded my luggage – always excessive – into his cream and green Ford Fairlane Ranchwagon and we set off for Coconut Cove. Bright lorikeets darted around a honeysuckled pergola as finally, just before 7 p.m., we pulled into the driveway, hedged with oleanders. It was then that I glimpsed, beyond a grove of tall palms, the inviting azure parapet of the Pacific.

In this Australian Shangri-La the low weatherboard bungalow, with its lopsided toupee of bougainvillea, looked idyllic. I stiffly alighted from the car, ready for a walk along the beach and perhaps a quick swim before dinner.

I was greeted by Colonel McConnichie, who also favoured the uniform of socks and shorts but, as befitted a retired soldier, his mufti was khaki.

'Welcome to the best-kept secret in Australia,' he said, grasping my hand a little too firmly so that I wondered if he was a Mason. 'Young Bryce called me from the airport warning us your flight was late, but Heather managed to put dinner on hold until 1900 hours.'

'Well, I'll have to wash and brush up a bit first,' I expostulated. 'I was hoping there might be time for a stroll, even a dip . . .'

'Plenty of time for that tomorrow, Barry,' said the Colonel. Did I detect a slightly imperious note in the voice of my host? 'The McConnichies guarantee you are going to have the *most relaxing time of your life* in Coconut Cove.'

Fastidiously he pinched a rather large mosquito off his cheek, ground it into a bloody pulp between thumb and index finger and resumed. 'Anything you need, within reason, ask Heather. It's Duncan and Heather, by the way. Remember that. We're one big happy family here and while you're at Coconut Cove you're one of us.'

I tried to look very, very pleased. 'Well, Duncan,' I said, 'I'll have a bath and join you a bit later on in the dining room.'

'You'll do better than that I hope, soldier,' rejoined the Colonel, and surely now there was a note of parade-ground menace in his tone? 'You'll get straight into your glad rags and join us for a quick drink on the verandah. Informality is the keynote at Coconut Cove but we like our guests to dress up a bit for dinner, and, let's face it, you're already bloody late and there's a very nice New Zealand accountant and his wife who are dying to meet you.'

With that, and an abrupt and martial 'As you were', Colonel McConnichie turned briskly on his heel and disappeared behind a hibiscus.

Was this holiday destination a disastrous choice, even before I met the New Zealand accountant or tackled the prawn cocktail and the chicken and pineapple? With a sinking heart I rummaged through my suitcase for something more formal than jeans and a T-shirt. Surely these people didn't expect me to appear at dinner dressed for luncheon at the Melbourne Club? I glanced around my 'suite', which was nice enough, although there was a great deal of rattan; indeed you could say the room was rattan-infested. A bottle of Australian champagne reposed in an ice bucket on a round bamboo table. An attached card said:

Welcome to Coconut Cove.
Your relaxation is our business.
Heather and Duncan

The New Zealand accountant, I reflected, would undoubtedly want to know how I dreamt up the idea of Edna Everage, how I remembered my lines and did I know Peter Sellers. I had only been at the place for twenty minutes and I was already entertaining murderous thoughts.

The meal was an ordeal. The Kiwis behaved predictably and McConnichie blustered away nonstop, pressing wines and spirits upon me even though I had, so I thought, made it very clear that I was a boring teetotaller. The Colonel talked a great deal about wine to the New Zealanders and, holding a bottle of some Australian vintage as if it were a priceless artifact, he launched into an oenophilic rhapsody. He was one of those men to whom one can say umpteen times, 'I don't drink', and yet will invariably reply, 'Not even whisky . . . or champagne? Perhaps just a beer, then?'

The next morning I skipped breakfast and made for the beach with my towel. I was at the water's edge and about to take a plunge into the caressing waves when young Bryce McConnichie nearly felled me with a flying tackle.

'For Christ's sake, mate, just as well I saw you or you'd probably be history by now. You can't go in the water, *it's the stinger season.*'

'The what?' I said. 'There was nothing about lethal jellyfish in your brochure.'

'Everyone knows you can't swim in northern Queensland between November and May. The water's full of box jellyfish. One flick from one of those bastards' tentacles and you could cop a heart attack,' he said, leading me back to the house.

'Well, Bryce,' I said, 'I'll just have to use the pool.'

'Tough luck, Mr Humphries,' replied the youth, indicating a large concrete pit by the side of the house. 'Our pool's empty this season while the blokes give it an overhaul. Sorry about that.'

Back in my suite I felt on the verge of tears. I must devise a plan of escape. I had already paid for a fortnight in advance, but perhaps that could be wriggled out of? I would get Clyde in Sydney to call me announcing a crisis of some kind that required my immediate return. It would have to be a pretty drastic excuse to convince Colonel McConnichie, who no doubt took a military view of deserters. But how could I telephone Sydney when there was no instrument in my room and the only phone was in the McConnichies' private lounge? 'Our home is your home, soldier,' he had said.

The next morning, after an insect-haunted sleep and in a delirium of anxiety, I borrowed a jeep in order to speed off for the nearest town, Cairns, six miles away, so that I could call the office and get myself sprung. It was difficult to escape the importunate McConnichies, who wanted to escort me, but I shook them off and was soon hurtling down a dirt road towards what I thought was the highway. The geography was puzzling, however, and after three miles I found myself definitely lost; but lost in alarming circumstances for I must have veered through the wrong gate into a sugarcane plantation. I had inadvertently driven into some kind of avenue, which dwindled towards a green infinity. On either side, hemming me in, towered an emerald palisade of cane. I made a sharp turn through another gap in what was apparently a vast plantation, and realised I was trapped in a maze of sugarcane, like a character in a Hitchcock film. *High green walls!* Mrs Liszt's prediction had come appallingly true.

It was only by chance that a youth on a tractor eventually appeared out of nowhere and guided me back to the road.

At length I reached the post office, made the call and explained the situation to Clyde's secretary. She must at all costs phone the McConnichies with a crisis – perhaps one of my daughters had fallen out of her tree house or Iris, my pianist, had broken a hip – something that would require my immediate return. Driving back to Coconut Cove I rehearsed the little speech I would make when the Colonel gave me the bad news. Naturally there would be crocodile tears at being so prematurely snatched from Paradise.

I was no sooner out of the jeep than the Colonel darted from behind a trellis and gravely informed me that there had been serious news from Sydney, and would I like a brandy? The office had certainly responded quickly, and with imagination. It seemed that the elderly and respectable Iris had been apprehended by store detectives in David Jones and was discovered to be wearing ten pairs of unpurchased pantyhose. She had fought with police and was now in custody. If this was not enough, the home of my manager, the Honourable Clyde Packer, had been raided by the Vice Squad and pornographic comic books and lewd paraphernalia had been seized. And one of my daughters had fallen out of her tree house and suffered multiple fractures. I would have to catch the next flight back home.

It was hard not to smirk as Colonel McConnichie gave me his deadpan recital of these ludicrous disasters. It was overkill, and Clyde's fingerprints were all over it.

The New Zealand accountant and his wife looked devastated, but all the Colonel said was, 'Hard cheese, soldier! Better report back to base, pronto.' Yet the curl of his lip suggested that he would be none too sorry to see the last of a person with my disreputable connections.

SOME years after I had been trapped between the high green walls that Mrs Liszt had foreseen, I was on another vacation, this time in Sicily. Although Mount Etna was rumbling forebodingly, I was assured by the concierge of my hotel that regular excursions to the 'medium risk zone' were still running and that it was all perfectly safe. In fact there was a cancellation that very day and he could get me on the last jeep before sunset. Accordingly I went, first by bus from Taormina and then, at a point halfway up the flank of the volcano, by one of the clapped-out jeeps that ran a shuttle to within 300 yards of an active vent – Bocca Nuova. Mine was indeed the last shuttle, and as the vehicle juddered up a narrow cinder track I could smell ever more strongly the sulphurous fumes of Etna, and was fervently wishing the experience over.

By the time we stopped it had grown grey and cold and there were smoking trails of ash on either side of the road. With the crater now glowing above me and the sun already setting, I decided I had had enough and asked my guide to turn around and take me back. But my driver had got out of the jeep and, with the aid of a flashlight, was peering at the engine and cursing loudly. Was there something the matter? 'Kaput' was the only word I recognised as he came back to me, mopping his face with a filthy rag. Was it possible? Could I really have entrusted my life to this peasant and his wreck of a jeep, which had now broken down at nightfall, at the very maw of an active volcano – one that was known to erupt and kill without warning? There were no walkie-talkies, no mobile phones, and my only companion – my only chance of salvation – this man with his incomprehensible dialect.

As the dusk deepened, the ashen trickles on either side of us began to glow, and deep in the earth beneath us I could hear a premonitory growl. Sometimes in morbid moments I have imagined the circumstances of my death: plane crash, drowning, choking on a vitamin capsule, driving off a cliff, defenestration or just a bad oyster. As I stood shivering at dusk with my Sicilian 'guide' on that perilous slope, I thought, So this is how it's *really* going to be: suffocated by igneous fumes, engulfed by pyroclastic dust and sucked into the fiery throat of a volcano!

Our only hope as far as I could tell was to sit it out until someone at the bus station missed us and sent up a rescue party. It seemed a forlorn hope as I huddled there, marooned on a slope of coarse black sand. *Black sand!* It hit me like a wave of . . . well, molten lava. Mrs Liszt's other prediction, fulfilled at last!

261

We had waited little more than an hour before the lights of a second jeep could be seen below, wobbling cautiously up the crater's flank towards us. I decided then that volcanoes were only interesting or picturesque on a very far horizon.

Perhaps Mrs Liszt's warning would have been proved more terribly prescient if I had made my excursion up Mount Etna only one week later. For on the twelfth of September 1979, at exactly the same spot, there was a thirty-second, vent-clearing, phreatic explosion, killing nine tourists and injuring twenty-three.

HOLD THE BLOSSOMS

~

*When people have been more than
usually disappointing, we turn with an
added tenderness to things*

HOWARD OVERING STURGIS

COLLECTORS are the last hunters. No obstacle appears insur-
mountable when a collector becomes obsessed with obtaining a
work of art at any price; moral scruples become meaningless.
Everything becomes secondary to the one goal and that is to
possess the desired object for yourself alone and no other.

On my first return visit to Australia from England in the
sixties, to present *A Nice Night's Entertainment*, I decided we
should travel on a Norwegian cargo ship, the *Talabot*, which
pursued a leisurely route from Rotterdam to Auckland via
Lisbon and Genoa. The long journey and the comparative luxury of a suite next to Captain Nielsen's spacious accommodation
seemed the perfect opportunity to write a show. After a farewell
lunch with John Betjeman and his companion, Lady Elizabeth
Cavendish, we took the train from Liverpool Street to Harwich,
and thence by overnight ferry to the Hook of Holland.

The *Talabot* was to sail a day later from the port of Rotterdam so there was time for me to visit Amsterdam and have a look around. It was on my rambles through this water-logged city, then unembellished by graffiti – the chubby aerosol scrawl that has become the universal autography of the moron and the chemically dependent – that I came upon the St Luciensteeg and the small bookshop of Leo Bisterbosch.

Mr Bisterbosch dealt in maps and prints of the topographical and devotional kind, but on entering the crowded and dimly lit premises I observed a number of drawings and objects from the art nouveau period in its more extravagant and sinuous Dutch manifestation.

This early-twentieth-century style had always amused me, and my friend John Tourrier had already designed at my request an art nouveau poster for my forthcoming Australian tour, on which I appeared like a moody daguerreotype amidst a flurry of olive-green arabesques. As the sixties progressed, 'that strange decorative disease known as *art nouveau*' (Walter Crane) underwent a huge and unforeseeable international revival; its tendrils seethed on wallpapers, lampshades and miniskirts, spreading from the sleeves of rock albums and invading the humid boudoirs of teeny-boppers.

The foremost Dutch exponent of art nouveau had been Jan Toorop, a versatile artist who seemed to have painted in every fashion from pointillism through symbolism to a realistic manner resembling the early Lucian Freud. Jan Toorop's formative years had been spent in Indonesia and his hybrid style lay somewhere between the wilting ladies of the pre-Raphaelites and the shadow puppets of Java. He was a kind of Balinese Burne-Jones.

Mr Bisterbosch appeared to have cornered the market in Toorop, whose reputation was then at a low ebb. The shop was filled with images by this artist: prints, drawings, a copper panel and even a stained-glass window. Already rather rashly anticipating the success of my forthcoming Australian tour, yet for comparatively little money, I bought a Toorop etching and a poster, but not before I had noticed, propped against the wall in a fuscous corner of the shop and partly hidden by tottering towers of books, an extraordinarily large symbolist drawing – so large indeed that it touched the ceiling – in which Toorop had traced a Rosicrucian allegory with some of his hieratic female marionettes framed by great manes of undulating vermicelli hair. It was the strangest drawing I had ever seen, and then and there I decided that I would one day acquire it.

For some years afterwards I returned to Amsterdam every summer, enjoying its transformation into a Mecca for the seductive and obliging flower children of Europe, and I always called on the old shop, which was slowly silting up with *objets d'art*. On each visit my Toorop drawing seemed to diminish, until it was all but occluded by a bookcase. A small, cobwebbed corner was the only evidence that it remained unsold or unsaleable. It was not until 1973, when after a period of monetary stringency my fortunes had improved, that I resolved that, if the picture was still *in situ* on my next visit, I would make Leo Bisterbosch an offer he couldn't refuse.

I had worked out in Dutch guilders the amount of money

that I thought the dealer would find irresistible; the major problem would be to extricate the picture and transport it to London, and thence to Australia, for my Toorop – in my imagination I already possessed it – had become such an integral part of the shop that it would take men younger and stronger than the frail Mr Bisterbosch to excavate it from beneath a drift of furniture, maps, books and bric-à-brac.

I had a friend called Brian who lived in South London and sold second-hand Volkswagen minivans to Australian tourists. These vehicles invariably broke down just outside Dover, but Brian, ever magnanimous, always included a length of rope in the trunk of every car he sold. Together we crossed the Channel and bought a large van at a second-hand car pool in Utrecht. It was a rust-bucket, a heap, but Brian reckoned it had one more trip left in it, and on a historic Tuesday morning in September 1973 we manoeuvred the juddering pantechnicon – Brian driving, I with my eyes shut – into the tiny cobbled cul-de-sac beside Mr Bisterbosch's canal.

Mr Bisterbosch gazed at the pile of readies uncomprehendingly. He had thought of a number and probably doubled it, and here was the exact sum, as if by magic, lying on his counter like a crisp salad. The picture had been for so long a part of his shop that he had forgotten when it had not been there and now, despite its invisibility, he thought of it almost as a structural necessity. Might not the whole building come down about his ears if the picture were removed? I assured him I had a friend who could assist in its careful extraction. He then raised the question of transportation, so I led him around the corner and, to his amazement, indicated the giant jalopy from which there still arose oily and ominous fumes.

The aged art dealer watched with incredulity as Brian and I laboured for several hours to exhume my prize from its dusty entombment. After an emotional farewell we were soon chugging towards Ostend and the ferry to Harwich and . . . home.

No sooner had we arrived at my London address than the transmission literally dropped out of the chassis onto the street, but within a week Toorop's long-missing drawing, *Divine Extase*, carefully swaddled in cardboard and tissue paper, was on its way to my Sydney flat in a big pine crate.

PRAGUE, like Amsterdam, is one of my favourite European cities, though I think – of all heresies – that I prefer some aspects of the Czech capital in the bad old days before McDonald's invaded Wenceslas Square, when few buildings in the city and suburbs had received a coat of paint since 1939 and when the best room in the art nouveau Hotel Europa could be obtained merely by interleaving the pages of one's passport with a couple of US dollar bills. The Europa employed the famous and venerable dwarf Rosco to drive their once-gilded cage lift, and it must have afforded this proud manikin in his patched and shiny uniform enormous satisfaction to close the concertina doors of his elevator and, at the touch of a brass button, grow six storeys tall.

When in the late eighties the Soviet invasion receded and the invasion by international film companies and fast-food purveyors took over, I visited Prague less often. I had come to know the city in desuetude, when the wattage was low and the streets and alleys were gloomy, mysterious and subfusc; when the most beautiful young whores in Europe gathered in the art deco cocktail bar of the Alcron Hotel along with KGB spies, left-wing Australian trade unionists with Bradford accents, drunken journalists and Bulgarian rock'n'roll bands. They were the days when for every tourist there was a personal 'shadow', so that once, having travelled by train and bus to far-off Karlsbad, I observed, seated on the other side of the bar or restaurant, or across the aisle at a concert of Suk or Janáček, or nonchalantly sauntering a few paces behind me in a picture gallery – the same little man. He wore a soiled raincoat over his threadbare suit and, like one's own reflection when it is accidentally caught in two mirrors, he turned away as I turned towards him.

Another time, however, I contrived to catch his eye. I was in a café in the old spa of Marienbad, that lovely, melancholy town of exfoliating stucco. I had glimpsed him come in and nonchalantly take a table in the far corner, unfold his tattered newspaper and order a beer from the infinitely derelict waiter. For a moment we looked at each other, the stalker and his quarry, and his face wore an expression of profound sadness, even regret, as if to say, 'I know you're just an eccentric tourist and I'm so terribly sorry, sir, but you see, I have my orders, and the man who gave me those orders had his from someone else who was merely obeying instructions from another, remoter authority, but you will have to get used to me, I am afraid. I am here until you leave Czechoslovakia.' He looked as if he might burst into tears.

Whenever I went to Prague it was to visit my friend Jiří Mucha, the writer and son of Alphonse Mucha, a famous exponent, if not the inventor, of art nouveau. Jiří lived in his father's thirteenth-century *palazzetto* up by the castle. Here, due to some abstruse arrangement with the authorities, he lived in a style that few of his countrymen enjoyed. With biographies and monographs he had rehabilitated his father's artistic reputation, and travelled to London, Japan and the United States lecturing and mounting exhibitions. At home Jiří's household seemed to be run by Marta, his Moravian mistress, a raven-haired hoyden who, when I first met her in the sixties, was dressed from head to foot by Courrèges, including white boots with windows in them. When I came to stay I always brought Marta cartons of Lucky Strike cigarettes and duty-free Johnny Walker and once, since I had come on to Prague from Bombay, a case of mangoes, a fruit that had possibly not found its way to Czechoslovakia since the thirties.

It was Marta, in her informal role as procuress, who arranged – even choreographed – those exotic soirées in which foreign visitors with libidinous tastes were entertained by some of Prague's more uninhibited young women, in search of whom she loyally trawled the bars and nightclubs of the city. It was on these occasions at Jiří's house, late at night and to the accompaniment of loud Beatles tapes, that the dim lights were dimmed still further and the tarnished *jeunesses dorées* performed their erotic charades. For these events Jiří would wear his wig, a curious headpiece like an old movie star's bob: that of Louise Brooks or Jiří's favourite prewar film actress, Colleen Moore. He was a spectator only, and would sometimes interrupt the illicit

Western rock music with a record of his favourite aria, an air that had haunted his childhood: the exquisite 'Song of the Moon' from Dvořák's *Rusalka*.

When my friend died in 1991 and the political wind had changed, Jiří's family reclaimed the Mucha house. In refurbishing it they found that the entire building was bugged, and hidden microphones were discovered in the most unlikely places. His faithful mistress, the handsome and tempestuous Marta, had disappeared before it was revealed that for many years she had been an agent of the KGB.

The city of Prague is particularly lovely in May when the cherry trees are in blossom. It is as lovely as Vienna in lilac time, and only less breathtaking than the seven hills of Lisbon when that most beautiful of all flowering trees, the blue jacaranda, blooms. In the early seventies my projected spring visit to Prague was slightly delayed, so I sent Jiří a jokey telegram:

Running late. Hold the blossoms.

When I finally arrived I naïvely failed to grasp why Jiří so reproached me for this innocent communication. I had not realised how suspicious my enigmatic message must have seemed to the evil ones who intercepted his correspondence, and this wire probably caused my friend to endure days of interrogation. Imagine life under a humourless totalitarian regime where your freedom could depend on explaining a joke.

I LOVED to explore the city and suburbs of Prague, once visiting the strange chapel at Sedlec, which is entirely decorated with the bones and skulls of long-dead monks, and stinks of garlic. I also liked to visit the studio – now a forgotten museum – of a symbolist sculptor at the turn of the nineteenth century. Entering by an elaborately wrought iron gate, one passes through a neglected garden and ascends to the stone terrace, its tiles loose and broken. Beside the huge front door, on the granite jamb, its palm outwards, fingers splayed, is a bronze hand of Christ. The nail that pierces His palm is the doorbell.

The Wiertz Museum in Brussels is a similarly neglected shrine, although one is rarely completely alone there since, with the revival of interest in the Belgian Romantic artists of the nineteenth century, a few adventurous amateurs of the byways of art sometimes make the journey to the Leopold district to visit this curious *atelier*. The canvases are huge, often depicting subjects of macabre horror, my favourite always being *The Mad Mother*. In this painting a deranged and laughing woman, experiencing what would be now called a serious midlife crisis, sits on her hearth stirring a cauldron of stew from which the principal ingredient, her infant's legs, grotesquely protrude.

Some years ago, in search of paintings by the then-forgotten artists of the symbolist school, as I had earlier sought pictures by Toorop, I used to make trips to Belgium to look up the aged relatives of these unfashionable painters. Alan Hollinghurst, in his novel *The Folding Star*, wonderfully evokes the mood of such tenebrous excavations. I liked particularly the works of Jean Delville, who was a real master of the mannerist genre, and the artist's charming son – in former days the tennis correspondent on *Le Soir* – invited me to his home one evening to inspect the few remaining works that the family was prepared to sell. It was a suitably gloomy night in Brussels as I moved around the ill-lit and overheated salon, peering at the canvases of writhing nudes and ecstatic angels. Every time I expressed a wish to buy something, the old man excused himself, moved quietly to the far end of the room and released a celebratory fart.

I have reached an age where I am the patron of various organisations: small theatres, chamber music societies and worthy charities. My duties are few, but those I have I discharge to the best of my ability. One of my titles, however, requires no more justification than a morbid imagination. I am the president of the Jan Frans de Boever Society in Belgium. It is a small society – its total membership is unlikely to exceed four persons – but all of us are united in our enthusiasm for the work of this neglected Ghentois artist. De Boever (1872–1949), who has at least one painting in the Museum of Fine Arts in Ghent (although sadly never on exhibition), specialised in erotic *memento mori*: pictures of chorus girls invariably accompanied by skeletons. The nudes are always provocatively posed with attentive cadavers, who ignite their cigarettes with bony fingers, grin from the shadows of their rancid boudoirs or attempt forms of congress more satisfactorily accomplished by the corporeally endowed.

My own de Boever collection consists of a mere seven or eight canvases, but our secretary acquires every picture that comes on the market and his small terrace home in Ghent is lined from floor to ceiling with capering skeletons and concupiscent trollops. At the society's last extraordinary general meeting there were no chairs on which to sit, since our secretary spends every spare euro on augmenting this unique collection. His young children, all strangers to the sedentary position and raised in this grotto of white-thighed and black-stockinged *filles de joie* and their osseous consorts, will carry into later life rich memories of bordello and charnel house.

'WHEN are you coming to Hamburg, dear, to see your girlfriends?'

The voice on the telephone was heavily Germanic and well fed. It belonged to my friend Wolf Uecker, gourmand, short-story writer, art dealer and regular contributor to German *Playboy*. I confess I had thought of those girls quite a lot lately and, although they were probably very expensive, they were irresistibly beguiling. A weekend at the Atlantic Hotel in Hamburg and a few long lunches and dinners with Wolf and Eva seemed suddenly imperative. He had introduced me to a local culinary eccentricity: the combination of oysters and cheese, which in a dockside Hamburg restaurant seems to work!

Wolf was a Berliner who, in the Second World War, had fought for the wrong general. He was the most amusing and generous of men, with a wonderfully rumpled face like that of a humourous bloodhound. It might be said of Wolf's countenance what an Australian wag once observed of W.H. Auden: 'He didn't get a face like that from eating strawberries.'

In the early eighties Wolf had an art gallery in that fine

Hanseatic city by the Alster, and dealt in art nouveau glass and Tiffany lamps, which were still expensively in vogue. He also sold furniture, erotica and German drawings and paintings of the twenties and thirties by George Grosz, Otto Dix, Rudolf Schlichter and other painters of that era whose work had been banned by the Nazis. I had learnt from my London friend Godfrey Pilkington that Wolf owned a masterpiece of this school by the former Dadaist Christian Shad, called *Die Freundinen* – 'The Girlfriends'. The picture had been painted in 1928 when the artist was at the height of his powers, but because of its – to say the least – confronting subject matter, it had been rarely exhibited, and the artist had kept it rolled up under his bed for nearly three decades. From time to time I would receive a summons from Wolf to fly over and look at the object of my infatuation. Although craftily he never positively agreed to part with it, one day perhaps it 'just might' be for sale. This may well have been an art dealer's ploy, and I was suitably tantalised; yet I really believed he loved the picture so much that he would only relinquish it under dire circumstances.

Die Freundinen is one of the greatest and most poignant portraits of the century, for Shad was a master of painting what can be seen as an expression of that which cannot be seen. One girl is sitting on the edge of the bed with her translucent black chiffon top partly raised, one strap fallen from her shoulder and her stockings pulled down. Between her spread thighs is placed an agitated hand. The face is detached, soft waves of hair cascading on her forehead. Behind her on the rumpled bed lies her naked friend.

Wolf had pursued this masterpiece from the day he first glimpsed it in the late sixties in the catalogue of a Milan gallery for an exhibition, Il Realismo in Germania. By the time he got to Milan, the work had been sold to a private Italian collector, whose wife, as it turned out, found the subject 'unacceptable'. Wolf tracked the painting down, but too late. It was already in the possession of an attorney and real estate agent, whom Wolf discovered lived only a five-minute drive from his gallery. Ultimately by good fortune and persistence it fell into the hands of my friend.

Eventually, however, after Wolf had owned *Die Freundinen* for ten years, circumstances obliged him to sell. I received a letter naming the price, and announcing that the same letter had been sent to three art museums and one private collector in Switzerland. The first to accept Wolf's terms won 'The Girlfriends'. I was at once on the telephone, and a few weeks later the Mona Lisa of the Weimar Republic and her friend hung on my wall.

This picture can now be seen at the Neue Galerie in New York City for, sadly, beautiful things of this kind are merely lent to us for a while and then pass on. Dire circumstances, which had forced my late friend Wolf to place those melancholy waifs in my custody, ultimately obliged me to surrender them to another, richer admirer.

With some of the profits from *Die Freundinen*, Wolf bought an old farmhouse in the flat rural district of Lüneberger Heide, about 45 miles south of Hamburg. Rustic without, the house was comfortable and sophisticated within, filled with polychromatic lamps and mordant drawings by Schlichter and Grosz. Here he wrote his books and cooked elaborate feasts for his friends, especially if a pig had been recently slaughtered. Unfortunately I once arrived to stay just after such a farmyard assassination, in time to see a peasant with a hose sluicing blood from the concrete floor of the barn.

Wolf was glowing with excitement as he told me in gruesome detail of the animal's fate. Zarah had been lovingly reared for several years and now, since her dispatch at dawn, nothing remained that had not been transformed into sausages, pâté, chops, ribs, steaks: everything within and beyond the *charcutier's* wildest imagination. He had loved that pig, yet in her new and various forms he loved her even more. However, I was not to know until the evening meal what special delicacy from the day's carnage had been reserved for me: a large plate of *roh Schweinefleisch* – raw minced pig. What had less than twelve hours before been cheerfully guzzling and shitting in its pen was now a quivering pink pyramid that I must eat, or seem to eat, beneath the eager scrutiny of my host. I muttered something about raw pork and tapeworms, and other such foolish superstitions, but these effeminate scruples were brushed aside with Teutonic scorn.

'Never vorry, my dear. It's the cleanest pig you'll ever eat. Remember, Zarah voss my friend!'

And with that, Wolf ladled a huge forkful of raw meat into his mouth and washed it down with schnapps. Closing my eyes and thinking of Australia, I managed, with the help of sauces, chopped onions and black bread, to choke down enough of this repellent delicacy to satisfy honour. But for many days after, I imagined I could feel the twitching of a newly hatched parasite enjoying his first swimming lesson in my intestines.

FOXHOLE PRAYERS

~

My career is hurting me

EUGÈNE IONESCO

MY FRIEND Clyde Packer went to live in California, and since then I have employed many agents and managers with varying degrees of ability and integrity. Some of them earnt their 10 per cent commission and some did not. I had, after all, joined the company of rogues and vagabonds and I always assumed that we, the actors, were the vagabonds.

In recent years there has arisen a new phenomenon: the gentleman agent. This is not to say there has not always been a small band of honourable men dedicated to the advancement of their clients: men whose love of literature and the theatre had driven them into this unlikely vocation. Some few theatrical agents are failed actors, stoically redirecting their frustrated and fragile gifts towards the promotion of more robust and lucrative talents. Others, however – especially those who today attach themselves to big international agencies – are philistine lawyers and accountants with all the vainglory of their brethren in the extra-theatrical world, inflated by their infatuation with show

277

business. Some agents become by osmosis as celebrated as their clients.

In the early eighties, still smarting from the depredations of an agent who had, amongst other impudencies, appropriated to himself in perpetuity the rights of my songs – and those of other writers – I offered myself on the rebound to Murray Wattles, a dull, but diligent fellow Australian from Brisbane. Here at last seemed the ideal person to manage my expanding career.

The firm of office stationers who had printed Murray's impressive embossed letterhead had suggested he style himself 'the Murray Wattles Organisation' or even 'the Murray Wattles Entertainment Group', but he liked 'system'. It was a new cant word of the period, which attached itself to everything from gramophones ('sound systems') to razors ('shaving systems') and shampoo ('hair-care systems'). Moreover it lent a spurious aura of the scientific to enterprises or products that might otherwise have seemed shambolic or deadly boring. Like 'laboratory tested', it inspired confidence. Thus my new and energetic business manager became the Murray Wattles Artists Management System.

Murray was a non-smoking, non-drinking, happily married man, and I could find no fault with him except perhaps his nail-biting and an irritating habit of larding his conversation with the phrase 'to be perfectly honest with you'. It was a locution that I would have gravely distrusted in a shifty British agent, but in Murray it seemed almost engaging.

In my trade it is a relief to totally trust someone; particularly if you have no interest in business, or if you feel that your artistic preoccupations place you on an exalted level, far above such mundane concerns. My new English accountant was likewise a man of total integrity. He radiated quiet dependability and a fastidious – if somewhat boring – attention to the dotted i's and crossed t's, which so charm the Taxman.

All the more surprising then that if, while on tour, I unexpectedly knocked on Murray's hotel room door to discuss a business matter, there might sometimes be a curiously long delay before it was opened. Did I imagine that I heard a woman's suppressed laughter in the background as my trusted agent, the married man, clutching his bathrobe around him, addressed me through a crack in the door? Did I detect the faintest whiff of booze, and could that cloud of acrid and nutty vapour debouching into the corridor be cigarette smoke? My abstemious manager had often regaled me with scornful stories of show-business idiots who gambled away all their money on cards and horses, so were those friends of mine merely malicious when they reported having spotted Murray at casinos and racetracks?

'Saw your mate out at Randwick racecourse last Saturday, Barry. He's a bit of a high-roller!' To these and other ominous signs I turned a blind eye and a deaf ear. It was impossible for this smiling little man, to whom I had personally entrusted my career and my small fortune, to be anything other than the slightly boring, conscientious paragon I needed him to be.

There are other instances in my life where I have projected roseate hopes and expectations onto the most unlikely characters, in the belief that they might, under my influence, magically conform to my idealised view of them. Once, in a hotel bedroom in an Australian city, I experienced more acutely than usual the touring malaise. I was in some miserable accommodation with its hideous appointments: its coat-hangers with nails instead of hooks, its too-short bathtub with Velcro strips on its bottom and on mine, the condemned chocolates on the pillow, the stink of cheap 'room fresheners', the television remote control still viscid from the grasp of a hundred lonely convention delegates with a penchant for the adult channel, and the polyester sheets infused with the odour of their nicotine breath.

Why was there not a head on the pillow next to mine? I asked myself. An attractive head; above all, a concupiscent head and all that extended restlessly below it. Was I not single, successful, moderately rich and not yet irredeemably past middle age?

I remembered someone, a girl, an artist – or so she thought of herself. She took Polaroid photographs of herself and her friends, slightly out of focus, and glued them to canvas with broken toys and scraps of fur and feathers adhering thereto. She had had a few exhibitions with the assistance of an arts council grant. She lived in another city in arty squalor, but had given me her number. I thought of her with a renewed interest and decided that if an epithet were to be attached to her, it would be 'obliging'. As I casually leafed through the pages of my pocket diary, I remembered a lewd smile and the phrase 'be my guest' that had preceded, rather surprisingly, my first and only encounter with her. I found the number. I was dialling it. What was her name? Thursday! What kind of a name was that? Would it be possible for me to contemplate an erotic tryst with a person named after the dullest day in the week, let alone solemnly arrange her airline ticket and invite her to join me immediately, this minute, *now*? Didn't a name such as Thursday go with green ink and smiley faces and – dared I contemplate it for more than a split second? – *trouble*?

Another voice inside my head was saying – whining actually – Why should a nice, interesting, fairly famous person like you be alone in a ghastly hotel room without any form of sexual recreation when the world out there is full of randy women called Thursday, Friday or for that matter Saturday, for Christ's sake! Whenever I was alone like this, my first thought was always, Who can I be alone with? Besides, I was in that somewhat rare state: unmarried. Most men have girlfriends between marriages; I usually had wives between marriages, so why not a brief deviation?

I could hear the phone ringing at Thursday's place. It was on a box covered with a shawl as I recalled, beside her tousled bed with its reasty sheets. Next to the telephone, between a packet of Drum tobacco with cigarette papers and an incense burner, lay a well-thumbed Sylvia Plath.

A voice in my brain, but slightly fainter, kept saying, Hang up now, this girl is a ratbag, a waif-adventuress. Put the phone down before it's too late. Be lonely. Enjoy your freedom.

The brief picture that had flashed across my mind of the artist's pungent boudoir and the promptings of my wiser, if cowardly self prevailed, and virtuously I began to lower the receiver to its cradle. But suddenly there was another voice, this time from the phone.

'Hello? Hello? Who is it?'

In a second the instrument was back at my ear. My heart was pounding dangerously and the foolhardy invitation was irrevocably extended. I had embarked on the road of no return, and there followed an episode that, while fortunately brief, was predictably costly and deplorable.

Although I sometimes arrogantly deluded myself into believing that I could assuage loneliness and my occasional bouts of accidie with a phone call or a snap of the fingers, and that I could, by the sheer power of my will, make another unpromising human being conform to my ideal, the results were always disappointing. But my denial was strong. You could show me a ratbag, and if necessary I would behold a saint; present me with a palpable scoundrel, and I would probably give him my power of attorney.

If your accountant, the custodian of your financial affairs, works for a large and venerable firm of chartered accountants in the city of London, it never occurs to you that he might be a nincompoop. However, if you are unable to reach him by telephone in the afternoons and his secretary actually says to you, 'It's always advisable to speak to Mr Oldham in the mornings. *He's better before lunch'*, you would be naïve or stupid not to smell a rat – or a few drinks – and yet I sailed blithely through one of the most professionally rewarding periods of my life with all these warning signs flashing and these minatory bells and sirens ringing in oblivious ears. It was my decade of hubris.

The two men to whom I had entrusted my prosperity were not vicious, merely human. They were exposed to irresistible temptations and whatever they may or may not have filched or misappropriated could be easily 'justified' by a gentle tweaking of the books.

In those days it was as well that I believed myself to be so punctiliously served by my agents and advisers because I was at the height of my success. There was the splendid apartment in Sydney with its incomparable view, an equally splendid house in London, and Diane, my young wife – a gifted artist – who had presented me with two sons, Oscar and Rupert.

As a child I had come to believe that whatever I wanted would be mine sooner rather than later, merely for the asking. In middle age it seemed that I had entered a second childhood of instant gratification. My devoted manager and my accountant saw to it that nothing disagreeable encroached upon my life or interrupted the steady flow of my just rewards – and theirs. My walls were embellished with fine pictures for I had expanded earlier collections, especially of the Viennese and Belgian symbolists. Packages from rare-book dealers arrived regularly on my doorstep, and secretaries, maids, housekeepers and chauffeurs were my cheerful minions.

It was when I discovered, quite by accident, that several hugely expensive Italian suits from a Bond Street shop, which even a rich Arab would hesitate to patronise, had been charged to me that I gently asked Murray if there had perhaps been some mistake. His countenance assumed an expression I had never before seen published upon it. It was the expression of someone who knows the game is up. That I should have so much as glanced at the books must, in itself, have given my manager some cause for amazement, but that I had also noticed such a minor irregularity – the matter of a few shreds of his apparel charged to me – must have surely induced a premonitory spasm of diarrhoea.

The truth dawned upon me slowly, but the cold hand of doubt had already reached into my breast and grasped my heart. I had heard a rumour, which needless to say I had instantly dismissed, that the office of the Murray Wattles Artists Management System, which I later learnt was rented at my expense, had been raided by the VAT inspectors, and files confiscated. I realised I might soon be obliged to explore the truth of this rumour.

Things went quickly from bad to worse, aided by my chronically thirsty London accountant. The fraternal relationship with smiling, straightforward, family-man Murray began to slide and crumble. It would be an absurd understatement to say it all ended badly. It ended calamitously, and I still feel a trace of rancour towards this unfortunate fellow. But he was, after all, as much in the grip of his gambling passion as was I in the grip of an egotistical indifference to reality. The tosspot accountant was certainly no help either; both men had pissed copiously in my soup.

I hope Murray will read this one day, but it is unlikely that he will recognise himself for by now, doubtless, he will have rewritten history. For by now I will be the villain: the slavedriver who worked him beyond the call of reasonable duty and paid him a pittance, which he was obliged to augment by an occasional delving into my pocket. No, he will not read this, for reading was never one of Murray's strong points; neither of contracts nor of the published requirements of Her Majesty's Inland Revenue. I recall the one occasion on which I caught him reading a book – was it a Tom Clancy? I can still see his gnawed finger laboriously tracing the words, the dunce's frown, and the tip of his tongue projecting between lips clamped in concentration.

On a long-distance telephone call my mother summed it all up, with one of her favourite apothegms. 'How many times have I told you, Barry?' she declared with her usual ruthless impartiality. '*A fool and his money are soon parted.*'

'I SINCERELY hope you will help us clear up this matter as quickly as possible, Mr Humphries.'

The man in the grey suit and maroon tie lowered his eyes to the papers on the table between us to allow his meaning to register.

'Most of the people we see find it much easier in the long run to tell us all they know. If they don't,' he added, with a wan, condolent smile, 'they can get sick, *very sick.*'

Did he mean syphilis or Ebola? I wondered. Or just nausea?

I sat in a bleak conference room in a building near Bishopsgate, being interviewed by this zealous man in his grey suit, and another: Mr Conroy and his associate, Mr Hughes. Mr Hughes was a small, nervous man, the few hairs on his scalp arranged in a courageous comb-over.

It would have been better if I had helped these two gentlemen with their inquiry single-handed, but I had foolishly sought professional advice from a very large firm of London accountants, who had assured me that one of their senior partners had once worked for the Grey Suits and could, to use his phrase, 'speak their language'. Consequently, when I attended the meeting that morning, I was supported by four overpaid city accountants whose method it was to exchange friendly banter with their brethren on the other side of the table, in a cringe-making attempt to lighten up proceedings. It failed, and Mr Conroy and Mr Hughes looked across at them with a proper contempt.

At this point in my career I had still not wholly apprehended the full infamy of Murray, my business manager, or the extent of his betrayal. It seemed I was responsible anyway for misappropriated money and slovenly accounts, but I am convinced the whole matter could have been quickly resolved if I had been left alone with my interrogators.

Suddenly, after a few routine questions, Mr Hughes raised his eyes from his voluminous file and asked me if I possessed a quantity of kruger rands. I suppose most people know what these are but I did not, and in some confusion I declared my ignorance. It was then, for one terrible moment, that Mr Conroy laughed. He must have been laughing quite a lot inside from the start of our discussion for I was already a well-known comedian and, in distress, the more risible. But the tension was broken and one of my accountants was actually mopping his eyes with a handkerchief. In fact everyone laughed except the senior partner and me. Instead he farted, loudly, and the small room filled with the feculent odour of the accountant.

As the air cleared I found myself grasping the true meaning of the Stockholm syndrome, where the hostages of terrorists find themselves in increasing sympathy with their captors, and hostile to their rescuers. After forty minutes in that conference room all those years ago, I had rather warmed to Mr Conroy and Mr Hughes and come to despise the clowns I had engaged to advise me.

In a subsequent interview I was surprised to see how much the Grey Suits knew about me; it was almost as if they had been ardent fans. It saddened me to think how little I really knew about *them*, and I decided I would have to conduct my own discreet investigations, if only to humanise these meetings and alleviate the Kafka-like atmosphere.

A quick perusal of a London telephone directory informed me that a P.J. Conroy (for my interrogator had signed a letter to me with those same initials) resided in north-east London in the suburb of Ponders End, at 15 Brookvale Terrace. Without quite understanding my motive, I drove very early one morning to this address, parking the car as close as I could to the Conroy residence, which was a pebble-dashed, two-storey, Tudor-style, twenties semidetached. In an upper window, between swagged net curtains, could clearly be seen the pinewood back of an old-fashioned dressing-table mirror.

It was still only 7.45 a.m. and cold. I knew I might have to lurk there for some time before the subject appeared at his front door, kissed his wife goodbye and walked down the street towards the tube station. I opened my *Financial Times* and, screening my face with it, settled in to wait. I felt like a gumshoe without a doughnut.

The subject did not leave for work that morning until 9.32 a.m. I recognised him instantly. He was wearing a red anorak but beneath it I glimpsed the familiar grey suit as he hurried to the gate and turned onto the pavement. From his right hand swung a large Samsonite briefcase and it was odd to think that somewhere within lay my dossier with his pencilled annotations. I buried my face in the paper as he strode past, a mere two feet from the car, and I watched his image dwindle in the rear-view mirror.

I staked him out for weeks thereafter, indeed for the duration of his investigation of me. I learnt what train he caught, what paper he read, where his wife shopped and where his children went to school. My feelings of anxiety and powerlessness ebbed away with every click of my stopwatch, every entry in my logbook and every surreptitious telephoto snap. Slowly, and to my great surprise, I began to feel an emotion resembling ardour towards this hard-working civil servant and family man, who bore me no personal malice and was after all only doing his job and seeking promotion. When he went to church with his loved ones at Our Lady of Perpetual Sorrows on Sunday mornings, I was there, heavily disguised, in a back pew watching and, let it be confessed, praying.

Although I had not been a regular churchgoer for some years, I did, from time to time, get on my knees and pray. But they were usually foxhole prayers: 'Lord, get me out of this one and I promise I'll never . . . et cetera, et cetera.'

At our last conference, by which time I had sacked my flatulent accountants and advisers, Conroy and Hughes outlined the terms under which our differences might be satisfactorily settled. A figure was mentioned that resembled not so much a sum of money as the population of a very small country. Mr Hughes's comb-over twitched. Mr Conroy fixed me with a steely and unblinking gaze, which I felt he must have been taught in some special College for Inquisitors. But I did not mind, and I smiled back. It was a smile that said, had he but known it: 'I hope you enjoyed the pot roast Helen, your wife, bought for you at Budgen's last Tuesday at 11.28 a.m., and I like her hair up, the way Barnaby did it on Friday night before you all went to see the Abba concert. And congratulations on little Sean's excellent arithmetic marks. One day he may grow up to be a famous tax inspector.'

PARNASSIANS

~

Poets, painters and puddings; these three
Make up the World as it ought to be
RICHARD HUGHES

WHEN I first came to London and established myself in a dank
basement at 2A Pembridge Gardens, Notting Hill Gate, it would
have been still possible for me to meet, in the flesh, most of the
English poets and painters that I had admired in my youth. All
the Sitwells were still alive and visitable, but I only met
Sacheverell, the youngest member of that terrible trio, at the
end of his life. Nor did I look up Siegfried Sassoon, whose books
I had devoured when young, in spite of their tedious digressions
into cricket and fox hunting. By 1959 Sassoon had declined into
mawkish old age. He was a reclusive and confused Catholic con-
vert, uncertain whether he was a hearty or an aesthete, a gentile
or a Jew.

This odd circumspection of mine, this reluctance to explore
even the foothills of Mount Parnassus, was part colonial cringe, part
old-fashioned shyness and part, too, a wish never to become the
Person from Porlock: the man whose unexpected visit interrupted

Coleridge in the midst of 'Kubla Khan', after which the poet completely lost his inspiration. In short, I was an untypical Australian, no good at turning up on strange doorsteps unannounced or barging in on the illustrious.

Augustus John – painter, not poet – I glimpsed in the distance at the Royal Academy, a marvellously drunken, bearded vision, and W.H. Auden I actually met several times: first, at a dinner in his honour at Wadham College, given by Ian Donaldson, when the poet looked like Spencer Tracy and mostly talked about Baron Corvo. In the early seventies at a South Bank poetry reading I met him again, this time on a panel that, bizarrely, consisted of Auden, Allen Ginsberg and Edna Everage, the last reciting naïve Australian verse in the McGonagall tradition.

After our performance, still disguised as the Moonee Ponds matron, it was difficult to engage Auden in a serious conversation, or even a frivolous one. He just stared at me as if I were one of the less frightening manifestations of delirium tremens. My wife Lizzie knew him well throughout her childhood and once even asked the great poet to write her a pop song. She played him a contemporary example. 'Where's the rhyme?' he objected.

When by the mid-sixties I had become a regular and accepted habitué of Soho, I began to meet rather a lot of writers and poets: the ones who frequented the bars and clubs of that gamey and heterodox neighborhood. Georgina, the daughter of the poets George Barker and Elizabeth Smart, was a particular friend, and I would often meet Lucian Freud and Francis Bacon in her company. (I last saw Bacon, not long before his death, in the vitamin and health foods department of Harrods, improbably, when he jumped out at me from behind a ginseng display.) It was in Soho in the sixties that I felt at last that this was the real world, which I had travelled 13,000 miles to inhabit.

JOHN WELLS and I had a number of mutual friends. Chief amongst them was John Betjeman, whom I think I had known longer than John had: since 1961 in fact. At first I used to visit Betjeman when he lived near the Church of St Bartholomew the Great, close to the Smithfield Meat Market. Later I would see him and Elizabeth Cavendish in Radnor Walk, Chelsea, in a small house filled with books and pictures. Here I met Cecil Beaton and Osbert Lancaster; and sometimes at dinner there would be Kingsley Amis and Philip Larkin, the latter always wearing odd socks.

'Kingsley is our Dickens; Anthony Powell, our Thackeray,' declared John.

I had admired Amis's writing since the fifties – his poetry even more than his fiction – but I was far from certain that my ardour was reciprocated. In later years I often saw him in the Garrick Club, but he steadfastly avoided eye contact and had adopted the prickly raiment of Old Curmudgeon. Perhaps without justification, I smarted at what I imagined to be a snub. Generally speaking, life is more conveniently arranged: the people we like often respond warmly to ourselves, given half a chance, and those we dislike usually can't stand us either.

Once, after lunch at the Garrick, I was standing in the vestibule looking for the porter to find me a taxi. The porter's lodge was empty and there was no one else around. Suddenly, behind me, there was a terrific and sickening thump. I spun around. On the stone floor at the foot of the stairs, like a beached porpoise, lay the author of *Lucky Jim*. It was evident that he was drunk and unconscious; possibly even dead. I looked around for help. No one. The writer's breath came back stertorously, so at least I knew he had returned to life. Single-handedly I tried to lug him across the floor to a chair by the front door, hoping, with assistance, to ultimately haul him into a taxi. Kingsley Amis was a dead weight and out for the count. But with another member's help I did finally manage to manoeuvre him into a cab, where he sat glassy-eyed, magenta-jowled and drooling slightly while we gave the driver a delivery address.

I never saw Kingsley Amis again, for soon after he yielded once more to the inexorable forces of gravity, this time at home, and died. Later *The Sunday Times* literary pages published the journals of Kingsley's latter-day Boswell, a writer who had stalked the famous author and recorded every trivial incident and *aperçu*. It seems that Amis, on being told of his fall and resurrection, had made inquiries to discover who had got him into the taxi. When given my name, he had apparently said, 'Good. At least he's not the type to ring *The Evening Standard.*'

Sometimes John Betjeman and I went down to Barnes to visit Abbott and Holder's art gallery in one of those big houses on Castlenau. On a summer afternoon we would sit under the enormous weeping beech in the garden, and Eric Holder would bring out bundles of paintings and drawings and spread them on the grass for our amusement.

'Art never lets you down,' said John, as if most other things did.

One day we chose about six pictures between us, all very fairly priced as they still are at Abbott and Holder's more recent premises in Museum Street, Bloomsbury. John bought a big seascape by Laura Knight, a breezy watercolour by Robert Anning Bell (given to me after John's death) and a nude boy on a rock in Cornwall by Henry Scott Tuke, who specialised in such subjects and was patronised by Edwardian schoolmasters and clergymen with Greek inclinations, and more recently collected by Sir Elton John.

In the sixties and seventies London underwent demolition on a scale that would have delighted the ghost of Hermann Göring. Developers, with the connivance of the City, finished the work of the Luftwaffe, and rebuilt as if Britain had never possessed an architectural tradition. Betjeman always used to say that there should be a blown-up photo of each architect plastered outside his erection so that we could actually behold the vandal's face.

'He's bound to have a beard,' said John, 'and probably a duffel coat.'

John Betjeman had been to Australia on a British Council tour in 1961 and longed to go back. When he finally did in 1973, to record a series of programmes for the BBC, his health had declined and bursts of ebullience and creativity often gave way to darker episodes of depression. Just as I had once treated my alcoholism with alcohol, so John was by then self-medicating dangerously. A doctor had prescribed him that fashionable drug of the period, that universal panacea, Valium. John was taking the Valium washed down with whisky and champagne, and the Australian programmes, in which his genius still sporadically flashed, petered out in Tasmania, where there were also temperamental clashes with the director, Julian Jebb. The tragic atmosphere that is almost palpable in some parts of Tasmania also affected him.

Once after his return to London I was travelling with him in a taxi, visiting a few of his favourite city buildings, when he realised that his supply of Valium had run out and he had mislaid his prescription. There was a terrible personality change as he slipped into a kind of desperate withdrawal.

The stroke that disabled him for the rest of his life occurred while I was on a long Australian tour, and for some reason the news only reached me months later. In spite of his incapacities he did another television series as a kind of rehab exercise, and I participated in a couple of episodes. It was nice to make my old friend laugh, and it is his laughter – a high, exultant cackle – that I best remember.

I HAVE always admired the writings of Herbert Read, but I once received a pretty nasty review of my novel *Women in the Background*, in *The Evening Standard*, by the poet's uppity grandson. Subsequently at a big party we were introduced. Unfortunately I had already clasped the hand of this young serpent before fully apprehending his name. All I could do in this unwished-for circumstance was blurt out an entire poem by

Herbert Read that I had memorised as a schoolboy and had no idea still lurked in the database of my unconscious.

John Betjeman had a number of *bêtes noires* whom he never forgave. One was the pompous C.S. Lewis; another, Geoffrey Grigson, a failed poet turned critic, who never missed a chance to belittle his fellow writers when they committed the unspeakable crime of achieving success and popularity. It was Grigson in *The Times Literary Supplement*, skulking behind the screen of anonymity, who attacked the Poet Laureate Cecil Day-Lewis as he lay dying. Grigson was a figure like Richard Flecknoe on whom Dryden had bestowed 'the laurel of dullness', or Alexander Pope's enemy Lewis Theobald, the hero of the *Dunciad*. The poets Roy Campbell and George Barker both knocked Grigson to the ground, and it is a miracle that he escaped from the Sacred Grove with his skin. Grigson also circulated, if not invented, the sarcasm that Stephen Spender was 'the Rupert Brooke of the Depression'. But it was a description that Stephen rather liked, somewhat taking the wind out of Grigson's grubby sails.

TRISTRAM POWELL, the film director, and I lunch together from time to time. Now, since I spend so much time in the United States, my friend and I have enjoyed this informal ritual less often.

Once I proposed that we meet at an Austrian restaurant I had discovered near St Paul's Cathedral. But when we got there after an awkward journey, we found it was under new management and less than *gemütlich*, so we decided to take a taxi to the

West End and eat oysters at Wilton's in Jermyn Street. Excellent though the oysters were, it seemed we should perhaps go elsewhere for our main course and thus we arrived, somewhat after 2 p.m., at Scott's in Mount Street, where we were soon trying to decide on a suitable place for dessert.

At another table I spotted a beautiful girl talking earnestly to a less than beautiful man. Tristram became aware of my distraction since, rudely, I was constantly angling myself at the table in order to get a better look at the tall, blonde diner across the restaurant.

'I know her,' Tristram announced. 'She's Lizzie Spender. I'll introduce you if you like.'

It was perhaps a year before I saw my future wife once more, at a party at the Groucho Club, and almost as long again before I proposed that we meet for lunch. But we were ultimately married in Spoleto, that lovely hilltop town in Umbria. Absent from the wedding was Lizzie's father, Stephen Spender, who at the time was too ill to travel, so Gian Carlo Menotti, a family friend, gave the bride away. For our wedding ceremony I asked a favourite modern French composer, Jean-Michel Damase, to compose a set of variations on Mendelssohn's Wedding March. I had commissioned him a few years before to write a rhapsody for horn and orchestra for Barry Tuckwell, which I hope will be recorded one day.

It was extraordinary to become a relative of the man whom I had admired since I first attended his lecture in Melbourne in 1954. Spender had been in Australia with his remarkable wife, Natasha Litvin, a concert pianist who was on a tour with Eugene

Goossens and the Sydney Symphony Orchestra. When, all those years before, Stephen had addressed the undergraduates at my university (or 'uni' as we prefer to abbreviate it in Australia) he had had to cope with a persistent communist heckler. I wrote a poem commemorating the event for his eighty-fifth birthday:

Remembering a far-off fifties day
You gave us all a talk at Melbourne Uni.
Your books were thirteen thousand miles away
From that bleak campus by the Ponds of Moonee.

Alone in the vast lecture hall you stood,
A Poet braving a tall cliff of faces.
I bet you wished you were in St John's Wood
Instead of putting hecklers in their places.

Since then, I've talked to students so I know
The need to win; I also know the fear.
I wonder would it help us through the show
If someone in the audience yelled: 'I'm here!
You're doing fine, you'll knock them all for six,
Just sock it to those smug provincial pricks!'

Instead I grinned and shuffled with the rest;
When you read Pylons, almost cried 'Encore!'
It's just as well that neither of us guessed
That in that mob there skulked a son-in-law.

Stephen Spender was like a friend I had sought all my life. I can never forget his smile: it was leonine, if one imagines a lion smiling. It was unreserved and unconditional and directed at us all. There was no English hint that the smile might have been an accidental benignity. It was the outward expression of a great and radiant nature.

Nothing had prepared me for Stephen's sense of humour, which pervaded so much of what he said. It was a quality that his unauthorised biographers have missed in their prim quest for sexual scandal. Life seemed to him a tremendous and sustained joke and, unlike some of his fellow poets, he never took himself very seriously, nor bore a grievance. Although there were many who did the dirty on him in the envious world of letters, Stephen never let any of them live rent-free in his brain.

Stephen Spender and I shared a passion for picture framers, and we most enjoyed excursions to the shops and workrooms of these dedicated craftsmen, carefully choosing the perfect frame and passe-partout for each drawing and painting. Stephen had faultless taste in these matters and his own remarkable collection, including works by Walter Sickert, David Hockney, Henry Moore, and his son, Matthew Spender, were all impeccably framed.

My interest in picture framers and their craft goes back a long way, and I must thank my mother for having actually given me an account with Dean's, a Melbourne framer, soon after I started painting in earnest. I must surely have been the only Melbourne schoolboy with such a rarefied indulgence. The company was in Little Collins Street, and was also an art supply shop. I would regularly take prints there – mostly of the post-impressionists and Paul Klee, a fifties favourite – and carefully choose their appropriate raiment.

Years later, at an auction in London, I bought very cheaply a beautiful silk fan painted by Charles Conder, that old favourite of mine, who was by then hopelessly out of fashion. It was the *Sanguine Fan*, one of his best: a transcription in watercolour of a *fête gallante* by Verlaine, and a painting that had inspired Edward Elgar to write a ballet of that name. When I bore my fragile treasure home, I noticed that the frame was badly worm-eaten and needed to be replaced.

Someone had mentioned a wonderful framer in Fulham called Mr Tice, so thither I went one morning with my precious Conder wrapped in a blanket. Mr Tice immediately turned the picture over and proceeded to remove the backboard, using the claw of a small hammer. One by one I heard the rusty nails grunt as he withdrew them. Then Mr Tice removed the picture. Before our eyes a terrible thing happened. The silk shivered, and a livid lateral rent inched across that exquisite crepuscular land-scape that had been so well preserved in its old frame since 1896.

'You clumsy fool!' I exclaimed, addressing the unfortu-nate Mr Tice. 'Look what you've done. The picture is ruined!'

We both stared at the spoilt painting. The framer looked as if he was about to cry. Hastily I apologised for my outburst. He claimed he knew a good restorer if I would leave the picture with him for a few weeks. I wouldn't know the difference, said Mr Tice in a desolate voice.

Two months later, when I had not heard a word from this

vandal and my telephone calls had gone unanswered, I went to Fulham and hammered on his door. No answer. A neighbouring shopkeeper approached me.

'If you're looking for Tice, you won't find him, gov'nor.'

'Where is he?' I asked.

'He's dead, sir. Done himself in with the gas.'

I was speechless and could only manage a faint, 'Why?'

'He was always a bit depressed, sir, but he had a business setback a couple of months ago. Something went wrong. Someone said something and then something must have snapped. Most of the dealers who left stuff with him have been round to collect it by now. Was he doing some work for you, sir?'

The next day I arranged to be let in and searched the basement for my Conder fan, or what was left of it. I noticed the faintest whiff of gas. At first the place seemed empty; stripped by every art dealer in London. Then, ominously beside the stove, I found it, wrapped up but unrepaired. As I climbed the stairs in some haste, with the Conder under my arm, I heard a rattle and a faint slap at the front door. There was a brown envelope with a window in it on the floor, just delivered. It was from the North Thames Gas Company – no doubt recording the cost of my picture framer's sudden departure from this world.

My painting has since been restored by a genius using, as adhesive, the spittle of a rare Chinese bird.

TOGETHER Stephen Spender and I went sketching and painting at Sintra in Portugal, where he had last been in 1935, with

Christopher Isherwood and W.H. Auden, in an ill-starred attempt to form a writers' colony. I realised that my father-in-law was an accomplished amateur artist. I usually painted alone, since a companion – especially a knowledgeable one – cramped my style. At Bundanon in New South Wales, the idyllic estate of my friend the great artist Arthur Boyd on the Shoalhaven River, I frequently went on painting expeditions. My host and mentor, Arthur, who even squeezed my paints for me, was so full of intemperate praise and encouragement that what slender talent I had ebbed away. I could do nothing but daub my canvas as if I had never held a paintbrush in my life.

Stephen Spender never stopped working. You could drive down Loudon Road, St John's Wood, at a late hour and see him in the front window writing and – towards the end – working at the computer, on which he had begun the novel about his childhood, 'Miss Pangbourne', unfinished at his death. When he was not writing, Stephen adored social life: dinners, lunches, suppers, concerts, plays. Because he loved art he loved visiting museums and galleries, and he was easy to find in a crowd – taller than most present, and usually laughing. He always liked my story about Adrian Silver's gallery in Melbourne.

In the seventies when Australian painting came to the fore, quite surprising people began to call themselves art dealers, many from the gown and mantle business and the used-car trade. In Melbourne there was a particularly vivid character called Adrian Silver who had made a lot of money selling automobiles and brought the same skills and terminology to the purveyance of fine art. I once entered his small gallery, which seemed to be thronged with visitors, or 'heads' as he called them since customers at a car lot are so called because their heads moving amongst the vehicles are all that the salesman generally sees of them.

'Looks like you'll be making a few sales today, Adrian,' I murmered encouragingly.

'Tyre-kickers, Baz,' the art dealer replied. 'Fucking tyre-kickers.'

Once when there was a particularly bustling group of art lovers on the premises, gazing at his heavily gold-framed wares, I spied my friend at the far end of the gallery talking on the phone. Placing his hand over the mouthpiece, he called to me as though there was no one else in the shop, 'I'm talking to Christie's in Sydney, Baz, about the last auction results.'

A hush fell briefly over the gallery. Adrian murmured a few more words into the phone, then once more placing a hisbid hand over the mouthpiece, he yelled, *'The arse has dropped out of Drysdale!'*

(Happily Mr Silver's melodramatic announcement proved to be inaccurate, although it is true that prices for works by Russell Drysdale, one of Australia's best artists, fluctuated in the seventies.)

Stephen was always a champion of David Hockney, whose genius he was one of the first to recognise. Hockney was a fellow spirit. One time, when David and I were visiting an exhibition of Entarte Kunst – art banned by the Nazis – at the Los Angeles County Museum, I said, 'How is it possible that after a catastrophe such as the Second World War some of these fragile drawings still exist?'

'Because somebody loved them,' Hockney answered simply.

It was the sort of reply Stephen might have uttered.

When Oscar was about twelve, he presented Stephen with 'Splattered Dreams', a collection of his own poetry. Stephen, who had been the friend of Edith Sitwell, T.S. Eliot, Virginia Woolf and W.H. Auden, read the work with sympathetic attention and found time to write an encouraging letter to the young poet.

I once had a suit made for my father-in-law by Sam, the famous tailor of Hong Kong. In the window of his shop Sam has photographs of himself posed with other eminent clients such as Presidents Ford, Clinton and both Bushes, Mrs Thatcher, Pavarotti and Kylie Minogue. Elaborate measurements were taken and sent off to Hong Kong, and months later the suit arrived. With tremendous excitement Stephen retired to the bathroom to try on this magnificent double-breasted garment. It was years since he had bought himself any decent clothes. He was in there a long time, but when he emerged – dismay. The suit seemed to have been built for a midget. Sleeves barely passed the elbow. Flies refused to zip and the trousers were the length of Bermuda shorts. Sam had bungled, or the measurements so carefully taken had been relayed in millimetres instead of inches. The disappointment, after such a long build-up, must have been acute; but Stephen, whose manners were perfect, smiled bravely and said, 'I might have put on a bit of weight!' His motto was always Disraeli's: 'Never explain, never complain.'

CAVITIES AND CROWNS

~

There are very few people before whom
one condescends to appear other than happy

LADY BLESSINGTON

SALVADOR DALÍ's wife produced a formidable pair of scissors
and clasping the nape of my neck very firmly with her left hand,
she attacked my scalp. Snip! Snap! The 'glittering forfex' did its
work, and a few stooks of mousy fibre fell into my lap. Dalí himself merely watched proceedings from an armchair, his head on
one side and his hands resting on an elaborate walking stick.

I had met the Dalís quite by chance at a famous bookstore
called the Gotham Book Mart on 47th Street in the heart of
New York's Diamond District. The year was 1963 and I was in
Manhattan for the first time, enlivening the cast of *Oliver!* at
the Imperial Theatre. Since I had left school, where long hair
was strictly forbidden, I had affected the lank locks of some old-
fashioned provincial aesthete; it was a look that suited the
Dickensian role I was playing at the time.

I was browsing in the New York bookstore when this
legendary couple entered – Dalí was currently promoting not

merely himself, but a new book about his work – and Gala Dalí's eye fell on this willowy young man perched on a ladder in the rare-book room. I was, of course, overwhelmed to see one of my idols in the flesh and I scuttled down the ladder and, somewhat obsequiously, introduced myself. A surrealist conversation followed in which Dalí expressed a great wish to visit Australia and examine the cave paintings of the Aborigines; he then broke into a kind of gibberish, which was his fanciful version of Aboriginal speech. The manager of the bookshop vainly attempted to intercede and bring the conversation back to business and the signing session that the artist had promised. Dalí's muse, Gala, had other plans it seemed, for she began to stroke my none-too-lustrous hair and proposed that we all go back to the St Regis Hotel immediately so she could make certain tonsorial adjustments.

Greatly excited by this unexpected encounter with the famous, after weeks of anonymity and theatrical drudgery – yet not a little apprehensive, for Gala's reputation as a sexual predator was legendary – I allowed myself to be swept off to this grand hotel on Fifth Avenue. For the whole journey Salvador maintained an unending stream of fluent 'Aboriginal'. When the door of the Dalían suite closed, Gala began her assault with the scissors for she was clearly anxious to establish her own credentials as an eccentric. Alas, rather like Yoko Ono, Señora Dalí lacked her husband's genius, and her surrealist postures were always rather humourless and uninspired.

Gala's gleeful assumption of the Delilah role was alarming and I managed to escape from her clutches without losing too much hair in the process. She then inserted a few of my severed locks into a copy of Dalí's autobiography, which they both inscribed. I had been in their hotel suite for about an hour when the artist and his wife became involved in an intimate and volatile argument, Dalí wildly gesticulating and shouting what seemed to be Spanish imprecations, while his wife ranted in French. Feeling somewhat *de trop*, I took my leave unnoticed, and descended to the hotel's entrance, on 55th Street, and the real world.

Elated by this dreamlike encounter with an idol of my youth, I rode back on the subway to my coldwater flat in Greenwich Village, hugging *The Secret Life of Salvador Dalí*, with the hirsute souvenir of my own secret life pressed between its pages. Sadly this precious volume vanished long ago, stolen by an envious person or lost in one of many upheavals and peregrinations.

BY MY next visit in 1977 the New York I knew in the *Oliver!* days had been transformed. The beatniks were gone, Marcel Duchamp and Jack Kerouac were dead and no one went to Harlem. The experimental painters were millionaires and the moral and cultural centre of the city was Studio 54. I was fresh from the success of *Houswife-Superstar!* in the West End and naïvely optimistic about my chances Off-Broadway. Like the city, I had changed too. I was even there with a new partner. Liza Minnelli was triumphantly singing that if you could make it in New York, you could make it anywhere, but as it turned out it was a chorus in which I was unable to join.

Alas, my Off-Broadway experiment, which had gone so well

during its previews, had struck the temporary theatre critic on *The New York Times* as 'abysmal'. Unfortunately, for its listings of current entertainments *The New York Times* picks a key word from its review and prints it below the title of the show every day and in every edition. Even the most intrepid Manhattan theatregoer was reluctant to make an excursion into the abyss!

An interesting girl called Cherry Vanilla interrogated me at length for Andy Warhol's *Interview* magazine. She was a celebrated 'Chelsea Girl' and a myrmidon of Andy's, and I am sure that I poured into her tape recorder a great deal of bilious invective on the subject of critics.

As the audiences dwindled, Diane or an assistant stage manager would run down the lane beside Theatre Four just before the curtain was due to rise, and peer up and down that dismal street in the vain hope that someone might be hurrying in our direction.

There is an unwritten theatre rule that a show need not proceed if the cast outnumbers its audience, but a one-man show must *ipso facto* go on. I decided then that if I ever plucked up the courage to try my luck once more with the Americans, I would wait until the critic on *The New York Times* was dead, or at least moribund.

Paradoxically it was that malevolent review in *The New York Times* that launched my return to England and the most successful years of my professional life there; and it was the similar critical reception of my West End extravaganza *Edna: The Spectacle* in 1998 that drove me, after so many years, back to Broadway.

I embarked on this latest American adventure with some trepidation. I felt exactly as I had as a schoolboy actor stepping for the first time onto the stage in *Ambrose Applejohn's Adventure* and gazing down at the expectant faces of all those parents and sisters and cousins in the school's Memorial Hall. It was an immobilising terror that I felt then and it said, 'Get through this, Barry, but never try to do it again.'

At the beginning of the nineties I had, however, done some television in Los Angeles and even rented a house there for a while so I could be near Oscar and Rupert, whose mother for business reasons had taken them to live in Beverly Hills. Our small production company made three Dame Edna interview programmes for NBC and a fourth for the Fox network, but the studio executives, always friendly, were nonetheless absurdly jittery about what Dame Edna might say or do on their programmes. Adlibs were frowned upon, and everything had to be carefully scripted and vetted for political correctness, which had become the new American disease.

On one occasion, as we were recording a show with Cher, there was a nearly disastrous technical problem when the lighting failed. While frantic repairs were underway, Edna stepped forward and apostrophised the studio audience in an attempt to keep the atmosphere buoyant.

'Sorry about the lighting, possums,' she said. 'I think the Mexicans in the basement must have stopped peddling.'

I learnt later that this extemporary remark almost caused a total walkout by affronted technicians, none of whom, incidentally, was Mexican. I had not realised the extent of the double standards in some quarters of the United States, which give noisy lip-service to the doctrine of equality and yet employ, for minimal wages, a huge subclass of Latino peasants as leaf blowers, dishwashers, chambermaids and hospital orderlies. Jest about this at your peril.

WHILE I was 'out west' I spent a whole month in Vail, Colorado, having my teeth fixed. The dentist had been fervently recommended by Anjelica Huston. The first question the dentist always asked me, after I had fallen into his chair, was, 'Baroque, Easy Listening or New Age?' He asked the question as though rejoicing in his musical scholarship and eclecticism, while at the same time subtly boasting of the equipment he possessed that could transmit these highly irritating forms of music into the defenceless ears of his patients.

If the story of my life were to be reconstituted as a piece of orchestral music – say, as a concerto – the solo instrument would be a dentist's drill. This merciless orthodontic tool has performed its whining obbligato sometimes *lento*, more often than not *tremolo furioso e strepitoso*, from my earliest youth to the present. Elsewhere I have related my experiences at the hands of Uncle Jack in the Victorian country town of Benalla, to whom my father took me in order that his dentist brother might conduct brutal experiments on my 'slightly prominent' front incisors. The oral device I was obliged to wear thereafter proved impossible to remove, until it was forcibly extracted from my mouth at my mother's insistence. It not only inhibited my

Above B.H. and Rhoze, 1974

Previous page A tribute to Christine Keeler

Iris Mason in New York, 1977, drawn by B.H.

Madge Allsop as
portrayed by
Emily Perry
(author's sketch)

Divine Extase, drawing by Jan Toorop, 1896

Phaline, gouache by Jan Frans de Boever, 1907

The author painting at Bundanon, as seen by Arthur Boyd

Painting on the Murray River

Overleaf Edna-boppers, Subiaco primary school,
Western Australia, 1994

Above Alexander Horace 'Sandy' Stone, after a little op

Opposite A patriot in repose: Sir Les Patterson in private

B.H. with Lizzie Spender

B.H. and Stephen Spender in Norway

Nicole Kidman and friend

On the set of *Ally McBeal*: (left to right) Jane Krakowski, Greg Germann, Dame Edna Everage, Calista Flockhart, Portia de Rossi, Los Angeles, 2002

Drawing of the author by David Hockney, 2002

speech but attracted a foul-smelling residuum of rancid food, impervious to toothpaste and mouthwash.

'That country quack', as my mother described my father's adored relative and the only professional on his side of the family, was replaced, and I made trips to a specialist who had rooms in the T&G Building on Collins Street. My mother and most people of her generation were unduly awestruck by specialists. 'He's not just a dentist, Barry – he's a specialist!' and then, as if to give force to her recommendation, she added, 'He did the Murdoch boy.' My mother was referring to the son of a local newspaper proprietor, whose teeth I did not then have an opportunity to examine at close quarters.

I had already been inducted into the curious mythology of specialists and I knew that they were 'misters', whereas ordinary, run-of-the-mill doctors were just plain 'doctors'. I never received a satisfactory explanation of this seeming anomaly.

Our local dentist, Dr Bremner – probably related to my piano teacher, Mrs Bremner – had his own method of tickling the ivories. He was fond of fillings and filled many of the cavities he created in my teeth with a blackish metal called amalgam, having first stuffed the holes with cottonwool soaked in oil of cloves. Thirty years later when a practitioner in Knightsbridge extracted this crumbling composite from a rotten molar, there was a sudden spicy whiff as of old-fashioned apple pie and a taste of Dr Bremner's surgery at Camberwell Junction.

'Who did this work?' exclaimed the dentist by appointment to Saudi princes and Lebanese arms dealers.

Indeed I was to hear the same incredulous words many

times over in the years that followed as I reclined in chairs ever more sophisticated, with my lips distended in an agonised rictus and with goggle eyes fixed on the Adam ceilings of Wimpole Street or the latest Adec overhead lights.

When my teeth were at their worst in London, I met a man I had known in Melbourne University days who had set himself up in a dental practice in Earl's Court, then the Australian ghetto and since invaded by even less desirable *émigrés*. Dr Darryl Blake had made a fortune cheating the National Health Service by charging his more credulous patients – mostly black or Arabic – cash, and then claiming the maximum cost of an entire dental reconstruction against the overloaded and ill-run government health service.

Over-prescribing was then a way of life for Darryl and his colleagues, and he boasted that he had invented a technique known as the 'Australian Trench' and even gave me a free demonstration of this lucrative operation. One day he beckoned me from the waiting room into his less than hygienic surgery. I saw, slumped in the chair in a drugged sleep, with his mouth clamped open, a man who looked as if he might have been a Nigerian warrior in full ceremonial robes. My Melbourne friend took up the drill and ran it around the entire set of perfectly white lower teeth, from wisdom tooth to wisdom tooth, and then did the same to the top set.

'We'll bung a load of crappy metal in there, Baz,' he said, not without a certain professional pride, 'and top it off with a veneer of cheap gold. These bush bunnies like to flash a bit of gold.'

He laughed. 'Nerida checked his wallet after she knocked him out and he's good for a *bundle of money*,' he added.

Nerida was Darryl's dental nurse, a buxom girl from Brisbane in a white overall and with a love-bite on her neck like sunset over Ayer's Rock. She gave me a conspiratorial smirk.

With a gesture towards the immobilised Nigerian, Darryl resumed, 'I'll charge this bastard about three grand in readies and then I'll bill the NHS.'

It was not difficult for dentists to persuade some newly rich peasant from the Yemen, with a Vuitton case stuffed full of cash, that his life-saving dentistry would only cost a few thousand pounds and that the balance, thanks to Her Majesty's beneficent health service, would be free. Often the dentist got a four-figure tip as well.

I must have looked mildly censorious.

'No sweat, Baz. We all do a bit of double dipping.'

I asked who 'we' were.

'All us Aussies in Pommyland,' the dentist replied, giving his exotic patient, who had groaned a couple of times, another soothing dose of gas. 'We're all members of a little flying club down in Surrey and once a month we take off for Spain where we've all got nice little places in the sun. We bring our wives or our hornbags too, not forgetting a sack or two of cash. There's at least fourteen Australian dentists I know working London at the present period of time with lovely villas down at Benidorm, all built by stupid nig-nogs like this.'

I believed him. A New Zealand girl had told me that there

was an Australian dentist in Fulham who did abortions as well. Darryl confirmed it.

'It's a breeze, Baz,' he declared. 'Just depends which way you tilt the chair.'

Two more Australian dentists, a married couple with impeccable credentials, later crowned my teeth, generously allowing me to live in a small flat next to their surgery free of charge while they did the work. Every morning I awoke with a start and in a cold sweat for it was no alarm clock or rooster that roused me, but the relentless buzzing of the drill as it made its matutinal excavations.

By way of thanks for their hospitality, with its concomitant moments of intense pain, I took my dentist friends for dinner and the theatre. The show was *Company* by Stephen Sondheim at Her Majesty's Theatre. It was far and away the best and most original musical I had ever seen, and is still one of my favourite shows. The star was Elaine Stritch, and her big number the famous 'Ladies Who Lunch'. I bought the LP and some months later back in Melbourne I thought I might play it to my mother, preferably when she was not in a position to turn down the stereo. (I always thought of parents as people who turned down the volume on one's life.) The moment I chose was during a visit by her hairdresser, Miss Eckersley, when my mother would be immobilised in a chair. Although my mother never went out, Miss Eckersley regularly came to the house and spent hours working assiduously on my mother's coiffure.

When I put on the record and turned up the volume, both my mother and Miss Eckersley listened patiently to the whole of Elaine Stritch's incisive rendition of this cynical hymn to the rich women of New York. Only when it was over did my mother give the hairdresser a signal to resume her ministrations, but not before saying, dryly, 'Very nice, Barry, but it's not *The Desert Song*, is it?'

A few years later I saw Sondheim's *A Little Night Music*, that flawless masterpiece of the musical theatre, so filled with melodies that catch the heart. It was a musical transformation of Ingmar Bergman's film *Smiles of a Summer Night*, and captured its poignancy, its eroticism and its regret. No one except Richard Strauss is so good at regret.

My own subsequent adventures in Scandinavia have been coloured by Bergman and Sondheim, and the long summer nights do indeed possess an almost supernatural magic. Once, staying with a house party in a hunting lodge on the Danish island of Fyn, we could barely sleep for the cicada-like din of nightingales singing in the forest, while at dawn we were woken by our fellow guests as through the thin walls came the yelps and expletives of amorous rapture.

In time Stephen Sondheim and I became friends, although we rarely saw each other. On my last big birthday he sent me an acrostic, shown overleaf.

In the years that followed my last dental appointment with the Australian couple I neglected my teeth, believing my magnificent new crowns were sufficient protection, but bad things were happening beneath the Royal Doulton surface of my smile and a New Zealand dental surgeon obliged me to spend a month in Auckland having a 'root resection', which was both painful

Barry –

Aging

Rather

Rapidly

Yet

Holding

Up

Miraculously,

Pumping

Hormones

Relentlessly –

Is

Edna

Sixty?

Happy Birthday and Congratulations!

And love,

Steve

(Sondheim, that is)

and costly. Since then I have spent further hours in dental chairs in London, Melbourne, Chicago, New York and Dallas, not to mention my month of implantations in Vail, Colorado.

The Vail dental practitioner was hopelessly stage-struck and occasionally scored a celebrity. Once he actually scored two at the one time. Shaking me violently awake from a drugged slumber, he introduced me to his other celebrated patient.

'Barry, wake up,' he cried. 'Meet Melanie Griffith.'

No doubt unwillingly cajoled, the lovely actress loomed over me.

'Hi, Barry,' she said, but I could only grin stupidly back with butchered gums, a crimson trickle leaking from a corner of the smile.

DURING my time in Los Angeles at the beginning of the nineties, I was approached several times to do theatre on the West Coast, and actor friends out there, such as Coral Browne, Vincent Price and Roddy McDowall, gave much encouragement to this idea. But still I had cold feet. The networks were hesitant to offer me a series, in spite of the success of the 'specials' they had commissioned, and an Edna film with Disney collapsed after endless meetings, adaptations of tired old scripts, and constant declarations of how 'excited' they all were. I have learnt in Los Angeles that as soon as a film or television executive expresses 'excitement', the project is doomed.

Coral Browne was a Melbourne girl, and a friend of my mother's actress friend Thelma Scott: the only theatrical person of our family's acquaintance. Coral had come to England to further her theatrical career in the early fifties at much the same time as Peter Finch, and she was not only a marvellous actress but an infamous wit and the author of many legendary exchanges. Her vocabulary was at once blunt and imaginative and she was at the height of her celebrity when she married Vincent Price, the star of many horror movies.

Vincent, with his honeyed Missouri accent and his erudition about such varied subjects as art and gastronomy, was the perfect foil for Coral. Once, at a slightly embarrassing reception given for my wife Lizzie and me by Zsa Zsa Gabor – embarrassing because the photographers stationed expectantly at the entrance to Zsa Zsa's Bel Air mansion failed to recognise the guests of honour – Coral, bored and already seriously ill, begged permission to leave early.

Drawing me aside, she said somewhat loudly, 'I hope you don't mind, Barry darling, but Vincent and I are fucking off!'

When she died in 1991 I wrote a scurrilous threnody in a style of which, I hoped, she might have approved. It ended:

Uniquely-minded Queen of Style,
No counterfeit could coin you,
Long may you make the angels smile
Till we all fuck off to join you.

BACK in London after my West Coast stay, I began planning *The Life and Death of Sandy Stone*, the compilation of all my Sandy monologues since 1958. It would be an arduous evening for an audience, but a funny one too, I hoped. The show opened at the Athenaeum Theatre, Melbourne, in late 1990 and toured the continent. It was one of the most enjoyable experiences of my career to impersonate a ghost and sit for the entire evening in an armchair, in a mood of sibilant reminiscence. (Try saying that with a loose denture.)

I published a first volume of my autobiography, *More Please*, in 1992 and in 1995 my novel *Women in the Background*, which a few mischief-makers insisted on describing as a *roman-à-clef*, for it is true that I may have unconsciously woven some autobiographical material into this fiction.

It was in 1997, soon after Sir Les had his own show, *Les Patterson Has a Stand-up: Live and Rampant*, at the Whitehall Theatre, that I had lunch with Jeffrey Archer, the best-selling novelist and politician. Jeffrey had been endlessly pilloried in the Edna television shows, but took it all with extreme equanimity; indeed he seemed to relish the punishment. From wary acquaintances, we became quite good friends and I admired his ability to deal with the hypocrites on both sides of the political fence who resented his extraordinary success and prosperity. Doing well was always his best revenge. I sometimes heard snobbish people in England describe Jeffrey as 'common', and I reflected on the amusing paradox that if he were suddenly transplanted to Australia he would be considered rather too posh!

One day at the Ivy restaurant Jeffrey asked me if I had another West End show in mind. I told him that I was writing *Edna: The Spectacle*, which would be a history of the Australian megastar's career, with a full cast of characters. The songs would parody famous shows such as *Chicago, Annie, Oliver!* and *Gypsy*. Beginning with her convict ancestor transported to the Antipodes for stealing a gladiolus, the narrative would move through the major events of her life. I envisaged an especially touching scene where a child actress – the young Edna – expressed her anguish on discovering that she was irretrievably 'different': the only kid in the world with *naturally* purple hair. Here a song suggested itself:

> *Why am I Mauve?*
> *What is it I lack?*
> *Where'er I rove*
> *I'm always lilac. (et cetera)*

The first act would take Edna to the present, just as she was about to step onto the stage of the Theatre Royal, Haymarket. The second half of the programme would be her solo act, ending with a big chorus number. As I described the show to Lord Archer, I got increasingly carried away. After all, I had spent some time collaborating with a brilliant lyricist, Kit Hesketh-Harvey, and an equally talented composer, James McConnell. All we needed was a backer. To my amazement, Jeffrey offered to finance the entire project. A suitable director was engaged and soon I, and a very large cast, were in rehearsal.

It was only then that someone began to do the necessary arithmetic. Supposing we filled the Haymarket to capacity every night, it would still be an enormously expensive show. Jeffrey, however, seemed unperturbed as the gifted young cast and orchestra prepared for our first out-of-town try-out at Guildford. But the show was long: too long. Cuts were made, songs dropped or truncated. By that time the show had toured to a vast theatre in Plymouth, which only made the sparse audiences look sparser.

We opened at the Haymarket with a special charity performance in the presence of Princess Alexandra. The rest of the audience consisted of parliamentary friends of Jeffrey's – not famous for their sense of humour – and people who had bought tickets to support the charity, not because they necessarily wanted to have a good night out. But it wasn't just the audience. There was something seriously wrong with the show itself. It was one of those events in every artist's life that 'seemed like a good idea at the time'.

The critics, whom I could see leaning forward in the stalls with notebooks and poised pencils, were almost unanimous in disputing the merits of *Edna: The Spectacle*. Nevertheless, and despite the show costing more than double its estimated budget, Jeffrey Archer insisted on supporting it through a hundred performances, although he was by then beleaguered with problems of his own. He was ungrudging in his generosity to me and to this flawed project, and I am pleased to here record my gratitude. We all, to some extent, reinvent ourselves. Jeffrey Archer just went to a lot more trouble, and the British never forgave him for it.

In the wake of these critical objurgations I looked at my career. Actually I had never really thought of it as a career, since a career suggests the idea of evolution and progress, whereas my professional life had been a series of advances and retreats: stagnations and renewals, lulls and surges, doldrums and typhoons. A career could be planned, but my life was the result of chance and improvisation. It was plotless.

Suddenly the idea of America became curiously attractive. Since many of my old television shows had appeared on cable there and John Lahr's backstage profile had attracted considerable interest, there had been inquiries from across the Atlantic. Why not do a modest show in a place such as San Francisco? – no spectacle, no grandiose musical elements, just an old-fashioned Edna tirade with a gladioli finale. But how to set about it?

I called my friend Joan Rivers in New York and told her what I had in mind and she gave me the name of her agent. Three phone calls later and thanks to Bob Duva I was booked for a short engagement in a small theatre off Union Square in San Francisco, where I decided to present, with local references added, a show I had tried out a couple of years before in the English provinces. It became *Dame Edna: The Royal Tour*. I felt fairly confident of a modest success even if the audience consisted only of row upon row of unnaturally healthy men in black leather. I knew I would look across the footlights and behold the Village People, but if I ran long enough they might even bring their mothers and sisters. Some people force themselves to have low expectations; mine come naturally. But by happy coincidence I was leaving London just as it was becoming expensive, dirty and dangerous: a melting pot where nothing melts.

A one-month-long season turned into a four-month run

and I was still playing to full houses. There were even women in the audience!

One evening the San Francisco chapter of the Australian Chamber of Commerce announced that they were coming to the show and made a large block booking. On the same night I was also informed that members of the local transvestites' society would fill the other half of the theatre, just across the central aisle from the Chamber of Commerce chapter. Since I always have the lights at 50 per cent in the auditorium in order to spot victims, the stalls presented a bizarre sight. On the left were the worthy Australian businessmen in suits and ties, with their nicely dressed wives; and on the right, an astounding group of exotic cross-dressers elaborately coiffed and in daring *décolleté*, in the guises of Mae West, Tina Turner, Marilyn Monroe and Judy Garland. They were accompanied by an assortment of androgynous walkers, gigolos and cicisbeos, who screamed and embraced their partners at all of Edna's jokes and joined vigorously in the songs, which they must have learnt by heart on previous visits to the show.

With audiences of this orientation in mind I had specially written a song for Dame Edna extolling the merits of her bachelor son, Kenny, who designs all her clothes and who is still waiting for Miss Right. Edna's song was a Ditty of Denial:

Mothers should never have a favourite
You have to love your children just the same
But I happen to be one with a very special son
And if I spoil him I hope I'm not to blame.

He was always slightly different from the others
And in Australia being different is a crime
He collected most of Melbourne's out-of-print
        Broadway albums
And took night classes in macramé and mime.

Yet as mothers do I worried and I fretted
That my darling and his roommate might be freaks
And my fears reached their zenith when my
        talented son Kenneth
Took an interest in the opera and antiques
But my worst forebodings quite evaporate
Now I'm in the city of the Golden Gate.

Chorus:
I never thought that I would see so many
Friends of Kenny
I never thought I'd see so many men
Exactly like my Ken
I always thought his peer group
Was a very slightly queer group
Members of a strange exotic clique
He's a favourite of the women's
Just like Richard Simmons*
And if you met him you would know
        he's not unique.

---

*A celebrated American television fitness guru, as yet unmarried.

To my amazement this simple music hall song, complete with sing-along choruses, became a gay anthem, and 'Friends of Kenny' T-shirts began to appear, proudly worn, in the Castro District. Such is the fate of the satirist.

ON THE strength of my success in San Francisco I received an offer to come to Broadway. Not Off-Broadway this time, but the Great White Way itself, and the ideal intimate theatre – the Booth on 45th Street – was proposed for the fall of 1999.

I had been busy writing a new show for Australia with a title inspired by one of my mother's more popular cautionary phrases: *Remember You're Out!* She often said this to my sister and me at public entertainments when it looked as though we might, just possibly, misbehave. I always liked to assail my theatre patrons with my mother's old, familiar admonitions, since in Australia, at least, parents spoke a common inhibitory language; and moreover it was an essential part of the infantalising of the audience.

My friend Harley Medcalf, who produced my Australian shows, begged me to exclude the character of Les Patterson from this offering, since Les had evolved into such a coprolalic misogynist that his presence in the show would alienate the Edna fans. It was with this in mind that I had given Les his own show at the Whitehall Theatre. However, the preparations for the Olympic Games in Sydney had produced many bureaucratic scandals, and a large number of Les look-alikes with influential friends on the Games committee were flying around the world on huge expense accounts, making fools of themselves. It was an irresistible opportunity to offer the Patterson point of view, so instead of putting him in the program I had him gate-crash the new show, with a brief outburst and song on the theme of perks, kickbacks and clandestine gratuities. He was then forcibly removed from the stage. It worked very nicely and the topicality of the interruption charmed even the most censorious old ladies.

At the conclusion of my Australian season I flew back to New York and began previews of *Dame Edna: The Royal Tour* in September 1999. The producer was convinced that two devices that had worked so well in England – namely, the invitation extended by Dame Edna to two audience members to enjoy a meal on stage, and the dressing up of other patrons as members of the British Royal Family – would be disastrous on Broadway. However, I bullied him into reluctant submission, and naturally he was proved wrong.

The mood, this time, was auspicious. After the first night the producers insisted on a party at Sardi's theatrical restaurant, a few minutes from the stage door. I had a chilling remembrance of the after-show party for *Housewife-Superstar!* in 1977, when I left a room of revelling strangers at midnight to read the reviews in the office upstairs and returned to find the restaurant had emptied.

This time around, it seemed, I had a success. Dame Edna's caricature, and mine, were added to Sardi's gallery of theatrical legends, and a touching poetic reflection appended:

I had my fame; ovations were my solace
Now fame is just a withered gladiolus.

Among those present at the first-night revels were the nonagenarian artist Al Hirschfeld and his wife, and the considerably younger actress Zoe Caldwell, whom I had not seen since we toured country Victoria together in *Twelfth Night* nearly half a century before.

On opening night things might have gone otherwise, for Dame Edna's eagle eye fell on a woman in the third row who was somewhat ostentatiously dressed and wore dark glasses throughout the performance. That evening Edna made innumerable jokes about pretentious people who insist on affecting sunglasses indoors, so that this unfortunate audience member became inducted into the Dame's little 'cast' of unpaid supporting actors. During the finale there is a moment when about four or five of these 'chosen ones' are summoned onto the stage for a profane benediction of embarrassment, at which time they are whisked into the wings and disguised as members of the British Royal Family, thereafter taking their bows to wild acclaim. When Edna beckoned little 'Four Eyes' – she of the dark glasses – a worrying silence fell on the previously jolly audience. The lady rose from her seat, but unsteadily, and made her way to the aisle. As she did so, I saw to my horror that she held a *white stick* in her grasp. Dame Edna begged her to return to her seat, but Four Eyes was not to be deterred and defiantly mounted the steps to the stage. By now the audience was deathly quiet and it was not a silence any comedian would welcome on a first night, or any other. I decided, since I had nothing to lose, that only some word or gesture of sublime effrontery or appalling taste could save the situation.

Happily the lady seemed to be having a good time as she wobbled across the stage towards Edna's frozen embrace.

'I know what you're all thinking,' said the Dame. 'How am I going to get out of this one?' (Sardonic titter from the audience.) 'Well, possums, I'm wondering just the same thing!' (Healthier titter.)

Dame Edna led Four Eyes gently towards the wings.

'Now be a good girl,' said Edna to her blind guest, who was by this time laughing, 'and one of my little Ednaettes will help you into a beautiful frock.'

Then, as Four Eyes gave Edna a sporting hug, I took the supreme risk. 'All I can say, Four Eyes, is: *thank heavens you didn't bring the dog*!'

The audience exploded with laughter and the show was saved. It was the closest call I have ever experienced in the theatre, and those present had the rare delight of watching Dame Edna squirm.

NOTAPROBLEM

~

It is a remarkable fact that
women often make sensible suggestions
when they least intend to do so
NORMAN DOUGLAS

AFTER a ten-month run on Broadway we went on the road, and I saw more of the United States and Canada in the subsequent year than most North Americans have. Well-intentioned people looked very worried when I said we were going to places such as Minneapolis, Clearwater and Detroit.

'It's a New York show,' friends said. 'Don't go to the Midwest because they *just won't get it.*'

Luckily they were wrong. I had heard those voices all my professional life, for hadn't they told me in Melbourne in the fifties never to play Sydney? And hadn't friends in Sydney advised me to avoid Perth because my show was 'too East Coast'? They had sometimes been right, those well-meaning folk, and it had taken me over ten years to catch on in England, and even longer in America. But I took the risk, and thought that if I spoke slowly, and loudly enough, even the sorely maligned Midwest of

America might like to laugh as heartily as anyone else.

As it happened there was nowhere on my itinerary that I did not hugely enjoy, with the possible exception of Atlantic City. I had not visited Toronto since the early sixties when I went there with little Davy Jones to join the cast of *Oliver!*, and I was amazed to discover a changed city. I was there in the month just before Christmas, as I had been on that far-off former visit. Then my producer, David Merrick, had put me in a small back room at a venerable hotel near the railway station. This time I had a suite in the front of the same building. But it is remarkable how excruciatingly uncomfortable even very nice hotels can become after a few weeks' sojourn. There are a thousand vexations that even regular ovations and the hyperbole of critics fail to ameliorate.

Every night after work I would climb into bed and find that the sheets and blankets reached just above my navel. This is because hotel housekeeping is staffed by charming Filipinas who make up the beds to accommodate their own diminutive proportions. I would yank at the bedclothes ferociously but they always seemed to be stapled to the bottom of the mattress. A final tug dislodged them completely and I would spend the rest of the night amidst vagrant bedding, prey to icy draughts.

This is not a criticism of a fine Canadian hotel. I am merely describing conditions that exist everywhere when one is living and working on the road.

I stopped remonstrating with housekeeping because they only parrot the standard and enraging 'Notaproblem.' Notaproblem is now a universal mantra and it absolves its user from any obligation to do a bloody thing. I prefer the more genial Australian usage 'No worries' because it doesn't patronisingly discount the fact that I have a problem. It merely suggests that I may have a problem but it's not worth worrying about.

Then there is always the mini-bar. Less-itinerant members of the human race may need to know that a mini-bar is a small locked refrigerator hidden in most hotel rooms and containing miniature bottles of alcohol, heavily chlorinated mineral water and tempting confectionery all priced at ten times their street value. Since I don't drink booze or devour nocturnal Mars Bars, I never visit the mini-bar. That does not stop the mini-bar inspector from barging in at inconvenient times to monitor my alcoholism and hyperglycaemia and to perform his noisy tally. In this Toronto hotel there is a $20 charge for clearing the mini-bar, which, being a stingy comic, I refuse to pay. Even if the mini-bar were empty at my request, they would still come around at inappropriate moments to verify the anomaly.

Like most people, I don't like to be woken by the telephone in the middle of the night, but I have a lot of friends who live in England, Australia and elsewhere, some of them quite clever people, who seem to think North America is in their time zone and blithely give me a tinkle at 4 a.m. In response to my croaked, 'Who's this?', they usually say, 'What time is it?', and then apologise at unnecessary length.

Most hotel phones have something called voicemail, which means that an untimely caller can record a message. A red light then starts flashing on your bedside extension, letting you know you've had a call. Did I say a light? It's a beacon; it is a warning to low-flying aircraft. It fills your bedroom with pulsating crimson; it's like sleeping with an ambulance.

I call the operator. Actually she's not an operator, she's Lori, the Customer Care Advocate.

'I know I have voicemail,' I say, 'but I can't sleep with that flashing light. I've tried draping it with socks and underpants but it beams through the cracks.'

'Notaproblem,' Lori replies.

'But it IS a problem. I can't sleep!'

The Advocate puts me on hold while she dials her supervisor. I listen to a robot-voiced woman telling me that my call is important to them. Loudly in the background is a lugubrious arrangement of 'Hey Jude' for cornet and synthesiser, badly off pitch.

After what seems to be an eternity, Luanda, the supervisor, comes on the line. She explains that the light will only go off after I listen to all my voicemail, beginning with the thirteen messages I've failed to erase over the past week. Most of these include the sound of people slamming down the phone because they've got my voicemail followed by ten minutes of accidentally recorded hold music. Each message is followed by a series of options: save, delete, replay, forward to another extension or press pound to return to the previous menu, requiring me to strike various buttons on the phone, hoping pound and hash are the same thing.

None of this is easy at 4.45 a.m. and if I have failed to jab the correct button through this long procedure, the red light continues triumphantly to cast its ruddy beams around the room like a revolving bordello.

I call the Customer Care Advocate once more.

'Is there a charge for destroying my telephone?' I gently ask.

Lori starts to say 'Notaproblem', but by then the morning light over Lake Ontario is knifing through the gaps in the curtain and I'm awake for good. Just as well, since there is someone thumping on the door wanting to know at what time did I intend to remove the 'Do Not Disturb' sign.

My dealings with the Customer Care Advocate reminded me of a Christmas vacation some years ago on the Cobourg Peninsula beside the Timor Sea. It was a very new resort owned by a consortium of Sydney lawyers, so I hoped it was losing money. The brochure informed me that I was a member of 'the Guest Community' and my room was called 'a habitat'. It wasn't solely mine, however, for a large number of animals, reptilian and arachnidan, also regarded it as theirs.

On Christmas Eve I called the front desk to ask if the housekeeping staff could please remove the huge iguana that had lodged itself in a cosy nook behind the mini-bar. The creature appeared to be absorbing a small wallaby and was preparing to light a post-digestive cigarette.

'No worries,' said Merv, the night manager. 'But we don't have "staff" here, mate. Give us your habitat number and I'll send around a member of the Host Community.'

My friend Amy Tan in San Francisco has offered me a few warnings about hotel rooms and their many health risks. Amy is a very clean girl and knows the perils of living in accommodations that many have shared. She tells me that the most germ-infested object in a hotel room is not the telephone receiver, the mattress or even the toilet seat. The instrument most pullulating with bacteria, fizzing with invisible contamination, is the television remote control! What unspeakable conjectures this information inspires, as with latex gloves I click from the adult channel to a midnight showing of *Springtime in the Rockies*.

FINDING somewhere decent to eat while on tour was always a nightmare, and I usually discovered the ideal restaurant about a day before I was due to leave town. I was lucky in Toronto and Minneapolis, less fortunate in Detroit, and in Atlantic City I starved. This once rather grand and romantic Lido of New Jersey is now Chernobyl-sur-Mer. The only attractive people to be seen are a few Russian waitresses who probably think Atlantic City is beautiful because it reminds them of a Black Sea resort in the bad old days. Hooters, a chain restaurant noteworthy for its large-breasted serving girls, is its classiest joint by far.

Elsewhere the touring comedian finds himself sitting glumly, and more often than not alone, in a pretentious, under-lit and overpriced brasserie, pleading for fish that has been cooked and not just thawed, for soup that is more soup than hot cream and, above all, for a drink without ice. In Fort Lauderdale I lived in a splendid suite facing the sea. The only vexation was a regular crashing noise outside my bedroom door. It proved to be a giant ice-making machine in the corridor, serving the entire floor and enabling guests to reduce the temperature of their drinks to freezing point at all hours of the day and night. It was a surreal fulfilment of Auden's ominous lines:

The glacier knocks in the cupboard,
The desert sighs in the bed,
And the crack in the tea-cup opens
A lane to the land of the dead.

Since I often had to seek restaurant guidance from the hotel concierge, I was frequently directed to fancy joints that went in for synchronised *cloches*. Just as the waiter was preparing, at a signal from his colleague, to lift the metal cover off my dish to reveal the miserable hand-arranged scraps of nouvelle cuisine 'presented' thereunder – *rillettes of Oklahoma corn-fed hare on a bed of baby Puerto Rican parsnips, perfumed with Nantucket fennel and with a dairy-free Roquefort and quince emulsion in a burdock and borage jus, and finished with a roasted garlic and white chocolate custard* – I took malicious delight in whipping off the lid myself, just to spite the waiters.

Alas, these little fits of petulance and borderline bastardry frequently assail the professional clown when he has been away from home too long. No one takes himself more seriously than a comedian.

ALTHOUGH I had toured many times in Australia, England and even Germany and Scandinavia, I had forgotten how many hours are consumed by the exigencies of publicity. The press conferences, the interviews and the radio and television shows are endless, often requiring a dawn colloquy in full costume at a remote TV studio, with a journalist in a bad toupee and his vivacious co-anchor, who hate each other off camera.

I had also forgotten how much research and rewriting was necessary in each city. There were local celebrities who must be substituted for the ones who got a laugh in the last town. Many of these names and topical references were woven into songs, so whole verses and choruses had to be reconstituted and new rhymes found for them. Then I had to relearn them, often as I travelled after a Sunday performance in, say, Houston to my next engagement on Tuesday in Denver. The reader will not be surprised to learn that not seldom I forgot where I was, and I once said 'Goodnight, Boston!' to a Seattle audience, and 'I'm thrilled to be in Florida' to the bewildered theatregoers of Detroit.

Opening nights are trying under any circumstances, but an opening night in a strange city every two or three weeks for ten months takes its toll. Sometimes a group of theatre-lovers, or a local charitable organisation that has bought a large block of tickets, invite me to join them in the foyer for an after-show reception. If I attend these functions as myself they are almost always disappointed, and occasionally resentful. This is understandable. They don't know who I am. It's Edna they want to see, so Edna sometimes graciously moves amongst them, posing for photographs with intoxicated aldermen, bedizened committee ladies and bored Corporate Sponsors who probably wanted to leave the show halfway through Act I.

We toured through heatwaves, blizzards and floods of biblical proportions. In Houston we had barely opened when it started to rain and after forty-eight hours it was still raining. A huge stormwater drain burst below the theatre, flooding the entire basement. Fortunately Dame Edna's exotic wardrobe was on the second floor, but the waters rose all over the city and a state of emergency was declared. It continued to rain for the next two weeks and the rest of the season was cancelled. The swollen bayous marooned our set in Houston and I got out on the first available plane to sunny Denver and another opening night with no scenery, just me in a followspot in front of the curtain. But thanks to my brilliant stage management, especially James Gibbs and Michelle Trimble, it was almost the best reception I received on the tour. So much for two truckloads of extraneous fripperies. What they don't see, they don't miss.

I enjoyed the variety of American cities, and their sudden surprises: the unexpected perfume of linden blossom that suffuses Denver in June and – intensely nostalgic for any Australian – the sweet reek of blooming pittosporum hedges, which in March spread their waxy fragrance over Beverly Hills and the hills of Holmby.

Amongst the towns I played in Florida, Palm Beach was the most amusing. It was still very much as it must have been in the thirties when Joseph Hergesheimer described it in *Tropical Winter* and Cecil Beaton sketched its wealthier inhabitants. New Yorkers who wintered there invited me to lunches at the Bath and Tennis Club, and parties at the Everglades. Many of the ladies attending the show outshone even Dame Edna in their finery, and more jewels and sequins glittered in the audience than ever coruscated on stage. When it seemed that the performance might soon be drawing to a close, many of the older, richer women rose and began to make their laborious way to the exits; but Dame Edna stopped them in their tracks by fixing them with a spotlight, accusing them of gross discourtesy and insisting that they must be hurrying off to their safe deposits to return their jewellery. It is unlikely that the cream of old Palm Beach society, which has never sat through a show to the end, was ever so publicly admonished.

Following our tour across North America, and sometimes appearing at every performance, were groupies and 'Edna-heads'. Most distinguished amongst the Dame's devotees, and one who appeared unexpectedly in cities as far-flung as Vancouver, and even waterlogged Houston, was that famous New York interior decorator and most charming of men, Mario Buatta: the Prince of Chintz. I began to look upon him as my lucky mascot, and he probably holds the record for having attended more performances than any other individual, beating the songstress Christine Lavin, actress Helen Hunt, composer Stephen Sondheim, comedienne Carol Burnett and Henry Kissinger.

ONE OF the delights of touring is the chance to visit out of the way used-book stores in the hope of some *frisson bibliographique*. In a glorified thrift shop in a suburb of Phoenix, Arizona, I came across a dusty set of *The Spirit Lamp*, the undergraduate magazine 'without news' that Lord Alfred

Douglas edited while at Oxford, several copies being inscribed by Douglas himself. In Philadelphia I discovered a scrapbook of unpublished articles by one of my favourites, Edgar Saltus, of whom Oscar Wilde once said to Amelie Rives, 'Passion struggles with grammar on every page.' Amongst these Saltusian gems was an account – hitherto overlooked by all 450 of Oscar Wilde's biographers – of a visit by Saltus and Wilde to a New York clairvoyant in January 1882, when her maid mistook the formidable Irish aesthete for Buffalo Bill! The psychic, scoring an impressive two out of three prophecies, predicted that Oscar would marry, write a very successful play and perform the role of Hamlet. Wilde, on leaving, expressed great doubts about his matrimonial prospects, but added that if he ever played Hamlet it would have to be in Australia. Alas, my great-grandparents were denied the pleasure of this performance.

A few months after Oscar was born in Sydney, my wife and I were at a gathering in London when a flamboyant woman sailed up to me and said with the trace of an Australian accent, 'I'm so pleased you've named your little boy after my father-in-law.'

'There must be some mistake,' I protested. 'I don't believe we have met, and I certainly haven't met your father-in-law.'

The lady laughed. 'Oh, he passed away in 1900. I never met him either, but I'm sure he would be pleased to hear that you had named your Oscar after him.'

I was still none the wiser, so she explained.

'My name's Thelma and I'm from Melbourne, like you are. In the late thirties I was a secretary – not a "personal assistant", a plain, honest-to-goodness secretary. Then I got a job in the Hill of Content bookshop in Melbourne. Did you know it?'

'I certainly did,' I averred. 'It's still there.'

She went on. 'Well, in early thirty-eight I went to the Old Country like we all did, and I got stuck there by the war. During the blackout we used to go to each other's places and huddle around the wireless in the dark, listening to Churchill's speeches. It was, well, rather cosy.'

I pictured the scene as she resumed.

'One night after the all-clear, we were listening in – still in the dark – when I felt a warm hand on my knee. No silk stockings then, not even black-market rayon. Well, for some reason I didn't mind. When the lights went on I saw this rather nice-looking older man – quite a bit older actually. I couldn't help laughing to myself when he said his name was Vyvyan. But he wasn't a sissy, Barry. Far from it. He was a fast worker too, and funny. We women go for funny men.' Thelma looked at me meaningfully. 'Only when we knew each other really well did he tell me that he was O.W.'s son.'

'O.W.?' from me.

'Yes, Oscar Wilde. Vyvyan changed his name to Holland when O.W. went to jail.'

I was gobsmacked. Could this nice Aussie woman in full bloom, if not the first bloom of youth, be the daughter-in-law of that legendary, almost mythological figure? Thelma Holland and I became friends, and when we lunched together in one of the new Knightsbridge brasseries the following week, she ordered an 'O.W. special' – one part green chartreuse and one part yellow chartreuse. Towards the end of our lunch she held my hand across the table.

'I can tell that you're like me, Barry,' she confided with a rush of frankness, no doubt inspired by the O.W. specials. 'You don't believe those horrible stories about O.W. either!'

I wasn't sure what Thelma meant. 'What stories?' I asked.

'Oh, you know. Those foul stories Montgomery Hyde put about saying that O.W. was *one of them*.' Thelma made an eloquent limp-wristed gesture.

'You mean,' I said, 'that you don't think that Oscar was homosexual? What about the trials? What about all the other . . . well . . . evidence?'

'All hearsay, Barry, as you well know. All slanders spread by that ghastly Monty Hyde. Let's have another special, shall we?'

I realised with amazement that this delightful countrywoman of mine, with her background of Melbourne and the Methodist Church, had throughout her long sojourn in London, and a happy marriage to the son of Oscar Wilde, remained impervious to all suggestions that her late father-in-law might not have been as most other men.

AFTER the show comes the 'third act', and in Los Angeles it always had a large and heterogeneous cast. The third act is that period after curtain fall when friends and acquaintances come backstage and mingle in the artiste's dressing-room. For the weary performer this is always the most arduous act of all, as his backstage visitors are still in a passive 'We're here to be entertained' mode, often standing in a semicircle saying nothing, while the actor, make-up only half erased, and in his dressing-gown, still feels obliged to give value for money.

In the old days when I had a full bar in the dressing-room and a fridge full of snacks, I would entertain for hours anyone who cared to drop by. A well-tipped stage doorman named Eddie or Dougie or Teddy would be happy to doze off in his small, overheated lodge for hours while the star and his guests caroused somewhere in the bowels of the theatre. At first I knew who the people in my dressing-room were, and they could always be sure of full glasses as they continued to lavish praise upon the show. Often, however, as the night wore on, I would notice that the 'friends' lolling on my sofa and enjoying my largesse were total strangers; and the later the hour, the less my guests seemed to like my performance. Some of them hadn't even been to the show.

Now my backstage hospitality is, to say the least, stingy, and I can never wait to get out of the theatre. However, on my American tour I decided it would be fun to relaunch that venerable institution the third act. On a typical evening after the show in Los Angeles my dressing-room contained Mario Buatta, Peggy Lee's daughter, my nephew's wife's brother, Larry Hagman and Linda Gray, Tracey Ullman, three unknown men as gay as New Year's Eve, and Goldie Hawn. Half a bottle of Edna Valley Chardonnay from a distinguished Californian vineyard did not go far.

MY Los Angeles season of *The Royal Tour* was memorable because of the film folk who attended. When one of Edna's female victims, a spry octogenarian, was summoned on stage at the end of the show to help with the finale, the audience applauded vociferously. The lady turned out to be Ann Rutherford, Scarlett O'Hara's younger sister in *Gone with the Wind*. Rarely does Dame Edna – or I – ever quite know what the fuss is about when television personalities, Broadway babes, veteran actresses and rock stars are enticed onto the stage. On numerous occasions in New York and on tour, Dame Edna picked out men and women whom the audience immediately recognised but she did not.

There was a decisive evening when Judy Badame, my dresser, told me that someone called David E. Kelley was in the audience. It was explained to me who he was – the creator of those television phenomena on legal themes, *The Practice* and *Ally McBeal*.

'Edna would be great on *Ally McBeal*,' declared Judy.

Taking her word for it, I persuaded the woman I inhabit, as Graham Greene described Edna, to mention on stage her litigation with her 'manager', Barry Humphries. 'I think I'll go to little Ally McBeal for an opinion.'

The Dame's seed fell, it seems, on fertile soil, and thanks to Mr Kelley I spent the first four months of the year 2002 playing a role playing a role. That is to say, Dame Edna has become an actress on an innovative television comedy–drama, and my own name is nowhere to be found in the credits. Perhaps this might properly be called 'meta-acting'. No longer a comic turn,

Dame Edna is an actress or, as politically correct actresses like to be called, an Actor.

The cast of *Ally McBeal* were young, gifted and thin; some, by the standards of Rubens and Renoir, might even have been described as spindly. Edna was by far the oldest and fattest participant and resembled a Botero that had strayed into an exhibition of Giacomettis. But she now feels sufficiently liberated to embark on a series of one-woman shows impersonating American female achievers such as Eleanor Roosevelt, Emily Dickinson and Oprah Winfrey, without neglecting her classical repertoire: Phaedra, Lady Macbeth, Medea and her *tour de force*, Edna Gabler.

DUSK

~

Everyone has loved and been
loved for a while. We lie about this and pretend
it was otherwise. We want some other
love than the one we had, some other history.
But we have loved and been loved

HAROLD BRODKEY

'HEY, Bazza, I seen on the TV yer goin' over pretty well with the Seppos!'

'The who?' said I, thinking I might have misheard my Sydney taxi driver.

'The Seppos – you know, the *septic tanks*. The Yanks!'

'I suppose so,' I said, pleased. 'Yes, I suppose I am.'

'Make the most of it, mate, while those bloody Seppos still reckon yer funny.'

The sardonic humour of an Australian cab driver almost always hits the nail on the head. A comedian is fortunate if his fame outlives him; too many fall by the wayside.

In my youth the most screamingly funny American comedian was Danny Kaye, whose films and recordings had us all in stitches. But when I listen to him today, although I can recognise his gifts and admire his slapstick energy and versatility, I rarely laugh. Similarly with the British music hall turns I would hear on the radio as a child. Recorded in the twenties and thirties of last century, the performances seem corny, even poignantly so; and no comedian really sets out to be poignant. Styles in comedy, as in eroticism, come and go. Last year's turn-on is often today's detumescence.

Having found my way into Madame Tussaud's, where Dame Edna's effigy has now reposed since the early eighties, I occasionally experience the nightmare of being melted down. When they first honoured the Dame by placing her on exhibition at that famous attraction, I wondered who had been summarily displaced. Perhaps a whole sixties rock group, a discredited politician or an insufficiently titillating serial killer? If one is reconstituted from the kneecaps of, say, the Pretty Things, Ho Chi Minh or Adolf Eichmann, what similar indignity lies ahead for me? It is a fine thing to be wax, but to wane . . . ?

My parents' bedroom door was almost always ajar, and at first I assumed this was because they could better hear their children calling for glasses of water or whimpering in the throes of a nightmare. When I was older, I supposed that this abandonment of their privacy was in order that they might more easily detect our tardy footfalls on the staircase as we returned later, and in my case *much* later, than the promised hour.

Every night, before retiring, touchingly unabashed and in

full view from the upstairs hallway, my mother and father would kneel on either side of their bed and pray. My father's prayers were always much longer than my mother's somewhat perfunctory communions with her Maker, and I egotistically believed that this was all due to me. Before the age of counselling, I imagined that my father was beseeching the Great Family Therapist in the Sky to intercede on behalf of his delinquent son.

My father was a member of the church vestry, and was constantly asked to contribute money and the services of his workmen to maintain the church's perpetually leaking roof.

'They're just using you, Eric. I hope you realise that. They're taking advantage of your good heart.' My mother had little time for Canon Hopkinson, whom she described as 'prosy', which we took to mean long-winded and sanctimonious. It was even whispered that life at the vicarage was less than harmonious, and belied the somewhat unctuous demeanour that the Canon displayed to us all on Sundays. In Norman Douglas's phrase, 'He was a good man in the wrong sense of the word.'

I came home from school early one day and was surprised to see Dennis Hopkinson, the vicar's eldest son, leaving our house. He must have been about twenty-five, and it was rumoured that he and his pious father, in particular, did not see eye to eye.

'What did Dennis want?' I asked my mother. I could see she was extremely irritated.

'Don't tell your father I told you, Barry, but he's after

more money. Your father is such a soft touch and that horrible boy knows it.'

'Is my father lending him money?' I asked disingenuously.

My mother explained that the vicar's son was a compulsive gambler and owed a great deal of money to some bookmakers, who were threatening him with violence if he didn't cough up. My father had apparently paid them off several times before, but the demands continued and my father was the only person the Hopkinson boy could appeal to.

'I've got a good mind to let that old hypocrite know what kind of a son he's got,' declared my mother. 'Don't forget, Barry, a gambler is far, far worse than a drinker!'

It was not only my father's benevolence to people outside the family circle that riled my mother, but that support he gave to his own siblings. Two of his brothers, Lewis and Leslie, worked for him in his building business, and my mother often spoke of them as idle freeloaders exploiting my father's good nature. 'Users' was the epithet she frequently applied to the recipients of my father's largesse. It must have been extremely difficult – even agonising – for him to bear this constantly reiterated complaint impugning the diligence, even the honesty, of his brothers, but he did. Not once did I hear him protest, although one could never tell what went on in the office.

Amongst my mother's large repertoire of phrases, both cautionary and inhibitory, was that admonition 'Stop drawing attention to yourself!' Once, as she sat on the beach rug staring fixedly at the sea, I heard her quietly observe, 'I'm afraid Eric is drawing attention to himself again.' I looked, yet all I could see was my father engaged in some innocent horseplay a little further down the beach, chasing Michael with a bucket of water.

I always vowed I would never inflict upon my own children any of my parents' discouraging platitudes, which no doubt they had inherited from their own parents. A favourite of my mother's, of course, was always: 'Barry [sigh], you used to be *such a nice boy.*' If there is anything to support the theory, popular in some academic circles, that Dame Edna derives from my mother, one of the Dame's characteristic remarks might well be cited. Addressing a mature woman in the audience she once said, as if bestowing a tremendous compliment, 'How lovely to talk to you. *I bet you were once quite an attractive woman too!*' Naturally my mother never made such a remark, but she just might have.

My mother certainly transmitted contradictory signals. On the one hand, she was parsimonious with her praise, so that I could never really be certain if what I did best met with her approval. Beneath this also lay the chilling doubt about whether I was really unconditionally loved. And yet she paid for special classes, including my art class at the George Bell Studio every Saturday morning – about which she asked no questions, although it was a life class and at every lesson I was confronted with a different, provocatively naked young model. She bought me a subscription to *Art News*, an expensive American periodical that championed the New York avant-garde. And she also subsidised my driving lessons without my father's knowledge. Not that my father did not indulge me too. Amongst other things he, who had in the past expropriated 'improper' books from my small library, provided me with an account at Robertson & Mullens, a venerable city bookshop, enabling me to order any book I wanted and charge it to him.

Christmas presents could be specified in advance, or at least firmly suggested, and I always knew where my parents concealed these expensive gifts. Often if one of my Christmas presents happened to be a set of gramophone records – in those days 78 recordings sometimes came in substantial albums – I might have secretly listened to the music several times before Christmas Day, rather spoiling my own surprise. Under the circumstances it is odd that I did not think of myself as a spoilt child, although such I was.

During the run of my Broadway show we lived in an Upper East Side hotel suite and for a time Oscar, then nineteen years old, stayed with us. There were certain house rules that he was meant to observe, but these were relaxed on weekends when he sometimes went clubbing with friends. Nonetheless a curfew of 1 a.m. was set for Friday and Saturday, which he did not always observe. Only as I sat up in bed trying to read at 2.30 in the morning, listening intently for the sound of a key in the front door or a footfall in the hall, did my mind flash back to my own adolescence. I recalled the agony of tiptoeing up the stairs and creeping past my parents' room. Would I make it to my bedroom without their light snapping on and my father's voice plaintively calling, 'Is that you, Barry?', followed by my mother's, 'Do you realise what time it is? Your father and I have been worried sick'? And then, inevitably, *'This is not a hotel, you know!'*

As I lay awake at the end of the twentieth century waiting

for my own son to come home, I felt myself reaching back through the years to my mother and father and begging their forgiveness. Now at last I know how you felt, dear parents.

The next morning I confronted Oscar at the breakfast table. In fact it was the luncheon table since he was rarely up by noon on weekends. I wanted to explain to him in a modern and civilised way how I felt and how I expected him to behave. After all, I was a very different person from my parents. I was a friend to my children, not a reproachful voice from the dark laying upon them some ineradicable burden of guilt.

I began to say, 'Have you any idea what time you came home last night?' But I stopped myself. I bit my tongue. 'We have a rule here, Oscar,' I said gently, instead, 'and if this is going to work, I want you to stick to it. Do you know what time it was you came home last night?'

Christ, I had said it! Or was it really me who had said it, or my father who inhabits me?

My son just looked down ruefully at his cereal. What could I say next that was firm, yet caring, something that could bring us closer, something helpful and 'appropriate', to use that repellent neologism?

'I hope you know that you can't come and go at all hours of the night. This is not a hotel, my boy.'

Oscar looked at me for a moment and then said, 'Actually, Dad, this *is* a hotel!'

I sat there speechless, immobilised. For verily in the shadows of that rented kitchen in Sutton Place stood Eric Humphries, the ventriloquial ghost.

Why all this anxiety over one's children?

Your mother's worried sick.

I hope you know you're killing your father!

My brilliant son Rupert is rambling around South America, before going to Edinburgh University to read philosophy. According to his enterprising itinerary, he ought to be in Uruguay now and I wonder when I might receive the ransom demand or the severed ear in the envelope.

They'll manage very nicely on their own soon enough, I gloomily reflect.

Had I forgotten that when I was a child I always half envied neglected kids? To be neglected was to come home at any old hour, to be thrillingly liberated, to run barefoot down mean streets with a rattling billycart. To be no longer spotless, and never, ever to be 'groomed'.

'You shouldn't play with that boy, Barry,' said my mother of a child known to live in a pejorative suburb. 'He's never nicely groomed.' She lingered cooingly on the 'oo' of that brushed and brilliantined word.

I MARVEL that my tastes in art and music, formed in earliest youth, persist until today. Sometimes they recede, go underground like certain streams, to re-emerge more strongly than before in later life. My old Melbourne bookseller Mrs Bird once sold me three blue volumes published in the twenties by Martin Secker, the collected poems of Arthur Symons, which I devoured avidly at the time. This English symbolist, friend of Verlaine,

Conder and Yeats, wrote verses of a hothouse eroticism that could not fail to intoxicate any adolescent, suburban aesthete. He inspired, in part, Max Beerbohm's wicked caricature of the 'decadent' poet Enoch Soames, whose name is an approximate homonym of Symons. Later, in my twenties and thirties, I repudiated this youthful appetite for Swinburnian langours, just as I ceased to enjoy the musical meanderings of Frederick Delius and the perversity of Beardsley's drawings. Then these passions – for such they were – connected me to a conjectural Europe; now they put me in touch with my past.

Today the seductive companions of my young self are my friends again. In my library hangs Augustus John's portrait of Symons, made before the end of the First World War. John in his memoirs tells us that Symons, who never fully recovered from a mental breakdown in 1908, was agitated throughout the sitting, dreading an imminent aerial bombardment. In my portrait the poet, who was to live for another quarter of a century, sits apprehensively listening for an enemy Zeppelin.

In an Australian suburb, at the age of eighteen, I played the music of Delius and Vaughan Williams on the gramophone and dreamt of England. Now, so often in reluctant exile, I hear 'Summer Night on the River' and it is Melbourne's Yarra I picture in my mind's eye, down by Macauley's boatshed at the end of Molesworth Street, Kew. Here, some way above Dight's Falls, breathing the mossy, mulchy riverbank smells, I would often trail my fingers in the purling, topaz-coloured water, as Mr van Senden, my friend Richard's father, vigorously paddled us upstream beneath tresses of willow and river gum. After such idyllic loiterings the journey home by lumbering tram was like being jolted from some exquisite dream.

I must have spent nearly a year of my life sitting, or standing, in a Melbourne tram. They were painted cream and green then, a colour combination suggested by a member of the public in the thirties when the Melbourne Tramways Board held a design competition. Today these comfortable vehicles still ply the city streets and rumble across town to distant suburbs, but their design has changed and their prize-winning cream and green is no longer.

We had a tram stop at either end of our street, indicated by a red and white tin sign that wrapped around the telegraph pole like the band on a cigar. It said 'CARS STOP HERE'. To a child this was a mysterious injunction – one of many – and I never understood whether it meant trams or cars, or both. Except in the brief peak hour, when the trams were packed with people crammed in their seats, uncomfortably strap-hanging or bursting like human dahlias from the doorways, they were ordinarily never too crowded. My mother always preferred me to go inside the compartment, where the lady shoppers sat, rather than occupy a bench in the breezy smokers' section by the tram's entrance, where the passengers were less nice.

These were usually manual labourers, deftly 'rolling their own' from a packet of Havelock Ready Rubbed and a Boomerang cigarette paper. They reminded me of Pat Baggot, my father's favourite gardener and odd-job man. In those days workmen all wore a kind of uniform: a fawn half-Norfolk jacket with a brown or maroon window check, over a fawn and maroon two-toned cardigan and an open-necked shirt. They wore grey or fawn trousers and boots, with a greasy grey or brown Akubra trilby always clamped on their heads. Like us schoolboys, they were never without a battered Gladstone bag: just the right size to carry home from the pub six chilled bottles of Melbourne Bitter.

Sometimes after a debating night at Melbourne Grammar or a concert in the Town Hall, I would travel home from town on the Wattle Park tram – inside the compartment, of course – with my friend Dennis Woodbridge, and on this thirty-minute journey I would bore him to death with my latest artistic theories and poetic enthusiasms. He was a patient listener.

After a dance or party I might catch the last tram, which seemed to travel at a snail's pace, rocking and juddering through the night until finally I could alight at Christowel Street and scuttle up the hill to our house to notice – ominous sign – a light still glowing in my parents' bedroom window. The people on the last tram seemed always to be sad. It was not unusual to see a young woman, or a woman less than young, in gloves and ball gown, sitting alone on her long ride home to some outer suburb. Around these uprooted wallflowers, with their unkissed lipstick, crushed finery and wilting corsages, I liked, in my imagination, to construct pathetic stories of unrequited love. Had they been to the Trocadero or the Palais de Danse? Whom had they hoped to meet? What dentist or accountant or polite commercial traveller might have rescued them forever from those long, lonely rides? Anyone with a car would have done.

Every famous visitor to Melbourne was, and still is, subjected to a publicised tram ride. Unlikeliest of passengers some years ago was Malcolm Muggeridge, journalist, lapsed atheist and sometime editor of *Punch*, who, as an old friend, I was conscripted to escort on this mandatory exercise. It failed to raise his spirits.

It was on the trams of Melbourne that one of the most publicised crimes of the early fifties was perpetrated. An unknown madman, whom the press called simply 'THE SPRAYER', hit the headlines and remained there, like Jack the Ripper, for several seasons. Women travelling by tram in the rush hour discovered, on alighting, that their dresses had been squirted with an indelible black substance by some unknown person. There were photographs of these appalled matrons in their stained frocks in the papers, and the public was urged, as it had been urged at the time of Jack the Ripper, to keep an eye open for the vile offender. Undeterred, the squirtings continued, and there were headlines such as 'SPRAYER STRIKES AGAIN' and 'HAVE YOU SEEN THE SPRAYER?'. But no witness came forward; he was never found and the story died.

In the ludicrous British Second World War propaganda film *A Canterbury Tale*, Eric Portman, acting as though under hypnosis, played the Glueman, a barmy village toff who prowled around at night in an air raid warden's outfit, squirting women's hair with glue. Poor Sheila Sim was the unfortunate recipient of one of these sticky nocturnal ejaculations, and she was only one of the many victims of this bizarre predator, a British country cousin of the Melbourne Sprayer.

Krafft-Ebing records the case history of a man who was compelled to furtively mutilate and maculate women's dresses.

The man would lurk in the crowded Kärntnerstrasse and the Graben when the Viennese crowds were at their thickest; then he would strike. It was his sole pleasure, and he was never apprehended.

The technical name for this behaviour, which political correctness demands that we describe not as a perversion, but rather as a 'stigmatised sexual practice', is 'saliromania' (from the French *salir*, to soil): a desire to damage or soil a woman or her clothes. Perhaps Krafft-Ebing's patient may have found his way onto a shipload of refugees fleeing Austria after the Anschluss. Arriving in Melbourne, after a period of internment, he may well have resumed his squid-like calling and become the first Melbourne Dadaist.

CHRISTOWEL STREET possessed an invisible chronicler in the person of Alf Dunn. Mr Dunn lived at number 24 in a Moderne house, designed and built by my father in about 1938. It had all the slightly nautical architectural mannerisms of its period. It was built of aubergine-coloured manganese bricks, with glass bricks illuminating the stairwell, steel-framed corner windows and a curved concrete 'eyebrow' over the other windows. On the inner sill of a picture window facing the street, beneath festoon blinds, a white marble puma prowled.

Alf had a 16-millimetre Bell and Howell movie camera, and from the late thirties right through to the early fifties he filmed the suburban world around him. Towards the end of his life Alf edited some of this footage and transferred it to video tape, but it was only after his death that I saw some of these extraordinary home movies. He liked to set up his camera in a fixed position in his driveway and photograph the street with its then sparse traffic and rare pedestrians. These films, which pre-figure in their uneventfulness the films of Andy Warhol and Yasujiro Ozu, possess a curious and hypnotic poetry, although Alf Dunn himself was the most prosaic of men. I have other tapes he made at his children's sports days. Again the camera is fixed and Mr Dunn's lens is rigorously incurious, even disdain-ful of people and events. It never seeks a subject or remotely follows a human action. Very rarely people, objects and incid-ents briefly trespass onto the screen, then disappear.

One evening in London I was watching one of Alf's films: an interminable view of the sea, probably taken some time in the very early fifties at the Melbourne beach resort of Sorrento. After five minutes of sparkling water, interrupted only twice by blurred children running between the sea and the camera, the top of a bald head appeared in the foreground, slowly rising up into full frame to reveal a man in bathing dress walking directly towards the lens. It was my father, still dripping from the sea. He looked at Alf, then at the camera, grinned sheepishly, and was gone. It is the only moving image of my father in existence and all the more touching since it culminates and redeems one of the most boring film sequences ever made.

On my last birthday my sister telephoned me from Mel-bourne. 'Do you realise that you've now outlived our father?' Barbara asked.

It was a chastening moment. Had she won a bet? I unkindly

wondered. Well, yes, I suppose I had become, by some sneaky process, what the world – and certainly the young – considers oldish.

I remember the first and last time I realised that my father was old. He had had what were called 'a few scares'. Nothing to worry about, but worth a check-up. We stood at the front door of 36 Christowel Street, with its Georgian porch, terazzo'd by the Angelo Brothers in 1937, and farewelled my father's doctor; or was it the doctor farewelling him?

The front lawn grew shadowy, but I suddenly remembered it as it had been in the sunshine of earliest childhood when I played there on the squeaky grass amongst the darting cabbage moths. I would stare into the faces of the snapdragons and the phlox and the zinnias and touch the round leaves of the nasturtiums on which the water rolled like beads of mercury. Then I recalled the lawn on winter mornings with its white tegument of frost bruised by my father's green footprints after he had made his morning pilgrimage to the front gate for *The Sun News-Pictorial*.

Together, as darkness filled the garden, we watched Sir Clive Fitts walk down the path, climb into his Mercedes and drive off. I had come home that evening to be told that my father was in the den having a 'routine' examination. He had certainly looked pale, even haggard, as he emerged from the consultation, and as we watched the doctor leave I stole a look at my father in profile and was shocked to see the sparse grey hair, the tufted ears and ragged dewlap.

I noticed the knotted veins on the back of my father's hand as it sought and gripped my own. In fear, as I now apprehend.

In love and fear. He was an old man, and I had never noticed it before.

My father always took his hat off in lifts, and so, in this hatless age, do I. In modern elevators, pressed between strangers who would not even notice, I doff to my father's memory.

Once, at a lookout in the Blue Mountains, I was alone and thinking aloud.

'This must be beautiful at dusk,' I said.

A boy and girl – sweethearts they might once have been called in a sentimental age – overheard me.

'What's dusk?' one of them said, too young for effete poetics. Far too young to remember hats or blotting paper or bank managers or a tuneful pursing of the lips.

Have I become Sandy Stone, the last repository of these quaint anachronisms, and with the word *dusk* still in my vocabulary? And so I set these things down before the onset of the first of a thousand small physical degradations as, in a still-distant suburb, Death strides whistling towards me.

ACKNOWLEDGEMENTS

~

THE AUTHOR wishes to give particular thanks to his friend Kim Zweig for suggesting the title of this book. He is also grateful to David Martin Bruson, who over the past year, at unusual times of the day and night and in many parts of the world, cheerfully typed the foregoing narrative into a legible form. Catherine Lambert has been unstinting in her assistance with illustrations and arcane historical details, as have Neil Munro, with his pristine memories of the Melbourne that is no more, and Nicholas Pounder, whose knowledge of my published ephemera exceeds my own. The author wishes to acknowledge the friendship and assistance of Renée Fleming, Markus Fokken, Thomas Goldwasser, Merlin Holland, Linda Hughes, Gavin Lambert, Christine Lavin, Rabbi John Levi, Charles Osborne, Tom Sanders, Stephen Sondheim, Amy Tan, Ken Thomson and Leslie van der Sluys. Janine Barrand at the Performing Arts Museum, Victorian Arts Centre, Melbourne, has been generous in allowing the author to plunder her archives. Joan Stanton Blank provided a rare photograph, long thought lost, and the author's sister, Barbara, and brothers, Christopher and Michael, excavated family photographs.

It remains for the author to thank all those who have helped in the process of publishing this book: his friend and publisher at Penguin in the UK, Louise Moore, and her assistant, Chantal Gibbs, for their devotion to these modest jottings; and especially his publishers at Penguin Australia, Robert Sessions and Clare Forster, their assistant, Cora Roberts, Deborah Brash, the designer, and the incomparable Lesley Dunt, the author's fastidious editor.

The writer is indebted to his old friend Lewis Morley for three arresting and historic photographic images, and to Polly Borland for her portrait of the sedentary Sir Les Patterson. To David Hockney the author is grateful for a remarkable evocation of himself in old age. He is also beholden to the great American photographer Greg Gorman for capturing the subject of this book at a cadaverous moment for the dust jacket of the Australian edition, and to John Swannell for the portrait on the dust jacket of the English edition.

Sources

~

The author and publisher wish to thank all copyright holders for permission to reproduce their work, and the institutions and individuals who helped with the research and supply of materials.

Text Sources

Verse on page 335: from W.H. Auden, 'As I Went Out One Morning', in *W.H. Auden: Collected Poems*, reproduced by permission of Faber & Faber.

Extract on page 238: from Alec Guinness, *My Name Escapes Me: The Diary of a Retiring Actor*, © the estate of Alec Guinness, reproduced by permission of Hamish Hamilton.

Parts of the author's accounts of the Jan Frans de Boever Society, *Edna: The Royal Tour*, and his friendships with Peter Cook and Spike Milligan have appeared in an earlier form in, respectively, *The Spectator*, *The Sunday Times*, *Something Like Fire: Peter Cook Remembered* (edited by Lin Cook), and *Spike Milligan: His Part in Our Lives* (compiled by Maxine Ventham).

Pictorial Sources

First Black and White Section

'Rosebud' and 'Barbara, Michael, Barry and Christopher': Maxwell Porteous.

'The Corner Shop': John Shirlow, 1869–1936, Australia, *The Corner Shop*, 1919, etching, 20.6 x 17.0 cm, Felton Bequest 1936, National Gallery of Victoria.

'Mrs Ellis Bird': courtesy Leslie van der Sluys.

' "Shoescape" ': courtesy Joan Stanton Blank.

'Dr Aaron Azimuth': front cover image from catalogue *The Art Works of Barry Humphries*, August 1958, Official Photographer Gerard Vandenburg, Performing Arts Museum, Victorian Arts Centre, Melbourne.

'Phillip Street players': Phil Ward Studios Pty Ltd.

'The young actor': Bruno Benini. Image kindly supplied by Malcolm Robertson, Performing Arts Museum, Victorian Arts Centre, Melbourne.

'Mrs Edna Everage': Laurie Richards Photographic Collection, Performing Arts Museum, Victorian Arts Centre, Melbourne.
'As Fagin': Anthony Crickmay, 1968.

Second Black and White Section

'A Conder fan': Lewis Morley, 1961.
'Salvador Dalí': Philippe Halsman, 1963.
'Barry with John Wells and John Bird': © BBC, London.
'Peter Cook, B.H. and Dudley Moore': Peter Carrette, 1971.
'Clyde Packer with the author': Janice McIllree, c. 1974.
'Colin "The Frog" Lucas': still from *Barry McKenzie Holds His Own*, courtesy of Grundy, from Screen Sound Australia Collection.
'Sidney Nolan' and 'Patrick White, B.H. and Manoly Lascaris': Ken Thomson.
'The apotheosis of Edna': Einar Nerman, 1976.
'Dame Edna on Broadway': © Al Hirschfeld, art reproduced by special arrangement with Hirschfeld's exclusive representative, The Margo Feiden Galleries Ltd, New York.
'Betjeman': © BBC, London.
'B.H. in Salamis': Lewis Morley, 1969.
'Rupert': Bruce Beresford.
'Oscar': Diane Millstead.

Colour Section

'Tribute': Lewis Morley.
'At Bundanon': painting by Arthur Boyd.
'On the Murray River': courtesy of David Dridan.
'Edna-boppers': *The West Australian*, 1994.
'Sir Les Patterson': Polly Borland.
'Sandy Stone': reprinted by permission of ABC.
'Nicole Kidman': Andrew Overgaard, © Vogue / The Condé Nast Publications Ltd.
'*Ally McBeal*': Mary Ann Valdes, 2002.
'Drawing of the author': reproduced courtesy of David Hockney, 2002.

Every effort has been made to trace copyright holders and we apologise in advance for any unintentional omission. We would be pleased to insert the appropriate acknowledgement in any subsequent edition.

Index

~